HOW TO WRITE

A Practical Rhetoric

HARRY M. BROWN
Midwestern State University

HOW TO WRITE

A Practical Rhetoric

HOLT, RINEHART AND WINSTON
New York   Chicago   San Francisco   Atlanta   Dallas
Montreal   Toronto

Library of Congress Cataloging in Publication Data

Brown, Harry Matthew
    How to write : a practical rhetoric.

    Includes index.
    1. English language—Rhetoric.   I.   Title.
PE1408.B857   808'.042   77-21524

ISBN 0-03-020881-5

Acknowledgments

"The Three New Yorks" by E. B. White. *Here Is New York* by E. B. White. Copyright 1949 by E. B. White. By permission of Harper & Row, Publishers, Inc.

"Love and an Apple" by Arthur Unger. Reprinted by permission from *The Christian Science Monitor;* © 1976 The Christian Science Publishing Society. All rights reserved.

"The Rebel and the Revolutionary" by Rollo May. Reprinted from *Power and Innocence, A Search for the Sources of Violence,* by Rollo May. By permission of W. W. Norton & Company, Inc. Copyright © 1972 by Rollo May.

"Harvest of the Seasons" by J. Bronowski. From *The Ascent of Man* by J. Bronowski. Copyright © 1973 by J. Bronowski. Reprinted by permission of Little, Brown and Company. Also reprinted with permission of the BBC Publications, London.

"The Driftwood on the Ice" by Harold A. Larrabee. From Harold A. Larrabee, *Reliable Knowledge.* Copyright © 1964 by Harold A. Larrabee. Reprinted by permission of Houghton Mifflin Co.

"The Dimension of Experience" by Peter Nowell. Reprinted by permission from *The Christian Science Monitor;* © 1976 The Christian Science Publishing Society. All rights reserved.

"The Emotional Woman" by Ashley Montagu. Reprinted with permission of Macmillan Publishing Co. From *The Natural Superiority of Women* by Ashley Montagu, pp. 106–108. Copyright © 1952, 1953, 1968, 1974 by Ashley Montagu.

"Surviving the Cities" by Carl Rogers. From "Some Social Issues Which Concern Me," *Journal of Humanistic Psychology* (fall 1972). By permission of the author and *The Journal of Humanistic Psychology.*

"The Open Window" by Saki. From *The Short Stories of Saki* (H. H. Munro). All rights reserved. Reprinted by permission of The Viking Press. Also, by permission of The Bodley Head, Publishers.

Preface

How to Write is a practical rhetoric designed to help students develop skills in writing expository and persuasive essays as well as special papers that may be required in their other courses and in their careers. Two main assumptions underlie the book. Writing is a craft that can be learned by almost anybody, and writing can be put to useful work.

It's true that some kinds of writing are not for everybody. To write a moving poem, to tell an imaginative story with plot and characterization, to describe an awe-inspiring scene in nature—these are beyond the powers of most people.

But there are two kinds of writing that are surely within the ability and the need of almost everybody. These are *expository* writing and *persuasive* writing. Expository writing might explain how to string a tennis racket or describe the traffic problems of a certain city or analyze the voting patterns of a specific community. Persuasive writing might argue that a woman's place is in a career or defend one community as safer to live in than another or insist that it is practical for people to help one another. We are also frequently called on to write such special papers and reports as business letters, reports on information gathered, and summaries of larger pieces of writing.

The materials of this book are selected and arranged to develop skills in these practical kinds of writing. There are three large blocks of material.

Part I, The Whole Composition, is the main unit. Chapter 1 covers the basic techniques of gathering and organizing material. Chapter 2 describes patterns of development—ten common overall patterns of structure and thought process (such as Method Analysis, Cause and Effect, Problem and Solution, Validating an Opinion). The thought process is emphasized in each case, as well as the formal structure. Each of the ten units includes a brief model essay and a list of writing topics. The units may be used in any order, in part, or in whole.

Part II offers some basic tools used in building compositions— developing various types of *paragraphs,* writing effective *sentences,* using precise and forceful *diction,* and following a logical and convincing *thought process.* The sections are not discursive, but they give abundant material to work with—brief explanations, examples, and exercises.

Part III, The Special Paper, provides a wide coverage of some very practical uses of writing outside the freshman English theme. There is substantial material to work with. Among the topics are rules of literary interpretation, the basic elements of short stories and poems, the principles of the scientific attitude, the techniques of writing specialized scientific reports, principles of writing examinations and summaries. Model writings are included. The chapter on business letters deals not only with correct format but also with the pyschology of effective business communication. The opening chapter on the reference paper is a total unit that includes a complete sample paper.

The book is flexible. The various sections of the book can be taught concurrently. The Whole Composition and The Special Paper are considered to be basic—the instructor can select from various writing units in them. The chapters on paragraph, sentence, word, and thought are tools to be applied as needed. They can be dealt with as units or used for reference.

An *Instructor's Manual* is available. It offers some general suggestions on using the book, a number of additional writing assignments, and additional exercises, including some covering Appendix material on punctuation, spelling, and grammar. Answers to many exercises in the text and to all the Appendix exercises are provided. The *Manual* may be obtained through a local Holt representative or by writing to English Editor, College Department, Holt, Rinehart and Winston, 383 Madison Avenue, New York, N.Y. 10017.

Thanks are due to the following students, who allowed me to use their writings: Catherine Alexander, Vera Anderson, Harriet Bird, Carl Campbell, Vikki Chaviers, Charles Colson, Mark Eller, Susan Galloway, Elizabeth Grauerholz, Matthew Harrison, Warren Houck, Laura Meux, Karen Rawlings, Cynthia Rushia, Walter Smith, and Kim Vaught.

I also wish to express my gratitude to those who read the manuscript and made constructive comments: Chris Antonides, Lansing Community College; Barbara Bixby, Brevard Community College; William G. Clark, University of Iowa; George Haich, Georgia State University; David Skwire, Cuyahoga Community College; Sally J. Smith, Brevard Community College.

H.M.B.

Contents

HOW
TO
WRITE
A Practical Rhetoric

PART ONE

THE WHOLE COMPOSITION: GETTING THE BIG IDEA ACROSS

When you are faced with the job of writing a composition of, say, two or three pages, there are two things you should remember:

1. Don't despair.
2. Don't just grab a pen and paper and start scribbling words.

You can avoid despair by getting rid of the false notion that writing is some lofty art or mysterious gift of genius completely beyond your power. It's true that some kinds of writing are not for everybody. To write a moving poem, to tell an imaginative story with plot and characterization, to describe an awe-inspiring scene in nature—these are beyond the powers of most people.

But there are two kinds of writing that are surely within the ability and the need of almost everybody. These are *expository* writing and *persuasive* writing. Expository writing explains. Its purpose is to transmit information. It may do such things as tell how to string a tennis racket, describe the traffic problems of a certain city, or analyze the voting patterns of a specific community. Persuasive writing defends a viewpoint, tries to change an attitude or an opinion. It might argue that a woman's place is in a career, defend one community as safer to live in than another, or insist that it is practical for people to help one another. These are some of the kinds of ideas and ways of thinking that all of us work with again and again in our lives.

Expository and persuasive writing is a craft and can be learned by almost anybody, at least anybody who has made it through to college. Don't despair. You can learn the craft of writing just as you can learn any other craft, such as driving a car or tuning a television set.

If you don't despair when asked to write a composition, don't jump to the other extreme, frenzied confidence, and grab a pen and paper and begin gushing words. With this procedure, one of two things will likely happen. Either you will end up in left field or some other nowhere of confusion and nonsense, or you will run out of words at about 50 and sit staring at the page with two and a half pages to go. Again, despair.

You can avoid the disasters of both gush writing and despair writing by realizing that writing is a craft. Developing skill in a craft is not easy, but if you follow certain practical principles and methods, you can definitely improve your skills in expository and persuasive writing.

To begin, you should concern yourself with two areas of skill: organizing the composition and using a specific pattern of development.

1

Organizing the Composition

Shaping the Material

CHOOSING AND LIMITING YOUR SUBJECT

Keep three things in mind in choosing a subject:

1. Your interest in the subject Pick a subject that appeals to you or one that you can develop interest in as you work on it. Don't merely try to write for the instructor's interest. You might guess wrong. You must finally write for the reader's interest, but if you yourself aren't interested, your paper will lack life, and the reader may not be interested enough to get your point.

2. Your knowledge If your composition is due in a week, you may not have time to do a lot of reading in a new field. You may instead wish to express well what you already know.

3. The reader's interest You are writing to an audience, real or imagined. A likely audience to consider is a composite of your instructor and your class. Write on a subject that is worth the reader's time. It may be some new insight (such as a new practical method for preserving student rights in college or preventing war in the world). It may be an old problem that always needs reiteration (such as women vs. men, society and the individual). Or it may be any subject—trivial and commonplace—if you treat it with interest or persuasion (such as what to do with a blind date). Keep the reader in mind. You are writing something to that person.

The scope of your subject is limited by the size of your composition. Most papers run from about 350 to 500 words. You must narrow your subject enough so that you can make it impressive or clear in these few

3

hundred words. If your subject is "Leisure Time," you can hardly say everything that can be said about the subject in two or three pages. You could narrow it down to "Hobbies" or "Outdoor Activities," then continue narrowing, at each step expanding the list of specific subjects. You might come up with a list like this:

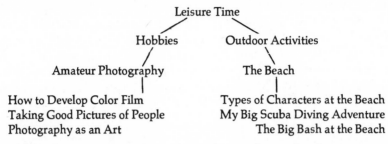

Leisure Time

Hobbies   Outdoor Activities

Amateur Photography   The Beach

How to Develop Color Film   Types of Characters at the Beach
Taking Good Pictures of People   My Big Scuba Diving Adventure
Photography as an Art   The Big Bash at the Beach

The final two lists are subjects limited enough to write about.

DECIDING ON YOUR PURPOSE

Before you select your final topic, you should consider your purpose in writing the composition. That is, just what do you want to do with your subject? What response do you want from your reader? In general, you will shape your subject toward one of the four main types of writing: *exposition* (to inform or explain), *argument* (to persuade or change an opinion), *narration* (to relate an incident), or *description* (to present a sensory impression). One of these general purposes will be dominant in a composition, but others may also be present. The examples of narrowed subjects under "Limiting the Subject" could have these purposes:

Exposition   "How to Develop Color Film" or "Types of Characters at the Beach" or "Taking Good Pictures of People" (probable purpose: to explain, to point out the kinds, to distinguish them)

Argument   "Photography as an Art" (probable purpose: to change an opinion, to get the reader to accept a certain attitude)

Narration   "My Big Scuba Diving Adventure" (probable purpose: to relate an incident)

Description   "The Big Bash at the Beach" or "Types of Characters at the Beach" (probable purpose: to make the scene so real that it is as if the reader were there)

You will shape your subject and your development of it according to what kind of response you want from your readers.

FORMING A CENTRAL IDEA: THE THESIS STATEMENT

A clear and forceful composition can be summarized in a single sentence called a *thesis statement*. You should not ramble *about* a subject. Write a sentence in answer to the question: What points are you making in your

The MAIN IDEA IN A SENTANCE

paper? Such a statement will guide you in gathering material and in arranging your paper, and it may be included in your finished introduction to guide the reader. Here are two helpful steps to forming a thesis statement:

1. Make a rough list of ideas about the subject Jot down ideas, opinions, assertions, facts, anecdotes—to make sure you can get enough material on the subject.

2. State the thesis statement Once you have gathered some material and have a general idea about what purpose you have for the subject and your readers, write the central idea to control your overall paper in the form of a complete sentence. This is important: a thesis statement must be a *complete* sentence. It may change later as you form your outline, gather more material, and write your paper, but you need a clear direction to begin.

EXAMPLES

1. **Purpose** To distinguish the kinds of people one usually sees at a public beach. (exposition)
   Title "It Takes All Kinds"
   Central Idea Most of the people at a public beach can be classified into one of four types according to their behavior: the sun-sleeper, the picnicker, the gangster, and the pilgrim. (thesis statement)

2. **Purpose** To tell an experience I had while scuba diving. (narration)
   Title "Never Trust a Shark"
   Central Idea My encounter with a shark taught me always to use caution and the proper equipment when scuba diving. (thesis statement)

3. **Purpose** To persuade readers that they should change their attitude toward photography. (argument)
   Title "Not Only Michelangelo"
   Central Idea The imagination and sensitivity and the aesthetic purpose of the photographer and the artistry of the product all indicate that photography is an art, not . . . (thesis statement)

EXERCISE 1-1
CHOOSING AND LIMITING THE SUBJECT

Narrow these broad, general subjects into subjects that can be treated in 350–500 words; in 750–1000 words.

Television	The individual in our society
Kinds of music	National leadership
What's wrong with our society?	Crime
Hobbies	The place of women in our society
Energy	Trial by jury in our country
Current fashions	Movies
America	Population
Americans in other countries	Trouble in Africa / the Middle East / South
Ecology	Sports America

Gathering the Material

You may have already gathered some material in shaping your subject. Now, with a central idea in mind, scribble down all you can think of on the subject—details, examples, descriptions, reasons, facts, ideas—anything related or near-related. This is not your composition. This is getting your raw material down in notes so that you can use it easily. Write yourself empty, and then look to see what gaps you need to fill in. Your limited subject and purpose will regulate how much and what kind of material you need in certain areas. Difficult or unfamiliar ideas need much explanation, with examples, analogies, and illustrations. Debatable subjects need evidence, facts, and sound arguments. Common ideas need vividness and originality.

With a tentative thesis statement and an abundance of scattered supporting material you can begin to organize to write the paper.

Arranging the Material: Outlining

You need a working plan before writing your paper. It may be that you clearly see the divisions of your paper and can begin writing with just a mental outline. But if you are not entirely clear on organization, prepare a formal outline. It is your working plan, your road map.

STEPS TO MAKING AN OUTLINE

1.   Read the thesis statement   It may already contain the main points of the composition. If your thesis is "The district game changed my attitude toward sports," you may have a three-part outline:

   I.   Description of earlier attitude
  II.   Pertinent events of the game
 III.   Description of new attitude

If the outline is not obvious from the thesis statement, use it as a guide in formulating an outline.

2.   Classify the material you have gathered

  1.   Distinguish ideas from details used to support ideas.
  2.   Group the ideas.

If you were considering writing on "Spectators at a Football Game," you might come up with a list like the following from just jotting down first thoughts, paying no attention to order or relevance.

Noise, banners, bright blue sky
A couple huddled close, wrapped in a blanket

Cheerleaders live in their own world
Just why do some people go to games?
The busy, busy action on the field
 The yeller who knows how to run the game—gets mad
Somebody always going for hot dogs
The scoreboard
Coach pacing the sidelines
Gang of 8–10 having their own boisterous party

From this list, you want to pick out the main ideas that fit your thesis statement. Now, ignoring the other details (you may want to use them for support later or discard them as irrelevant), group the main ideas. You may see one or two ideas becoming subpoints under a larger category. Here, six categories of people at a football game may be regrouped into three main types. For instance. You may end up with a list that looks like this:

The couple
The gang (including the hot-dog person and the yeller)
Cheerleaders and coach

3. Adjust the thesis statement You may need to eliminate some subpoints or shift your central idea to cover them.
4. Make an outline The two popular types of outlines are the topic outline and the sentence outline. Use whichever form is best for you.

KINDS OF OUTLINES

1. Topic outline The main points are written in brief but meaningful phrases or words, using a consistent numbering system.

College Misfits

   I. The Intellectual
      A. Concern with odd information
      B. Social ineptness
  II. The Athlete
      A. Concern with the fads
      B. Conceit
 III. The Anti
      A. Eccentricity
      B. Self-centeredness
 IV. The Socialite
      A. Interest in group activity
      B. Shallowness

2. Sentence outline A sentence outline differs from a topic outline in that you write each lead as a full sentence. The sentence outline is more informative, because it states ideas more fully.

The Crisis of American Masculinity

   I.   The American male lacks confidence in his masculinity.
  II.   This unsureness is caused by a man's uncertainty about his identity in general.
 III.   The American man can recover his sense of individual spontaneity by development in three areas.
      A.   He can develop his comic sense through satire.
      B.   He can develop his aesthetic sense through art.
      C.   He can develop his moral and political sense through vital engagement in political life.

RULES OF OUTLINING

1. Use the *standard* lettering system   It begins with the capital Roman numeral I, and alternates through letters and numbers:

   I.
     A.
        1.
           a.
           b.
        2.
     B.
  II.

2. Make logical divisions   Since an outline is a division, you must not use single subheads. Divide into two or more items or not at all. If you use an *A* under a Roman numeral, use a *B*. If you put a *1* under an *A*, use a *2*, and so on.

3. List ideas only   Do not list supporting material. For instance, "Example" or "Illustration" would not be written as a subpoint.

4. Use parallel grammatical form   Make the form consistent. Use single noun headings throughout, or noun plus verbal, or prepositional phrases, and so on. Consistent form gives a sense of consistent thought and makes writing and reading easier.

EXERCISE 1-2
CORRECTING OUTLINE FORM

Correct the form of the following outline.

How to Study

   I.   Setting the scene
      A.   Getting rid of people
      B.   Arranging the desk and light

    1. The best kind of lamp
  C. Lining up subjects
    1. Put the interesting subject first.
    2. The hardest in the middle
II. Concentrating
    1. Think of one subject at a time.
    2. Use your will power.
    3. Noise
    A. Radio
III. Sticking with it
    1. If you can stick with it for 15 minutes, you've probably got the whole thing made.
IV. Conclusion.

Writing the First Draft

Get started. Don't bog down over a title or the right introduction. You can do these last. Develop your idea. If you do have an introduction in mind, it is a good idea to write it halfway down the page. Then after your ideas have clarified in writing you might want to go back and cross out your first introduction and write a better one in the space you left blank. Most first introductions are wordy and clumsy and have to be rewritten. Write fast and rough, if need be. Don't delay over grammar or spelling. If you are uncertain, put parentheses around that word or phrase, and check it later. Try not to go out for a break. If you keep your ideas going and write a little under pressure, your mind will be sharper, and your paper will have more snap. If you write when your mind is at rest, your paper will be at rest.

Make the first draft as full as possible. You may even include extra material. It will be easier later to take out than to put in. Revision will put it all into shape.

Writing Introductions and Conclusions

INTRODUCTIONS

A good introduction has two purposes: to interest the readers and to lead them into your subject. Avoid aimless, vague generalizations and mere decorations. If you can't work up some special device, just make a sharp, direct statement of the point you are going to develop in the paper. Here are some of the methods that may be used:

1. A direct statement of the thesis

The largest single step in the ascent of man is the change from nomad to village agriculture.

2. A curious statement

The little man wearing a stocking cap stood in the middle of the Fifth Avenue bus, drinking from a jar.

3. A startling statement

When Grandma introduced me to scuba diving . . .

4. A vital question

What has happened to the American male?

5. An anecdote

There is a story, possibly apocryphal, about a psychologist who shut a chimpanzee in a soundproof room filled with dozens of mechanical toys.

6. Repetition of title

Title: "Americans Are Strange
First line: Americans are strange: they can't rest.

7. A startling fact

The U. S. statistic of one divorce per every four marriages is all too familiar.

CONCLUSIONS

The first common error in ending a paper is just to stop, without any conclusion. The second common error is to bring in a new idea. The function of a conclusion is to clinch the development of the ideas and to bring it to a natural, definite resolution. Several methods may be used. Here are some samples:

1. **Climax**   If the paper has a logical, climactic buildup, and the preceding ideas would be clear in the reader's mind, you may simply stress the final point of a developed discussion. You may clinch the conclusion by making reference to the relationship of the last idea to the preceding main points or by indicating that you have reached the end of the thought process you started out with. In "Radioactivity and the Future" (p. 201), the author traces the consequences of radioactivity in germ cells. He begins with the causes of radioactivity, atomic bomb explosions, and atomic energy waste. He then moves through the cumulative effect of radioactivity to end with the climax of the thought process, the "dire consequences in the human race."

2. **Restatement**   You can also effectively conclude your composition by restating or summarizing the central idea. In "The Dimension of Experience" (p. 35), the author opens with a curious statement:

There is a distinct possibility that I will be sitting in a boat in the middle of the Indian Ocean six years from now.

After defending this strange opinion with some very sound reasoning, the author concludes with a restatement of the opening thesis and a list of the arguments used to develop it.

> So, my going to the Indian Ocean is not subject to chance nor is it a predetermined event. It is as possible as any other event that is in line with my thinking. For my experience is as wide, as exalted, as fruitful, as happy, as full of compassion, as my thought.

3. Application You may wish to conclude with some application of the material you have presented. As long as you do not introduce a new idea for development, you may end with a challenge, a suggestion of importance, or a provoking question. In "Surviving the Cities" (p. 40) the author describes the problems of the cities and offers a solution. The final paragraph challenges us to apply his solution to the problem:

> We know how to carry out every aspect of this. The only element lacking is the passionate determination that says, "Our cities are inhuman. They are ruining lives and mental and physical health at a devastating rate. We are going to change this, even if it costs us money!"

Checklist: Revising

First-draft writing is seldom satisfactory. Excellent ideas and sections may be there, but revising makes it all effective. It is best to let some time elapse between writing and revising. Then you can come back with perspective. Test for effectiveness in four areas: (1) subject matter, (2) organization, (3) style, and (4) grammar and mechanics.

1. Subject matter There are three main areas to check.

a. *Accuracy of ideas.* Are your facts right? Carefully check opinions, interpretations, and arguments for soundness.

b. *Adequate development.* Look for gaps and vagueness. Have you used enough details to make clear explanations and give convincing support? Remember, the ideas are clearer to you than they are to the reader. Don't leave the evidence or explanation in your head. Your reader may need them.

c. *Unnecessary material.* Irrelevant and unnecessary material must be pruned out. Check your ideas first against the topic sentences and then against the thesis statement. Remove excess.

2. Organization Check the overall structure in five areas.

a. *Thesis statement.* Is your central idea directly stated or clearly implied? Is your purpose clearly indicated?

b. *Main points.* Does each paragraph or main point develop an aspect of the thesis statement? Are the ideas in logical order?

c. *Transitions.* Are the transitions clear? Can the reader follow your movement from one idea to another? Do you need to insert a "first" or a "second," repeat a key word, or restate the idea of one paragraph as you move into the next?

d. *Introduction.* Does your introduction really introduce? Is it necessary? Pertinent? Interesting: Or is it off the subject, stilted, or "cute"?

e. *Conclusion.* Have you ended, not just stopped the paper? Is the idea you developed in your paper neatly rounded off? Or have you gotten off the subject by bringing in a new idea?

3. Style Style is not a matter of correct grammar, but of effective expression. Check to see if you have expressed your ideas in the best way possible to make them clear and forceful. Try rewriting weak passages to improve them. Especially check these weaknesses in style:

    a. Cumbersome sentences
    b. Wordy passages
    c. Imprecise vocabulary
    d. Dull, lifeless words
    e. Vague pronouns

4. Grammar and mechanics Correct all errors in grammar and mechanics. The worst errors are usually in these areas:

    a. Typographical errors
    b. Spelling
    c. Sentence fragments
    d. Run-on sentences
    e. Agreement of subject and verb
    f. Case of pronouns
    g. Use of adjectives and adverbs
    h. Punctuation
    i. Capitalization
    j. Abbreviations

Checklist: Preparing the Manuscript

Your instructor may have special instructions for preparing the finished draft. If not, the following will serve:

1. Ink and paper For longhand, 8 ½ x 11 inch lined theme paper; blue, blue-black, or black ink. For typing, typing paper. One side only.

2. Spacing Single space in longhand. Double space in typing. No extra space between paragraphs.

3. Margins About an inch and a half at the top, an inch and a half at the left, an inch at the right, and an inch at the bottom.

4. Title In longhand, center the title on the top line of the front page. Leave a line between title and text. In typing, center the title about two inches from the top of the first page. Leave about an inch between title and text.

Capitalize key words in the title, but do not underline the title, and do not put it in quotation marks unless it is an actual quotation.

Use an exclamation point or a question mark at the end if necessary, but not a period.

The title is not part of the body of the paper. Don't open with a "this" which assumes the words of the title, such as "This has been a growing problem."

5. Page numbers Number each page after the first one in arabic numerals (2, 3, 4) in the upper right-hand corner.

6. Signature Fold the paper and endorse it near the top to the right of the fold. Put down the following information:

Name

Title of paper

Date

7. Corrections in copy Eliminate typographical errors. Retype if there are major errors; make minor corrections in the text if they can be done neatly.

    a.   Delete words by drawing a straight line (~~a straight line~~) through them.

the

    b.   Add words by using a caret and writing them over∧line.

    c.   Indicate a paragraph beginning in a solid text by putting the paragraph symbol in the margin and drawing a right angle where the new paragraph begins.

. . . Add words by using a caret and writing them over the line.   ⌐Indicate a paragraph beginning in a solid text by . . .

    d.   To indicate that what you have written as two paragraphs should be written as one, write No ¶ in the margin to the left and draw a line from the end of the first paragraph to the beginning of the second paragraph.

This is is the way to join two blocks of sentences into a single paragraph.⌐
 ⌐Write No ¶ in the margin and . . .

If corrections are much more elaborate than these, it is better to retype the page. The manuscript must be clean, correct, and legible.

2

Using a Pattern of Development

Establish a thought plan for your composition. When we think meaningfully about a subject, we don't just run through our minds a jumble of bits and pieces about the subject. We usually have some angle—something special we want to do with the information. We have some underlying thought process and purpose. Figure out just what your overall idea structure is, so that you can have a framework for your composition.

The four general rhetorical purposes of composition are guides—exposition, argument, narration, and description. From these general purposes, our minds run to several standard, specific thought processes and purposes. Some of the patterns that could be the organizing principle of your composition are these:

1. Comparison and contrast
2. Problem and solution
3. Tracing causes and effects
4. Backing up an opinion
5. Classification and division
6. Exposing error and clarifying the truth
7. Pro and con
8. Telling a significant event
9. Describing a scene
10. Interpreting the meaning of evidence
11. Defining terms
12. Telling how something is done or made
13. Telling how something works, functions, or develops

There are other thought patterns, but these are the most common.

You will get greater control of your writing project if you make it clear to yourself just what general purpose you have in mind and which specific thought process you want to build your composition on.

Some of these patterns are defined and illustrated in the following pages.

Classification and Division

Grouping and analyzing into parts are common thought processes. We frequently have to take a mass of things or ideas, sort them out, and arrange them into categories according to their common characteristics. This thought process is called *classification.* A companion thought pattern is *division,* by which we take one complex thing or idea and break it into its component parts. According to our particular interest at the time, we may classify a group of items or divide one thing into its parts differently at different times. For instance, the whole group of students at a college may be classified as freshman, sophomore, junior, or senior. The principle of interest is the class in college or the number of credit hours acquired. With academic emphasis as the principle of interest, you could classify students as being in the areas of science, education, business, or liberal arts. Another principle of interest could be attitude toward study or favorite activity. With these principles you might come up with something like athlete, socialite, activist, and scholar.

Whatever principle of interest you use, follow two rules:

1. *Be complete.* Don't leave out an important part or kind. You don't have to discuss all, but you must justify your limits if you leave out an important part or type.
    Complete   Spring, Summer, Autumn, Winter
    Incomplete   Spring, Summer, Winter

2. *Be consistent.* Don't cross-classify or use two different principles of interest.
    Consistent: Freshman, Sophomore, Junior, Senior
    Inconsistent: Freshman, Sophomore, Senior, Loafer

The thought process of classification and division provides an easy, workable plan for a whole composition. Simply, if you can count and if you can tell one thing from another, you can write a well-organized composition. The dimensions are set. You know where to begin and where to stop. The big job is to get the initial thinking clear.

After sorting out the kinds and making a thesis statement, you can see the pattern of the composition as inevitable. There are two easy choices.

First, you can describe each type in turn—perhaps a paragraph for each—possibly pointing out similarities and differences as you go. A second overall structure is to classify the several kinds and then concentrate on a larger description of one of them.

The following essay, "The Three New Yorks," uses the second plan. Sentence 1 states the classification. The rest of paragraph 1 describes and contrasts the three kinds of New Yorkers.

Paragraph 2 focuses on one type—the commuter. The final paragraph resolves the discussion by tying the commuter in with the other types through the resident.

The Three New Yorks

E. B. WHITE

There are roughly three New Yorks. There is, first, the New York of the man or woman who was born here, who takes the city for granted and accepts its size and its turbulence as natural and inevitable. Second, there is the New York of the commuter—the city that is devoured by locusts each day and spat out each night. Third, there is the New York of the person who was born somewhere else and came to New York in quest of something. Of these three trembling cities the greatest is the last—the city of final destination, the city that is a goal. It is this third city that accounts for New York's high-strung disposition, its poetical deportment, its dedication to the arts, and its incomparable achievements. Commuters give the city its tidal restlessness; natives give it solidity and continuity; but the settlers give it passion. And whether it is a farmer arriving from Italy to set up a small grocery store in a slum, or a young girl arriving from a small town in Mississippi to escape the indignity of being observed by her neighbors, or a boy arriving from the Corn Belt with a manuscript in his suitcase and a pain in his heart, it makes no difference: each embraces New York with the intense excitement of first love, each absorbs New York with the fresh eyes of an adventurer, each generates heat and light to dwarf the Consolidated Edison Company.

The commuter is the queerest bird of all. The suburb he inhabits has no essential vitality of its own and is a mere roost where he comes at day's end to go to sleep. Except in rare cases, the man who lives in Mamaroneck or Little Neck or Teaneck, and works in New York, discovers nothing much about the city except the time of arrival and departure of trains and buses, and the path to a quick lunch. He is desk-bound, and has never, idly roaming in the gloaming, stumbled suddenly on Belvedere Tower in the Park, seen the ramparts rise sheer from the water of the pond, and the boys along the shore fishing for minnows, girls stretched out negligently on the shelves of the rocks; he has never come suddenly on anything at all in New York as a loiterer, because he has had no time between trains. He has fished in Manhattan's wallet and dug out coins, but has never listened to Manhattan's breathing, never awakened to its morning, never dropped off to sleep in its night. About 400,000 men and women come charging onto the Island each week-day morning, out of the mouths of tubes and tunnels. Not many among them have ever spent a drowsy afternoon in the great rustling oaken silence of the reading room of the Public Library, with the book elevator (like an old water wheel) spewing out books onto the trays. They tend their furnaces in Westchester and in Jersey, but have never seen the furnaces of the Bowery, the fires that burn in oil drums on zero nights. They may work in the financial district downtown and never see the extravagant plantings of Rockefeller Center—the daffodils and grape hyacinths and birches and the flags trimmed to the wind on a fine morning in spring. Or they may work in a midtown office and may let a whole year swing round without sighting Governors Island from the sea wall. The commuter dies with tremendous mileage to his credit, but he is no rover. His entrances and exits are more devious than those in a prairie-dog village; and he calmly plays bridge while buried in the mud at the bottom of the East River. The Long Island Road alone carried forty million commuters last year; but many of them were the same fellow retracing his steps.

The terrain of New York is such that a resident sometimes travels farther, in the end, than a commuter. Irving Berlin's journey from Cherry Street in the lower East Side to an apartment uptown was through an alley and was only three or four miles in length; but it was like going three times around the world.

SUGGESTIONS FOR WRITING

Write a composition using classification or division as the overall pattern of thought and structure. You may describe each type or each part fully, or you may follow the pattern of "The Three New Yorks" and emphasize one type. Your purpose likely will be exposition—to make clear.

SUGGESTED TOPICS

Popular TV shows
Kinds of people on a bus or subway/waiting in a line/shopping in a grocery store
The different "cities" that make up your community
Kinds of pollution
The different reasons people have for going to college
Requirements for being a good athlete / golfer / tennis player / shortstop
Marks of a radical / liberal / conservative
TV watchers
Kinds of automobile drivers
A mature person

Narration

Often we want to tell about the things that happen to us. Sometimes we just narrate the event for entertainment's sake. If so, the purpose is straight narration. More often, we see the incident as making some point, as illustrating or revealing some principle of life. If so, the purpose is exposition or argument. We relate the event, but the significant thing is the point made. The event itself is explanation or evidence.

Our concern here is to use narration to make a point. In writing a composition, in processing your own experience, keep two principles in mind.

1. Relate the incident Don't just tell *about* the event. Make it happen before the reader. Tell the event itself by lining a series of small events in a time sequence and relating them with vivid details. You may wish to use dialogue, but you don't have to. You may use a strong narrative line, as in the following narration, "Love and an Apple," or you may take a milder biographical approach, as in "The Watermelon" (p. 19). The incident may be autobiographical, something that happened to you; or it may be observational, your observation of something happening to somebody else.

2. Make a point Don't stop at telling what happened. Point out an insight, a realization, a principle of general human experience. Your first purpose is to be expository or persuasive—to get across an idea. The narrated event is secondary; it offers further explanation or gives evidence.

The point may be direct or indirect. You may comment at the beginning, the middle, or the end as to the meaning of the incident. Or, if you arrange your details carefully, you can let the meaning just be suggested by the narration.

In "Love and an Apple," the meaning is suggested by the tone and arrangement of details. We can formulate the central idea something like this: "Though a man tries to reach out to people with love, most people are so alienated and afraid of difference that they reject the offer." In "The Watermelon," an incident is related first, and the central idea is stated in the last sentence: "All animosities were buried and the simple fact of meeting a familiar face . . . was sufficient to make us forget. . . ."

The thought process of narration provides a manageable plan for a whole composition. Once you've thought through your personal experience, your composition follows a chronological order. You tell the event and you make a point either directly or indirectly. If you can tell time and if anything has ever happened to you, you can write a well-organized composition.

Love and an Apple

ARTHUR UNGER

The little man wearing a stocking cap stood in the middle of the Fifth Avenue bus, drinking from a jar. He sighed, then placed a cover loosely on the jar.

"Pure spring water," he reassured the other passengers. "Unless, of course, they're now putting something in it."

He began to shake the jar, sprinkling the floor of the bus with his pure spring water.

When he looked at me, I turned away. After all, the recommended treatment for big-city "crazies" is: never let them catch your eye.

"Wet down the dust . . ." he muttered to himself as he sprinkled.

Nobody in the bus dared look him straight in the eye, although he kept trying to make eye contact as he wandered about. The passengers didn't even dare look at each other for fear there would be smiles and laughter which might encourage an intimacy, provoke an incident.

Out of the corner of my eye, I saw the little man remove an apple from a brown paper sack, carefully wash it with the spring water, then cut it into edible bits. He ate the pieces with loud sighs of joy and appreciation.

Then, he took a seat by the door, his arm dangling in the exit trough like a child preparing to reach for the golden ring on a carrousel.

When the bus stopped within range of a litter basket on the street, as the door opened he managed to toss the apple core into the basket without moving from his seat.

He smiled to himself as he applauded his own markmanship.

"Littering is a dirty habit," he muttered.

Then, he stood up and began to jog slowly around the bus, every now and then stopping to look deeply into the determinedly unseeing eyes of the non-spectators. Nobody offered him any direct-contact satisfaction so he jogged back to the center of the bus.

"Exercise," he observed, "exercise to keep in shape."

He grasped two handles hanging from the ceiling railings on either side of the bus and managed to lift his whole tiny body up in the air, extending his legs gymnast-style, trying desperately to make a complete 360-degree flip, finally giving up and lowering his legs.

"That should discourage the muggers," he said, undiscouraged.

Suddenly, a look of despair came over his face and he bent down, tightened the lid of the jar and placed it in the brown paper bag. As he walked to the exit door he seemed to be making one last effort to contact the other passengers . . . but still nobody acknowledged his visibility.

The bus stopped, the door opened, and he stepped down onto the city street. Just before the door closed, he doffed his cap in a dramatic sweeping gesture and softly communicated a message.

"Love . . ." he said.

The bus moved on.

I turned to watch him on the street. It seemed safe to see him at this point. He was opening his jar to take one last sip.

Inside the bus there was a communal sigh of relief. All the "sane" people went back to reading newspapers and the graffiti on the walls, once again safely isolated in their hard plastic seats.

When I got up to leave, I noticed the dust was not flying about the floor anymore. And there was a sad, crisp smell of apple in the air.

The Watermelon

MARK TWAIN

On the summit we overtook an emigrant train of many wagons, many tired men and women, and many a disgusted sheep and cow. In the woefully dusty horseman in charge of the expedition I recognized John ———. Of all persons in the world to meet on top of the Rocky Mountains thousands of miles from home, he was the last one I should have looked for. We were schoolboys together and warm friends for years. But a boyish prank of mine had disrupted this friendship and it had never been renewed. The act of which I speak was this. I had been accustomed to visit occasionally an editor whose room was in the third story of a building and overlooked the street. One day this editor gave me a watermelon which I made preparations to devour on the spot, but chancing to look out of the window, I saw John standing directly under it and an irresistible desire came upon me to drop the melon on his head, which I immediately did. I was the loser, for it spoiled the melon, and John never forgave me and we dropped all intercourse and parted, but now met again under these circumstances.

We recognized each other simultaneously, and hands were grasped as warmly as if no coldness had ever existed between us, and no allusion was made to any. All animosities were buried and the simple fact of meeting a familiar face in that isolated spot so far from home, was sufficient to make us forget all things but pleasant ones, and we parted again with sincere "good-byes" and "God bless you" from both.

SUGGESTIONS FOR WRITING

Narrate an incident which revealed or demonstrated to you something about yourself, or others, or life in general. You can either state your point directly as in "The Watermelon," or you can so arrange the details as to let the incident speak for itself, as in "Love and an Apple."

SUGGESTED TOPICS

I realized how much people really need others when . . .

Observing two people having an argument

When I faced an emergency

Learning the hard way

A person shows another side of himself under pressure / in a restaurant / on an airplane

The difficulty of understanding parents

An incident in my childhood that is still with me

Method Analysis

Method analysis explains how something is done or made. We ask the questions: "How is it made?" "How do you do it?" At its simplest, it gives instructions or directions on how to accomplish a certain end. It may tell how to play a game, how to get to Jonesville, how to dress a wound, how to transplant a kidney, how to develop a backhand in tennis, how to win an election, how to win a war, how to develop a good memory, how to make friends.

Method analysis usually follows one of two patterns, according to your specific subject.

1. A sequence of events This traces definite steps that follow one another in chronological order, such as "How to Make a Cake."

2. A list of actions or techniques This is a set of methods made up of different actions or techniques which may take any order, such as "How to Make Friends."

With either pattern you may have to group or classify many small actions or steps into a few large ones. For instance, making a jacket may take 30 to 60 separate actions, but the process will probably be clearer if you think in three blocks:

1. Cutting out the pattern (with substeps)
2. Sewing the basic jacket (with substeps)
3. Making finishing touches (with substeps)

In the following essay, "All Choked Up," the author starts with an introductory paragraph to indicate the importance of the method he is going to explain. Paragraph 2 describes the method in two large blocks: (1) getting the proper hold and (2) exerting the proper pressure. Paragraph 3 gives two variations of the method for different situations.

In structure, method analysis is a combination of the two preceding patterns—classification and division and sequence in time. It provides a workable plan for the whole composition. The conclusion is inevitable. You know where you are going and when to stop. The usual purpose is expository. If you can count, if you can tell time, and if you have ever done or made anything, you can write a well-organized composition.

All Choked Up

ANTHONY WOLFF

Even these days not all medical advances involve sophisticated laboratory research or high technology. Indeed, a recent addition to the arsenal of do-it-yourself first-aid remedies promises to save as many lives as do some of the more elaborate examples of medical magic offered in modern hospitals. Called the "Heimlich maneuver" after Dr. Henry J. Heimlich, the Cincinnati surgeon who developed it, the simple new technique offers immediate aid to a victim who is choking on a foreign object and might well die before professional help arrives.

The traditional anti-choking procedure prescribed pounding the victim soundly on the back in the hope of knocking the offending object loose. Instead, Dr. Heimlich recommends that the person rendering aid put both arms around the choking victim from the rear, with one hand in a fist against the choker's upper abdomen between the navel and the bottom of the rib cage. With the other hand on top of the fist, a quick bear hug, by which the fist is pulled upward into the abdomen, will raise the victim's diaphragm, compressing the lungs and forcing a burst of air through the trachea to expel the offending object.

If the victim has collapsed, the Heimlich maneuver can be performed by turning him on his back, kneeling astride his thighs, and placing the heel of one open hand on the upper abdomen with the other hand on top of it. A sharp push upward with both hands will expel the foreign object. If necessary, a choking person can even perform the maneuver on himself, pulling his own fist sharply and forcefully upward against his abdomen. In any case, the procedure should be repeated until the foreign object is ejected from the throat.

SUGGESTIONS FOR WRITING

Write a composition telling how to do or make something. Following the two basic rules of the thought process: (1) determine which structure is appropriate for your subject—a sequence of steps or a set of techniques; (2) then group the many steps or actions into a few large blocks.

SUGGESTED TOPICS

Operating a motion picture projector
How to develop a backhand
How to meet an emergency (snakebite, loss of a job, etc.)
Selling a person what he doesn't want
The making of a modern doctor
Training a dog
Overcoming an undesirable habit
A simple process of making enemies
How to tell a believable lie
Getting rid of an undesirable person
How to conserve energy
How to make friends

Comparison and Contrast

One of our most common thought processes is noting how two things are alike or different. We use comparison and contrast for three basic purposes:

1.   To explain two items   We may want to give information about both, such as comparing Italian films and Swedish films. The purpose is likely to be expository.

2.   To explain one item   We may want to clarify something unfamiliar by comparing it with the familiar, such as comparing puberty rites in New Guinea with a high-school graduation in Illinois. Here one term is used merely as a tool to shed light on the other. The purpose is likely to be expository.

3.   To show one item as better   We may want to show the superiority of one thing over another, such as the emotional control of men and of women. With this form the purpose is probably persuasive. Making choices and establishing values require comparison and contrast. We use these methods when we decide which record to buy, which course to take, or which career to pursue.

When you use comparison and contrast as a structure for a whole composition, there are two basic patterns of arranging the materials. You may describe all the features of item A and then follow it with all the similar or differing features of item B. The pattern is $A_{1,2,3}$—$B_{1,2,3}$. The second pattern is to alternate the points of comparison between A and B. The pattern is A_1, B_1, A_2, B_2, and so on.

In a detailed comparison of two automobiles, for example, you might describe the Ford in terms of cost, comfort, performance, and durability, and then do exactly the same thing for the Chevy. Or you might compare the cost of the Ford with that of the Chevy, then the comfort, the performance, and the durability. The two simple outlines would be like this.

FORD AND CHEVY

I. Ford
   A. Cost
   B. Comfort
   C. Performance
   D. Durability

II. Chevy
   A. Cost
   B. Comfort
   C. Performance
   D. Durability

FORD AND CHEVY

I. Cost
   A. Ford
   B. Chevy

II. Comfort
   A. Ford
   B. Chevy

III. Performance
   A. Ford
   B. Chevy

IV. Durability
   A. Ford
   B. Chevy

Whichever pattern you use, check these points.

1. *Stick to the same principle of comparison* Be consistent. Give both subjects similar treatment. Points discussed for one subject should be discussed for the other.
2. *Select significant points* The points of comparison should be significant. That is, they should contribute to your purpose.
3. *Be complete* All of the significant points should be discussed. Don't leave out a main point of comparison.

The following essay, "The Rebel and the Revolutionary," uses comparison and contrast to show that one thing is superior to another. The author contrasts the revolutionary and the rebel to show that the rebel is better for society. The author's purpose is persuasive.

The pattern here is $A_1 B_1$. The rebel and the revolutionary are compared through one principle of comparison: the attitude toward political change.

The two introductory paragraphs assert the value of the rebel. Paragraph 3 describes the revolutionary, and paragraph 4 describes the rebel. Paragraphs 5 and 6 bring the two together to argue for the superiority of the rebel.

The Rebel and the Revolutionary

ROLLO MAY

In the present day, when multitudes of people are caught in anxiety and helplessness, they tend psychologically to freeze up and to cast out of the city walls whoever would disturb their pretended peace. Ironically, it is during just those periods of transition when they most need the replenishing that the rebel can give them that people have the greatest block in listening to him.

But in casting out the rebel, we cut our own lifeline. For the rebel function is necessary as the life-blood of culture, as the very roots of civilization.

First I must make the important distinction between the rebel and the revolutionary. One is in ineradicable opposition to the other. The revolutionary seeks an external political change, "the overthrow or renunciation of one government or ruler and the substitution of another." The origin of the term is the world *revolve,* literally meaning a turnover, as the revolution of a wheel. When the conditions under a given government are insufferable some groups may seek to break down that government in the conviction that any new form cannot but be better. Many revolutions, however, simply substitute one kind of government for another, the second no better than the first—which leaves the individual citizen, who has had to endure the inevitable anarchy between the two, worse off than before. Revolution may do more harm than good.

The rebel, on the other hand, is "one who opposes authority or restraint: one who breaks with established custom or tradition." His distinguishing characteristic is his perpetual restlessness. He seeks above all an internal change, a change in the attitudes, emotions, and outlook of the people to whom he is devoted. He often seems to be temperamentally unable to accept success and the ease it brings; he kicks against the pricks, and when one frontier is conquered, he soon becomes ill-at-ease and pushes on to the new frontier. He is drawn to the unquiet minds and spirits, for he shares their everlasting inability to accept stultifying control. He may, as Socrates did, refer to himself as the gadfly for the state—the one who keeps the state from settling down into a complacency, which is the first step toward decadence. No matter how much the rebel gives the appearance of being egocentric or of being on an "ego trip," this is a delusion; inwardly the authentic rebel is anything but brash.

True to the meaning of the rebel as one who renounces authority, he seeks primarily not the substitution of one political system for another. He may favor such political change, but it is not his chief goal. He rebels for the sake of a vision of life and society which he is convinced is critically important for himself and his fellows. Every act of rebellion tacitly presupposes some value. Whereas the revolutionary tends to collect power around himself, the rebel does not seek power as an end and has little facility for using it; he tends to share his power. Like the resistance fighters in France during the last world war, the rebel fights not only for the relief of his fellow men but also for his personal integrity. For him these are but two sides of the same coin.

The slave who kills his master is an example of the revolutionary. He can then only take his master's place and be killed in turn by later revolutionaries. But the rebel is the one who realizes that the master is as much imprisoned, if not as painfully, as he is by the institution of slavery; he rebels against that system which permits slaves and masters. His rebellion, if successful, saves the master also from the indignity of owning slaves.

SUGGESTIONS FOR WRITING

Write a composition using comparison and contrast. You may wish to show the superiority of one thing over another, or you may want to clarify one or both items. Choose and shape your subject accordingly.

SUGGESTED TOPICS

The working conditions of two jobs
The value of two careers
Two kinds of home life
Two different people you know
How the actor and the athlete are alike
The liberal and the conservative
The practical person and the idealist
The traditional woman and the liberated woman
The ghetto and the suburb
Two towns

Description

Effective description brings a subject to life as if the reader were there. The subject can be a sports arena, a bug, a person, a restaurant full of people, a thunderstorm, a traffic accident, or anything that can be perceived by the five senses or imagined. It is as if the writer were saying, "I have seen something worth seeing and I want you to see it too and feel what I felt about it."

To bring a subject to life, description makes use of two techniques:

1. Using concrete details It is the use of the five senses which puts the reader on the scene. In the examples below, notice what difference is made by sense words and specific, concrete details.

She worked in her flower bed, digging around in it and looking over the plants. She always saw to it that no bugs or other pests got into her flowers.

She took off a glove and put her strong fingers down into the forest of new green chrysanthemum sprouts that were growing around the old roots. She spread the leaves and looked down among the close-growing stems. No aphids were there, no sowbugs or snails or cutworms. Her terrier fingers destroyed such pests before they could get started.

—John Steinbeck, "The Chrysanthemums"

2. <u>Creating a dominant impression</u> Don't try to tell everything about a subject. Instead select details and arrange them to give a specific impression, a particular point of view, or a controlling idea.

The following essay, "River Scene," illustrates the two principles of using concrete details and creating a dominant impression. Twain describes the same river scene in two different ways to give two different impressions.

The details in paragraph 1 create an impression of romance and beauty. The same scene is described in paragraph 2, but the details are shaped to give an impression of danger.

Description in general is used in two different ways. Sometimes it is used independently to recreate a scene that is worth sharing for itself alone. More often it is a part of a composition in which another type of writing dominates—exposition, persuasion, or narration. "River Scene" uses the contrasting descriptions to support the author's controlling idea that one loses a sense of "romance and glory" by "learning his trade." Notice that the central idea is expressed throughout—in paragraph 1, sentences 1–4; in paragraph 2, sentence 3; and in paragraph 3, the first and last sentences. The contrasting descriptions are examples to prove the point.

Writing effective description is not easy. It is not the work of a lazy mind. It takes an alert mind, sharp perception, and the willingness to search for the concrete word to described the subject. But if you can see and hear and if you can keep your mind awake, you can write effective description.

River Scene

MARK TWAIN

Now when I had mastered the language of this water and had come to know every trifling feature that bordered the great river as familiarly as I knew the letters of the alphabet, I had made a valuable acquisition. But I had lost something, too. I had lost something which could never be restored to me while I lived. All the grace, the beauty, the poetry, had gone out of the majestic river! I still kept in mind a certain wonderful sunset which I witnessed when steamboating was new to me. A broad expanse of the river was turned to blood; in the middle distance the red hue brightened into gold, through which a solitary log came floating, black and conspicuous; in one place a long, slanting mark lay sparkling upon the water; in another the surface was broken by boiling, tumbling rings, that were as many-tinted as an opal; where the ruddy flush was faintest, was a smooth spot that was covered with graceful circles and radiating lines, ever so delicately traced; the shore on our left was densely wooded and the somber shadow that fell from this forest was broken in one place by a long, ruffled trail that shone like silver; and high above the forest wall a clean-stemmed dead tree waved a single leafy bough that flowed like a flame in the unobstructed splendor that was flowing from the sun. There were graceful curves, reflected images, woody heights, soft distances, and over the whole scene, far and near, the dissolving lights drifted steadily, enriching it every passing moment with new marvels of coloring.

I stood like one bewitched. I drank it in, in a speechless rapture. The world was new to me and I had never seen anything like this at home. But as I have said, a day came when I began to cease from noting the glories and the charms which the moon and the sun and the twilight wrought upon the river's face; another day came when I ceased altogether to note them. Then, if that sunset scene had been repeated, I should have looked upon it without rapture, and should have commented upon it inwardly after this fashion: "This sun means that we are going to have wind to-morrow; that floating log means that the river is rising, small thanks to it; that slanting mark on the water refers to a bluff reef which is going to kill somebody's steamboat one of these nights, if it keeps on stretching out like that; those tumbling 'boils' show a dissolving bar and a changing channel there; the lines and circles in the slick water over yonder are a warning that that troublesome place is shoaling up dangerously; that silver streak in the shadow of the forest is the 'break' from a new snag and he has located himself in the very best place he could have found to fish for steamboats; that tall dead tree, with a single living branch, is not going to last long, and then how is a body ever going to get through this blind place at night without the friendly old landmark?"

No, the romance and beauty were all gone from the river. All the value any feature of it had for me now was the amount of usefulness it could furnish toward compassing the safe piloting of a steamboat. Since those days, I have pitied doctors from my heart. What does the lovely flush in a beauty's cheek mean to a doctor but a "break" that ripples above some deadly disease? Are not all her visible charms sown thick with what are to him the signs and symbols of hidden decay? Does he ever see her beauty at all, or doesn't he simply view her professionally and comment upon her unwholesome condition all to himself? And doesn't he sometimes wonder whether he has gained most or lost most of learning his trade?

SUGGESTIONS FOR WRITING

Describe a scene to bring it to life. You may use many kinds of concrete details about objects, activities, or people, but select them to give some dominant impression to support some idea.

SUGGESTED TOPICS

A busy street corner
Then and now: returning to a place after a long absence
A pet
Downtown at six in the morning and at five in the afternoon
The characters in a hotel lobby / a restaurant / a waiting room
A scene in nature
A person you know
A holiday dinner / surprise party / picnic

Tracing Causes and Effects

Among our most frequent questions are "Why?" "What brought this on?" and "What is going to come out of this?" In more specific terms it is "What drove Jane Bond to drink?" "Why did Tom Hooper beat up his wife?" "What makes the sky blue?" "What is going to happen to the world if we don't decrease the population growth?"

The thinking process behind these questions is causal analysis. We are seeking to locate and explain the causes or consequences of a given act, feeling, idea, condition, or event. We are trying to make sense of our world.

Tracing causes and effects may take any of several patterns. You may classify a list of causes or effects. You may establish the cause and effect connection between two events, showing how one directly caused the other. Or you may trace a whole chain of events in which A is the cause of B, which is the cause of C, which is the cause of D, etc. Or you may show how several otherwise unrelated events converge to cause something.

Analyzing causes and effects can be very complex. A given event, such as young man's robbing a gas station, may have a chain of causes reaching back several generations and may have consequences reaching far into the future. Also, a given event may have several causes or consequences, not just one. What looks at first like a significant cause may be very minor or might not be a cause at all, such as the old medical belief that letting blood was a cause of a person's recovering health.

Check these guides to help you think clearly about causes and effects.

1. Distinguish immediate cause from remote cause　What caused the death of Tim Johnson, who died in an automobile accident? The most immediate cause was brain concussion. A less immediate cause was the oil slick on the road that caused the car to slide out of control. Another less immediate cause was his heavy drinking, which led to an argument with his wife, which shook him up so much that he couldn't control his car. An even more remote cause was the pampering he received as a child from his mother, which made it difficult for him cope with the problems of adult living, including his wife, and so on. A written analysis might logically stop at any point, of course, depending entirely upon your purpose.

2. Look for several causes　As you analyze causes and effects, don't fasten immediately on the first one that comes to mind and decide there is only one cause or one effect. There are probably several, all at once or in a sequence. It is likely hasty thinking to conclude that a young man took up hard drugs for one reason—to gain acceptance with the group. It is likewise shallow thinking to say that a divorce was caused by the wife's heavy drinking.

3. Don't leave out any links in a sequence　If you leave one link out of a chain of causes and effects, the reader may be lost. For example, a cause and effect series could run something like this.

Business losses depress the boss; boss nags secretary; secretary nags husband; ugly home scene drives son to gang; gang tests son; son robs gas station; police catch son; son ends up in jail.

If we leave out one link, such as "ugly home scene drives son to gang," we could not get a true account of the important events and conditions that led to the boy's ending up in jail.

4. Don't confuse causal relationship with time relationship　In logic, this error is called the *post hoc ergo propter hoc* fallacy. ("after this;

therefore because of this.") Just because one event happened at the same time or just after another event does not necessarily mean that the one caused the other. Your losing your wallet shortly after a black cat crossed your path was not likely to have been caused by the black cat. Many an incumbent politician campaigns by saying, "These glorious things occurred because I was in office." The truth of the matter is often that those things occurred not because but *while* he was in office, and he himself had little or no causal connection in producing them.

The following article, "Harvest of the Seasons," traces a sequence of causes of the change from nomad life to village agriculture. The big stages are from wild wheat to Emmer to bread wheat to agriculture. The wild wheat with its small 14-chromosome grains that scattered in the wind crossed with a goat grass of 14 chromosomes to make Emmer, a larger 28-chromosome grain that still scattered in the wind. Emmer crossed with another 14-chromosome goat grass to make bread wheat, an even plumper 42 chromosome grain that did not scatter in the wind, but had to be planted. The need for planting and harvesting brought about the need for permanent settlement. Hence village agriculture.

Harvest of the Seasons

J. BRONOWSKI

The largest single step in the ascent of man is the change from nomad to village agriculture. What made that possible? An act of will by men, surely; but with that, a strange and secret act of nature. In the burst of new vegetation at the end of the Ice Age, a hybrid wheat appeared in the Middle East. It happened in many places: a typical one is the ancient oasis of Jericho.

Jericho is older than agriculture. The first people who came here and settled by the spring in this otherwise desolate ground were people who harvested wheat, but did not yet know how to plant it. We know this because they made tools for the wild harvest, and that is an extraordinary piece of foresight. They made sickles out of flint which have survived; John Garstang found them when he was digging here in the 1930s. The ancient sickle edge would have been set in a piece of gazelle horn, or bone.

There no longer survives, up on the hill or tel and its slopes, the kind of wild wheat that the earliest inhabitants harvested. But the grasses that are still here must look very like the wheat that they found, that they gathered for the first time by the fistful, and cut with that sawing motion of the sickle that reapers have used for all the ten thousand years since then. That was the Natufian pre-agricultural civilisation. And, of course, it could not last. It was on the brink of becoming agriculture. And that was the next thing that happened on the Jericho tel.

The turning-point to the spread of agriculture in the Old World was almost certainly the occurrence of two forms of wheat with a large, full head of seeds. Before 8000 BC wheat was not the luxuriant plant it is today; it was merely one of many wild grasses that spread throughout the Middle East. By some genetic accident, the wild wheat crossed with a natural goat grass and formed a fertile hybrid. That accident must have happened many times in the springing vegetation that came up after the last Ice Age. In terms of the genetic machinery that directs growth, it combined the fourteen chromosomes of wild wheat with the fourteen chromosomes of goat grass, and produced Emmer with twenty-eight chromosomes. That is what makes Emmer so much plumper. The hybrid was able to spread naturally, because its seeds are attached to the husk in such a way that they scatter in the wind.

For such a hybrid to be fertile is rare but not unique among plants. But now the story of the rich plant life that followed the Ice Ages becomes more surprising. There was a second genetic accident, which may have come about because Emmer was already cultivated. Emmer crossed with another natural goat grass and produced a still larger hybrid with forty-two chromosomes, which is bread wheat. That was improbable enough in itself, and we know now that bread wheat would not have been fertile but for a specific genetic mutation on one chromosome.

Yet there is something even stranger. Now we have a beautiful ear of wheat, but one which will never spread in the wind because the ear is too tight to break up. And if I do break it up, why, then the chaff flies off and every grain falls exactly where it grew. Let me remind you, that is quite different from the wild wheats or from the first, primitive hybrid, Emmer. In those primitive forms the ear is much more open, and if the ear breaks up then you get quite a different effect—you get grains which will fly in the wind. The bread wheats have lost that ability. Suddenly, man and the plant have come together. Man has a wheat that he lives by, but the wheat also thinks that man was made for him because only so can it be propagated. For the bread wheats can only multiply with help; man must harvest the ears and scatter their seeds; and the life of each, man and the plant, depends on the other. It is a true fairy tale of genetics, as if the coming of civilization had been blessed in advance by the spirit of the abbot Gregor Mendel.

SUGGESTIONS FOR WRITING

Write a composition in which you analyze a causal relationship. You may organize your ideas in any of several ways. You may work from cause to effect, or from effect back to cause. You may trace a long sequence, work with single causes or effects, or analyze several causes and effects. Observe the four principles for clear thinking about causes and effects.

SUGGESTED TOPICS

Polluting our waters
Buying a particular car
What causes a headache?
What makes the colorful sunset?
Student cheating
Increase in crime
A dispute between two people
Losing a job
Getting sick
Current general attitudes toward political leadership / voting
Alcoholism
A teenager's running away from home
The popularity of a certain fad or fashion

Interpreting the Meaning of Evidence

As beings with perception, imagination, reasoning power, and curiosity, we are constantly looking around us and drawing conclusions from what we see. Interpreting the meaning of evidence is a special form of exposition. It works with information and attempts to set forth a clear explanation as to what the information means. The purpose is to clarify.

The conclusion about the meaning of the evidence is also like argument in that it is an opinion or judgment, even though sound and unemotional. We accept the argument or the conclusion on the basis of evidence and a sound thought process.

There are three main rules of evidence:

1. Consider the evidence itself You must not start with a ready-made notion or conclusion and then dredge up evidence and force it to fit. Follow the evidence wherever it leads. To be reliable, evidence supporting a generalization or hypothesis must be (1) known or available, (2) sufficient, (3) relevant, and (4) representative.

2. Take the simplest interpretation The simplest conclusion that accounts for all the evidence is most likely to be correct because it is most like the interpretation that has before explained similar evidence. The odds are all for the simplest.

3. Consider all likely alternatives The simplest will probably be it, but it might not. Don't jump to conclusions. All likely explanations must at least be considered.

For further guides to interpreting the meaning of evidence, check Chapter 6 on "The Thought" (p. 114).

The following narration, "The Bicyclist," shows Sherlock Holmes making interpretations of the evidence he sees. It is a typical situation and thought process that all of us continually experience as we observe other people.

The next essay, "The Driftwood on the Ice," uses a more extensive thought process. It proceeds in an objective, scientific manner. Beginning with the evidence of a piece of driftwood on an ice floe off the coast of Greenland, Nansen's mind moves from observation, to hypothesis, to elimination of alternatives, to experimental verification. He makes use of other knowledge to support his interpretive process. Following his careful thinking, we tend to agree that his interpretation of the evidence is valid.

The Bicyclist

ARTHUR CONAN DOYLE

With a resigned air and a somewhat weary smile, Holmes begged the beautiful intruder to take a seat, and to inform us what it was that was troubling her.

"At least it cannot be your health," said he, as his keen eyes darted over her; "so ardent a bicyclist must be full of energy."

She glanced down in surprise at her own feet, and I observed the slight roughening of the side of the sole caused by the friction of the edge of the pedal.

"Yes, I bicycle a good deal, Mr. Holmes. . . ."

My friend took the lady's ungloved hand, and examined it with as close an attention and as little sentiment as a scientist would show to a specimen.

"You will excuse me, I am sure. It is my business," said he, as he dropped it. "I nearly fell into the error of supposing you were typewriting. Of course, it is obvious that it is music. You observe the spatulate finger-ends, Watson, which is common to both professions? There is a spirituality about the face, however" —she gently turned it towards the light—"which the typewriter does not generate. This lady is a musician."

"Yes, Mr. Holmes, I teach music."

"In the country, I presume, from your complexion."

"Yes sir, near Farnham, on the borders of Surrey."

The Driftwood on the Ice

HAROLD A. LARRABEE

While on a voyage in the sealing ship *Viking* to the Arctic Ocean in 1882, Fridtjof Nansen, then an ambitious twenty-one-year-old naturalist, who had gone along to learn something at first hand about the methods of marine research, noticed a piece of driftwood on a floe off the coast of Greenland. To the rest of the ship's company, the log meant nothing. To an Eskimo, it might have meant an added stick of valuable firewood. But to young Nansen's mind it posed a problem: What kind of wood was it? Where had it come from? Before Nansen stopped thinking and investigating, he had become the last man in history "to discover an ocean"; he had come nearer the North Pole than any other human being up to that time; and he had helped mightily in the founding of a new science, that of oceanography.

His first question about the driftwood was easily answered: it was some sort of pine. That ended his concern with that particular log of wood. For this simple step of classification made available a large amount of accumulated botanical information concerning the localities where pine trees do and do not grow. Nansen now had a basis for framing a number of possible answers to his second question. He knew, for example, that there were no pine trees on Greenland, Iceland, or Spitzbergen; so those points of origin could be eliminated. There were, however, plenty of pine trees in North America, Norway, and Siberia. But the question remained: from which of these three countries could the driftwood have come by the aid of an ocean current and borne on *top* of a cake of floating ice? From his personal knowledge of the normal behavior of driftwood and floes, Nansen was reasonably sure that the log had not climbed aboard the floating ice. Therefore, it must have fallen upon the ice from somewhere along the shore. That meant, he deduced, that it had come from a land with pine trees growing near the shore, and with offshore formations of floating ice.

His next step was to try out successively in his mind the North America, the Norway, and the Siberia hypotheses. He knew that the Gulf Stream came northward from the southern coast of North America, where there were pine trees, but no ice. Norway's shores were likewise pine-clad but ice-free; so both of those hypotheses could be eliminated. That left Sibera, which had both pine trees and offshore floes. The log, he conjectured, must have been brought from the eastern Siberian coast to Greenland by a hitherto-unknown drift current across the Arctic regions, which might well be one great ocean. Nansen's theory was scoffed at as absurd, although it was soon powerfully reinforced by other evidence, especially by the finding of unmistakable relics, on floating ice off the southwest coast of Greenland, of the American polar ship *Jeanette*, which had been wrecked north of the New Siberian Islands three years before. In an address before the Christiania Geographical Society in February, 1890, Nansen summed up his reasons for believing that "a current flows at some point between the Pole and Franz Joseph Land from the Siberian Arctic Sea to the east coast of Greenland"; and announced his plan to prove his theory in a spectacular fashion by drifting across the polar sea in a ship carried only by the slowly moving ice pack. This "illogical scheme of self-destruction" was hailed as "sheer madness" by most of the contemporary authorities on Arctic exploration; but they were silenced by the famous voyage of the *Fram* (1893–96) from the coast of Siberia to a point near Spitzbergen, propelled solely by the ocean current beneath the ice in which the stout ship had been frozen fast. Few men have seen their theories more triumphantly vindicated than did Nansen. His train of thought and observation, starting from the driftwood on the ice, not only revolutionized the technique of polar exploration; but also established the essential characteristics of the Arctic Ocean, thus paving the way for wholly unforeseen results of great practical importance in solving the future problems of weather prediction, of the sealing industry, and of Arctic transportation.

SUGGESTIONS FOR WRITING

Describe some experience you had in forming a hypothesis about the meaning of evidence.

SUGGESTED TOPICS

A person with a contradictory item of wearing apparel
A rickety automobile in the driveway of a luxurious house
The police escorting someone out of a department store
A person's certain way of life or peculiar habit
How a crime was solved
What was making the noise at night?
What was wrong with the car?
Why is a certain person depressed / elated / angry?
The cause of an illness
The commotion on the ball field
One quiet person in a noisy gang
An abandoned car

Validating an Opinion

"But that's just an opinion," we hear, as if opinions in themselves were bad. True enough, an opinion is not a fact, and facts are definite and fairly easy to come by, while a valid opinion is hard to come by and is never actually positive.

Nevertheless, we must form good opinions if we are not to make a mess of our lives. The actions, situations, and conditions of our lives are governed primarily by opinion. Is that a fair price? Is this a good buy? Is this a good person to marry? Is that the right job to take? Is this the proper treatment for the illness? We must form opinions and act on them. But there are good opinions and bad opinions, or, rather, sound opinions and shaky opinions.

In trying to persuade others of the validity of your opinion, you must avoid such pitfalls as prejudice, wish-fulfillment, hope, and other emotional considerations. You must avoid irrelevant thought processes. You might momentarily persuade emotional people by bombast and appeal to their prejudices, but with intelligent and alert people, you must use precise terms, solid evidence, and sound reasoning.

1. Precise terms Vague, ambiguous terms will leave the reader vague. Useful discussion is impossible unless there is a clear agreement on the meaning of terms. When a shrewd car dealer has just cheated a car buyer and excuses it by saying, "Business is business," we are not persuaded of his purity. The word "business" is ambiguous, and the car dealer is using it to mean two different things. The first "business" seems to mean the practice "buying and selling for profit" and the second seems to mean something like "anything you can get away with."

In a thinking process like the following, the thinker has lost control of the meaning of the terms.

> People should change their prejudiced attitudes towards race since no race is inferior; in fact, some are superior.

2. Evidence A large number of verifiable and relevant facts, carefully interpreted, must be used to form a reliable opinion or generalization. The following opinion as stated is unreliable because so far there are no verifiable or relevant facts to validate it.

> UFOs are ships from outer space.

The following opinion is not based on sufficient facts to be reliable.

> Puerto Ricans are no good. I know because there was a Puerto Rican family in our neighborhood for two years until we moved out.

You can't make a valid judgment on the basic of one family.

3. Sound reasoning The thought process underlying an opinion must be logical. The connection between your supporting ideas and the opinion you are validating must be clear and actual. The logic of the following opinion breaks down because no connection is established between the "third time" superstition and the skills required to pass a driver's test.

> Mary did not pass her driver's test the first two tries, but she'll pass this time because the third time's a charm.

Making careful use of precise terms, abundant evidence, and sound reasoning will not guarantee that others will accept your opinions, but you will certainly make your opinions valid enough that they cannot be overlooked easily.

In the following essay, "The Dimension of Experience," the author states a very unusual opinion, and then proceeds to make it quite believable by careful use of terms, evidence from experience, and sound reasoning. He distinguishes such important terms as "possibility," "chance," "fate," and "basis." He cites unforeseen experiences that he has been drawn to and shows that they are representative and typical of what could happen to all of us. His main line of reasoning is that because we have been drawn to such unforeseen experiences in the past, it is likely that we will be drawn to many similar unforeseen experiences in the future. We are drawn not because of fate or chance, but because we choose to follow what opens to us on the basis of its being loving, joyful, and universal.

From the author's use of terms, his evidence, and his sound reasoning, we are persuaded of the validity of his opinion: There is a distinct possibility that six years from now he will be sitting in a boat in the middle of the Indian Ocean.

The Dimension of Experience

PETER NOWELL

There is a distinct possibility that I will be sitting in a boat in the middle of the Indian Ocean six years from now. Six is a nice number, don't you think? It could just as well be two days or *fifty-six* years. Why the Indian Ocean? Well, I looked in my Atlas and determined that it is the farthest place from New Hampshire anywhere on the globe (which somehow makes it seem more un-likely). I have no particular desire to travel there. Nor do I have the slightest idea what I would be doing there. All I know is that it is a *distinct possibility.*

Sound ridiculous? I would be hard pressed to chart a series of events that would lead me to that remote corner of the earth. And, if I succeeded, the results might seem as absurd as the effort. So I will not insult your intelligence with such speculation.

The logic lies elsewhere. It is to be found in your own experience. Let's approach it this way:

Think back over the course of the last five years. Would you have imagined five years ago that you would experience all that you have since then? Do you have strong interests now in areas towards which you were once indifferent? Has a new job caused you to move across the country? Are there new friends in your life who have challenged some of your most cherished convictions? I'm sure you can think of many other such changes. Even if your outward circumstances have not changed appreciably, your ideas, goals, or desires may have changed a great deal.

Now, take the same sort of look at this last week, yesterday, or even the last hour. If you had spent two more minutes working in the garden instead of going shopping when you did, would you have missed meeting the "chance" acquaintance with whom you have now shared deep insights and far-reaching experiences? On the other hand, what you were thinking about in the garden might have led you into a totally different realm of experience—one equally rich and varied.

When I look back on my own life, I realize that it could have gone in any number of directions. There is the time I learned to play chess. A friend had been after me to play him a game for weeks before I finally agreed to try it. After he taught me the moves, there was rarely a day in the next four years that I did not either play or study the game. And then, just the other day, someone I just met mentioned the possibility of my working on an archaeological dig in Israel for six weeks. When I look at such an opportunity and think about the ideas, situations, and people that I would likely encounter, the ramifications are mind-boggling!

At various times in my childhood I considered becoming a baker, the President, an architect, and a writer. Only my interest in writing survived college and I might have made a career of it had not one of my college professors just happened to pull a little slip of paper out of his shirt pocket during a group discussion. He read from the slip about a job opening in a community-based rehabilitation program. I immediately felt right about this job even though I had never considered that line of work before. That is where I am working now. But where will I be next year?

I do not know. I do know that there are no doors closed either behind or ahead of me. Architecture and writing are as much a part of my experience as they ever were. Only my *focus* has changed.

Oh, I almost forgot. I have yet to explain how I could seriously imagine myself in the middle of the Indian Ocean. First, however, there are two nauseous notions I must dispel: chance and fate.

As chance would have it, such a possibility would be unlikely—to say the least. But what are the odds based on? How can one determine the likelihood of an event when there are an infinite number of possibilities? Chance is merely the belief that experience is limited in one way or another.

As for the theory of fate, I believe it was founded on fear of chance. Chance is a kind of chaos and it is little wonder that we would rather regard the events of our lives as part of a master plan. To be sure, there is a plan. But it is not a plan of human events. More accurately, it is a *basis*—a basis for our experience. We are not drawn to a particular experience: we are drawn to what is loving, joyful, and universal. And there are many experiences that fit that bill—not just one predetermined path. The options that we choose show how well we understand that basis.

So, my going to the Indian Ocean is not subject to chance nor is it a predetermined event. It is as possible as any other event that is in line with my thinking. For my experience is as wide, as exalted, as fruitful, as happy, as full of compassion, as my thought.

SUGGESTIONS FOR WRITING

Formulate an opinion and validate it through use of exact terms, abundant evidence carefully interpreted, and sound reasoning.

SUGGESTED TOPICS

American society is / is not dominated by women.
Welfare is wrong / right.
It makes sense to trust other people.
Ownership is not the way to happiness.
A wholesome society is based on cooperation, not competition.

Worry does no good.
To develop yourself is the reason for life.
The reasons for the breakdown in communication in our society
The values of formal learning
The values of practical experience
What good are sports?
Why music / art?
There is life on other planets.

Error and Truth

Pointing out error and putting truth in place of it is a special form of either exposition or argument. Much of our thinking deals with trying to distinguish error from truth, and much of our communication deals with exposing error and putting truth in its place. "That's wrong. Let me tell you how it really is." Errors may be of two kinds: errors of fact or errors of judgment.

Errors of fact, such as the belief that summer is hotter than winter because the sun is closer to the earth, can be easily cleared up. A new fact or a clear explanation may do it. You could point out that distance has little to do with it when we are talking about 92 million miles. You could explain that the earth is colder in winter mainly because the sun's rays come from a lower angle and therefore have to travel through more atmosphere which absorbs or lessens the degree of heat which gets through to the earth.

Errors of judgment, opinion, and attitude are harder to dislodge. Over a long time, they may be compounded on inaccurate information, twisted thinking, fantasy, and desire. For instance, some people have a hard time giving up the opinion that women are more emotional than men or that only men and not women are capable of running world affairs, although sound knowledge and valid thinking refute such errors. People resist giving up such errors of judgment because they are deeply rooted in emotions and twisted thinking.

The process of exposing and correcting errors in judgment requires forceful persuasion. You must use facts and information, careful interpretation, sound reasoning, and precise language.

The following essay, "The Emotional Woman," has a two-part structure. Paragraph 1 describes the common error that men control their emotions better than women do. Paragraphs 2 and 3 argue that the opinion is false—"All this is nonsense." Notice that the author does not merely restate his opinion or make forceful assertions. He uses careful explanation of terms, such as "emotional" and "control." He uses comparative figures on drinking, violent actions, and other emotional expressions. And he makes sound interpretation of the factual material.

The Emotional Woman

ASHLEY MONTAGU

The notion that women are emotionally weak and that men are emotionally strong is based on the same kind of reasoning as that which maintains that the female is physically inferior to the male because of the latter's greater muscular power. Trained in repression, or in the art of "schooling his emotions," as it is sometimes called, the male looks with disdain upon the female who expresses her feelings in tears and lamentations. Such behavior is in the male's estimation yet another proof of the female's general inferiority to the male; her greater emotionality is proof of her "lack of control." His own ability to control his emotions the male takes to be a natural endowment in himself which the female lacks.

All this is nonsense. In the first place it is more than questionable that women are less able to control their emotions than men. What most men—and, I fear, women, too—have overlooked is that men and women are taught to control and express different kinds of emotions. Thus, girls are taught that it is perfectly proper for them to cry but that they must never lose their tempers, and if they do they must on no account swear: it isn't ladylike. Boys, on the contrary, are taught that it is unmanly to cry, and that while it is not desirable to fly off the handle or to cuss, well, men have always done so. Girls may not express their emotions in violent ways; girls may not fight. Boys may—and do. Nineteenth-century ladies permitted themselves to swoon or call for the smelling salts; their twentieth-century descendants are likely to swear instead, and if they call for anything it is for a stiff drink. But then these twentieth-century descendants are obviously not ladies. Twentieth-century ladies still do not curse, and if they drink, though they are today at perfect liberty to drink what they wish, they still do not drink as men do. Though it is considered "manly" for men to drink, it is not considered "womanly" for a woman to do so. Women, in fact, don't drink nearly as much as men do, and, by comparison with the rates for men, they are seldom drunk. Alcoholism and deaths from alcoholism are enormously more frequent in men than in women. Here, indeed, is a very significant difference in emotional expression, for men drink—whatever they may claim to the contrary —largely for emotional reasons, much of the time because they are unhappy; and an enormous number of them are unable to control their drinking. Whatever the reasons may be, women are able to, and do, control their drinking incomparably more successfully than men. It is interesting to observe that about the only time many men are able to cry is when they are drunk, and it may be suspected that some of them get drunk in order to be able to do so. Crying is such a good way of letting off steam. The poor things obviously don't want to be as "controlled"—by masculine standards—as they must be when they are sober.

Women don't fight, don't curse, don't lose their tempers as often as men do; they seldom get drunk and exceedingly rarely commit acts of violence against other persons. Though quicker on the uptake, they do not jump to conclusions as hastily and unconsideredly as men. Women tend to avoid the trigger response of the male; as a result, they do not to off half-cocked as frequently as the male does. Women tend to keep their emotional balance better than men do. In short, women use their emotions a great deal more efficiently than men, and not in the "emotional" manner that men imply when they use the word disparagingly in connection with women. In this sense women are positively *less* emotional than men. In the accurate sense of the word, women are more emotional and have their emotions more effectively under control than do men. I am speaking, of course, in terms of the generality of women and men. There are exceptions to most rules in both sexes.

SUGGESTIONS FOR WRITING

Select what you consider some commonly held false opinion, expose the error, and point out the truth. Remember that with many opinions, it is possible to argue either way. Take a stand and state your case. Keep yourself on solid ground.

SUGGESTED TOPICS

Men are stronger than women.
Competitive sports build character.
The women's liberation is / is not a trivial movement.
The present educational system adequately educates.
Crime does not pay.
Honesty is the best policy.
A successful society must be based on competition.
All parents love their children.
Athletes are not good students.
Making money is the way to happiness.
Dogs / horses are among the most intelligent of animals.

Problem and Solution

Presenting a problem and offering a solution is a special form of argument, that is, of validating an opinion. It is used so frequently that it deserves special attention. The record player won't work; you need more money for clothes; your neighbor's barking dog keeps you awake at night; you are making low grades in mathematics. We continually have problems to solve. In solving problems, we should keep in mind five principles.

1. See the problem clearly Make sure you have pin-pointed the right problem. For instance, you complain to your dormitory supervisor that you have a sore throat because of the uneven temperature of your room. The supervisor sends you to the health center and you tell the doctor what you think your trouble is. He grunts and checks nose, throat, chest, pulse. He clarifies your problem not as a sore throat because of the temperature of your room, but as throat irritation from too much cigarette smoking. The problem clarified, the doctor can work out a solution with you—give up smoking, cut down on smoking, switch to a milder brand, get some throat medication.

2. Consider alternate solutions Don't settle right off for the first solution that comes to mind. Consider all possibilities to arrive at the best.

Dropping the course is not the only solution to the problem of your low grade in math. You should consider such other likely alternatives such as studying more, attending class, and getting a tutor.

3.   Figure the consequences   Before you put a certain solution into operation, you must consider the possible consequences or side effects in order not to produce new problems worse than the original one. A solution to the problem of your lack of money for new clothes is to rob an all-night food store. A solution to the problem of the neighbor's barking dog is to poison the dog. These solutions would solve the problems of finance and sleep, but the consequences would probably create new and worse problems.

4   Be sure the solution is real   You would not solve the problem of snakebite by killing the snake or by bandaging the wound. Again, it is not a real solution to say that the problem of the fighting among members of a family would be solved if they just loved one another more. Not fighting is one of the things that loving means. You would just have to work at the problem of how to make the people concerned more lovable and more loving.

5   Find a solution that's workable   A solution to the problem of your broken record player is to buy a new record player. That would solve the problem. But it's not a workable solution if you lack money to buy a new record player. You will have to find another solution that is feasible.

For a composition on problem and solution, a single two-part structure is usually easiest. First, state the problem and give enough details to show that the problem exists. Then state the solution, indicating that it would indeed be a practicable solution.

The following essay, "Surviving the Cities," uses a basic two-part structure. Paragraphs 1 through 4 state the problem and its significance, using an analogy of an experiment with rats. Paragraphs 5 and 6 give a solution, with enough details for us to see its workability.

Surviving the Cities
CARL ROGERS

Our large urban centers are seemingly ungovernable, choking on their own traffic, becoming insufferable garbage-littered ghettos, and rapidly becoming financially as well as psychologically bankrupt. Yet, according to the British economist Barbara Ward, by the year 2000 some 80 percent of us will be living in such cities.

In this incredible influx into the cities, it might be well to consider some lessons learned from a study of rats. John Calhoun designed an experiment in which one dominant male rat could keep any others from entering some sections of the experimental area. But no rat could dominate the central section. All the rats in every area had sufficient food and water and could breed as they wished.

The rats multiplied, of course, but in the areas controlled by a dominant male, overcrowding was not excessive. In the central uncontrolled area, there was serious overcrowding accompanied by poor mothering, poor nest building, high infant mortality, bizarre sexual behavior, cannibalism and often complete alienation. More ominous still, the central area, with all its bad conditions, had a certain magnetic pull. The rats crowded together in it. Females in heat would leave the protected areas and head for the central area; many never returned.

The resemblance to human behavior is frightening. In humans we see poor family relationships, lack of caring, complete alienation, magnetic attraction of overcrowding and lack of involvement so great that it permits people to watch a long drawn-out murder without so much as calling the police.

We have not availed ourselves of the alternatives. we need to turn loose some of our city planners or, better yet, to unleash creative innovators like Buckminster Fuller, scrap our obsolete building codes and instruct these people to build small urban centers, designing them for human beings and human life. We could build smaller cities with great park and garden areas, with neighborhoods of all races and all economic levels. The human planning—both before and during the building of such a community—would be fully as important and as well financed as the architectural planning.

We know how to carry out every aspect of this. The only element lacking is the passionate determination that says, "Our cities are inhuman. They are ruining lives and mental and physical health at a devastating rate. We are going to change this, even if it costs us money!"

SUGGESTIONS FOR WRITING

Write a composition in which you clarify a significant problem and offer a workable solution.

SUGGESTED TOPICS

A plan for making cities livable
The breakdown in communication
Spoiling nature
Surviving technology
Prison conditions
Crime in the streets
Power failure
Handling a crisis (car accident, snakebite, somebody hurt, man overboard,
    somebody lost)
Televisionitis
Individualism in a bureaucratic society
The world food shortage
Pornography
Inflation

PART TWO

BUILDING A COMPOSITION: THE TOOLS

Our first aim is usually to put across an idea, a block of thought, a whole composition. But we don't just switch on, press a key, and receive a whole composition print-out. A composition is not a sudden product. Rather, writing an effective composition is a craft, a gradual piece-by-piece shaping that can be worked at by means of several tools and building materials. These are paragraphs, sentences, words, and thoughts.

We normally start with the big idea in mind, but we build our development of it through component blocks of thought, or paragraphs. In turn, we build each paragraph through separate sentences, and each sentence through individual words. Underlying it all is the clarity and force of the thinking process.

Developing skill in working with paragraphs, sentences, words, and thought processes will help you in building the whole composition.

The paragraph The paragraph is the basic idea unit and structural unit of prose. It is two things at once: It is a unit of thought, several sentences developing a single topic; and it is one phase of a larger subject, a logical subdivision of the whole composition. As a portion of the whole, it may have its own thought pattern and structure different from those of the whole essay. Attention to structure and development of the paragraph will help you see its place in the larger composition.

In materials and structure, the usual paragraph is a kind of essay in miniature. The three kinds of materials and the structure that make up the paragraph are the same as those that make up the larger essay. Just as the main idea of an essay is usually expressed in a thesis statement and developed by the various ideas of the paragraphs, so the central thought of a paragraph is usually stated in a topic sentence and developed by details. Various words and devices are used to connect the parts.

If you can become proficient at developing the individual paragraph parts, you can become proficient at building the whole composition.

The sentence   The sentence is the minimum statement of an idea, and so a clear, forceful sentence builds toward a clear, forceful paragraph and a clear, forceful composition. You must manage the tools of sentence structure to express your ideas clearly and consistently, give them the proper weight, relate them precisely to one another, and give them the final force.

The word   One word is worth a thousand pictures, if it is the right word. Individual words, of course, are the ultimate building blocks. The effective writer must carefully select and place each word for the greatest precision, directness, and vitality.

The thought   Some say the basis of writing is not the whole composition, the paragraph, the sentence, or the word, but the thought. That is, if you get a significant thought and see it clearly, you will find the right words, sentences, or whatever to express it. Certainly there is a lot of truth to the idea. If your thought is muddled or trite, your writing will be muddled or trite.

In your whole composition, you are putting across a big idea. To do it effectively, you must follow a clear and valid thought process. To your thought process, you must be able to apply the tools of logical, convincing thought—the rules of evidence, the principles of reasoning, and the techniques for spotting emotionalisms and logical fallacies.

This section of the book gives materials for working with paragraphs, sentence structure, words, and thinking. These units do not have to be studied in the order given. They can be worked with in any order or concurrently. In whatever way learned, they are necessary tools and building blocks for the whole composition.

3

The Paragraph:
A Minimum Idea Unit
with Supporting Material

While your big idea or thesis is developed through a whole composition composed of several paragraphs, the composition builds one paragraph at a time. The paragraph is the minimum unit of idea development. The sentence may state the idea, but the paragraph is the group of sentences used to explain the idea, to open it up, to put it across.

The main purpose of this chapter is to get you to analyze paragraphs. Use your pencil, mark in your book, and dissect the paragraphs. If you can discover that a paragraph has parts and structure and that it builds from a central idea, then you will gain skill at developing your own paragraphs and building them into a whole composition.

A paragraph is not just an assemblage of words and sentences. The usual paragraph is made up of three distinct kinds of materials. There are central ideas, details to clarify or confirm the ideas, and devices to connect the parts. If you distinguish these kinds of materials, you can keep control of things as you construct a paragraph.

Checklist: Kinds of Materials in a Paragraph

1. Ideas   The point that is to be put across.
Topic sentence or topic idea
Restatement
Summary
Clincher

2. Supporting material   Any kind of material that will explain, clarify, validate, or undergird the central idea of the paragraph. These are the workhorses.

COMMON KINDS

Facts	List of kinds or types
Statistics	List of component parts
Examples	Points of comparison
Definitions	Points of contrast
Explanations	List of causes and effects
Qualifications	A sequence of events
Illustrations	A sequence of steps or stages
Specific instances	A sequence of causes and effects
Analogies	Reasoning
Anecdotes	

3. Connective devices Words and phrases that connect and show relationships between the parts. These are the bridges, the glue, the links.

COMMON KINDS

Repetition of key words
Synonyms
Pronouns and demonstratives (such as *this* and *that*)
Transitional expressions (such as *first, next, however*)
Restatement
Summary
Logical arrangement of parts

The following paragraph illustrates the three kinds of material that make up the usual paragraph:

Overt Behavior

In psychology behavior refers to any overt action on the part of an animal organism. The action may be simple or complex. At one extreme, it may be	*Idea:* topic sentence Development: qualification *Connection*
blinking an eye, flexing a finger, tilting the head, swallowing some water, taking a step, uttering a sound, or putting a mark on an answer sheet. At the	Development: examples
other extreme, it may be singing a song on a television show, attempting a ten-foot putt on the eighteenth hole of a golf tournament, bargaining for an automobile on a used car lot, taking a final examination in a freshman history course, painting a still life in an attic studio, or piloting an ocean liner from	*Connection* Development: examples
New York to Liverpool. In psychology behavior is used to designate an overt action.	*Idea:* restatement

—William S. Ray, *The Science of Psychology*, Macmillan, 1964.

It will be helpful to look at each of these three kinds of materials in turn.

Central Idea

An effective paragraph is usually built around one central idea with enough details to put the idea across. This controlling idea is often put into a single sentence called the *topic sentence.* It usually comes first or near the beginning of the paragraph, but it may be placed in the middle or at the end. The topic sentence may be implied rather than stated, especially in narrative writing. Occasionally the paragraph will be built on a sequence of ideas, and the topic idea will progress throughout the paragraph.

Topic sentence first

Prehistoric Affection

Many prehistoric finds suggest attitudes of affection. A Stone Age tomb contains the body of a woman holding a young child in her arms. Caves in North America that were occupied some 9,000 years ago have yielded numerous sandals of different sizes; those of children's sizes are lined with rabbit fur, as if to express a special kind of loving care for the youngest members of the community.

—René Dubos, "The Humanizing of Humans," *Saturday Review/World*, December 14, 1974.

Topic sentence last

Curious Chimpanzee

There is a story, possibly apocryphal, about a psychologist who shut a chimpanzee in a soundproof room filled with dozens of mechanical toys. Eager to see which playthings the ape would choose when he was all alone in this treasure house, the scientist bent down on his knees and put his eye to the keyhold. What he saw was one bright eye peering through from the other side of the aperture. If this anecdote isn't true, it certainly ought to be, for it illustrates the impossibility of anticipating exactly what an animal will do in a test situation.

—Frank A. Beach, "Can Animals Reason?" *Natural History*, March 1948.

Topic sentence in middle

Male Dominance

During the last 50 years American women, chiefly through inheritance, have come to possess a formidable amount of economic power. This is a country of rich widows. The extent of their influence has helped to create this legend that women are in charge. But this does not go down to the roots of American society, does not change its fundamental character: <u>It is still dominated by the masculine and not the feminine principle.</u> How do I know? Well, here is a quite simple test. At the present time America possesses sufficient instruments of destruction to kill every man, woman and child on earth. This macabre achievement, which has demanded an astonishing amount of technical skill and superb organization and the expenditure of billions and billions of dollars, not only represents the masculine principle triumphantly asserting itself but also suggests the male mind coming to the end of its tether. Where is the feminine principle, where is Woman, in this madness? Where is the feminine emphasis here upon love, on the happiness of persons? Is this how women want their money spent? We have only to ask the question to know the answer. Here is a society shaped and colored by male values. It is about as much like a matriarchy as the Marine Corps.

—J. B. Priestley, "Women Don't Run the Country," *The Saturday Evening Post,* December 12, 1964.

Topic sentence implied

(The Indians used buffalo in many ways.)

Indians and Buffalo

The meat was eaten fresh, or dried in the sun, pounded, and mixed with berries to make pemmican. The tanned hides were fashioned into moccasins and leggings, dresses and shirts, and summer coverings for beds. The thick robes made snug blankets for winter, and the scraped hides were stitched together to cover tepees. Rawhide was used in trunks and containers, cooking pots, ropes, quivers, and saddles. Warriors took the thick, tough hide from a bull's neck to make shields. Hoofs were boiled to obtain glue; horns provided spoons and ladles. Rib bones formed sled runners; other bones served as tools; sinew made bowstrings. Thick woolly bison hair stuffed medicine balls, and the beard decorated bows and lances. Nothing was wasted—even the tail found use as a whip or fly swatter.

—Robert McClung, *Wild Animals of North America,* National Geographic Society, 1960.

Topic sentence progressive

Ugliness

The country itself is not uncomely, despite the grime of the endless mills. It is, in form, a narrow river valley, with deep gullies running up into the hills. It is thickly settled, but not noticeably overcrowded. There is still plenty of room for building, even in the larger towns, and there are very few solid blocks. Nearly every house, big and little, has space on all four sides. Obviously, if there were architects of any professional sense or dignity in the region, they would have perfected a chalet to hug the hillsides—a chalet with a high-pitched roof, to throw off the heavy winter snows, but still essentially a low and clinging building, wider than it was tall. But what have they done? They have taken as their model a brick set on end. This they have converted into a thing of dingy clapboards, with a narrow, low-pitched roof. And the whole they have set upon thin, preposterous brick piers. By the hundreds and thousands these abominable houses cover the bare hillsides, like gravestones in some gigantic and decaying cemetery. On their deep sides they are three, four and even five stories high; on their low sides they bury themselves swinishly in the mud. Not a fifth of them are perpendicular. They lean this way and that, hanging on to their bases precariously. And one and all they are streaked in grime, with dead and eczematous patches of paint peeping through the streaks.

—H. L. Mencken, *A Mencken Chrestomathy*, Alfred A. Knopf, 1949.

EXERCISE 3-1
FINDING THE TOPIC SENTENCE

Find the topic sentence in each of these paragraphs. If the central idea is not directly stated, formulate your own wording of it.

Logic Is Fun

If you enjoy working out the strategy of games, tit-tat-toe or poker or chess; if you are interested in the frog who jumped up three feet and fell back two in getting out of a well, or in the fly buzzing between the noses of two approaching cyclists, or in the farmer who left land to his three sons; if you have been captivated by codes and ciphers or are interested in crossword puzzles; if you like to fool around with numbers; if music appeals to you by the sense of form which it expresses—then you will enjoy logic. You ought to be warned, perhaps. Those who take up logic get glassy-eyed and absent-minded. They join a fanatical cult. But they have a good time. Theirs is one of the most durable, absorbing and inexpensive of pleasures. Logic is fun.

—Roger W. Holmes, *The Rhyme of Reason*, Appleton-Century, 1939.

Restless Americans

One of the generalities most often noted about Americans is that we are a restless, a dissatisfied, a searching people. We bridle and buck under failure, and we go mad with dissatisfaction in the face of success. We spend our time searching for security, and hate it when we get it. For the most part we are an intemperate people: we eat too much when we can, drink too much, indulge our senses too much. Even in our so-called virtues we are intemperate: a teetotaler is not content not to drink—he must stop all the drinking in the world; a vegetarian among us would outlaw the eating of meat. We work too hard, and many die under the strain; and then to make up for that we play with a violence as suicidal.

—John Steinbeck, "Paradox and Dream," from *America and Americans*, Viking, 1966.

Language Limits

"A name is a prison, God is free," once observed the Greek poet Nikos Kazantzakis. He meant, I think, that valuable though language is to man, it is by very necessity limiting, and creates for man an invisible prison. Language implies boundaries. A word spoken creates a dog, a rabbit, a man. It fixes their nature before our eyes; henceforth their shapes are, in a sense, our own creation. They are no longer part of the unnamed shifting architecture of the universe. They have been transfixed as if by sorcery, frozen into a concept, a word. Powerful though the spell of human language has proven itself to be, it has laid boundaries upon the cosmos.

—Loren Eiseley, *The Invisible Pyramid*, Charles Scribners' Sons, 1970.

Don't Blame It on Me

"It's not my fault! it's not my fault! Nothing in this lousy world is my fault, don't you see that? I don't want it to be and it can't be and it won't be." This outcry comes from Kerouac's Sal Paradise, but it expresses the deep conviction of multitudes of irresponsibles in the age of self-pity. It is a curious paradox that, while the self is the center of all things, the self is never to blame for anything.

The fault is always the fault of someone or of something else. This is implicit in all the letters which are addressed to Abigail Van Buren. "Dear Abby: This is my problem . . . My husband . . ." "Dear Abby: Here is my problem . . . My wife . . ." Or it may be my son, my daughter, my mother-in-law, my neighbors. It is never Me.

Blame it on God, the girls, or the government, on heredity, or on the environment, on the parents, on the siblings, on the cold war, on the pressures toward conformity, on being unloved and unwanted. But don't blame it on me, the very center around which the whole universe revolves. This me is like the innocent and apparently unmenacing Dennis, who stands before an accusing mother, in the middle of the parlor, with his body twisted about as he looks back on the carpet at some curious mud tracks which lead right up to his heels. Says Dennis, in bewilderment, "I don't know what that stuff is . . . it just keeps following me."

—Robert Eliot Fitch, *Odyssey of the Self-Centered Self*, Harcourt, Brace & World, 1961.

Cycle of a Tree

A tree in the forest, old with too many springs, is conquered by flourishing fungal parasites; on a day of high wind, it falls. The saprophytes slowly devour the log's tissue, and, themselves decaying, feed other saprophytes. The bacteria take over, many linked species, each reducing the dead stuff to forms more elemental, until at last the nitrifying bacteria, both by their living and by their multitudinous dying, release nitrates to the soil. Rain and soil water dissolve them. The roots of bracken, sprung where the old tree grew, absorb them, and they are life again.

—Donald Culross Peattie, *Flowering Earth*, G. P. Putnam's Sons. 1939.

Methods of Support: Building an Idea

After you have clarified a central controlling idea for a paragraph, you must say enough about the idea to put it across. So the next step in writing is to select materials—according to your purpose and the best methods of accomplishing that purpose.

SELECTING MATERIALS ACCORDING TO PURPOSE

In selecting and arranging materials to develop your idea, you are likely to have one of two purposes in mind for your reader—*to inform* or *to persuade.* If your purpose is to *inform,* then you must use clarifying details, such as definition, analytical parts, explanations, descriptive details, examples, analogies, illustrations, and so on. If your purpose is to *persuade,* you will make use of evidence, statistics, specific instances, examples, reasons, reasoning, and so on. The materials for the two purposes overlap, of course. The point is to gather appropriate material to back up your idea.

Inform In the following paragraph, in order to inform, the author clarifies by using definition, analysis into types, and examples.

At the end of the paragraph we are ready to say, "Yes, you have made it clear. I understand what you mean by 'needs.'"

Needs

By "needs" I mean the inherent demands that men make because of their constitution. Needs for food and drink and for moving about, for example, are so much a part of our being that we cannot imagine any condition under which they would cease to be. There are other things not so directly physical that seem to me equally engrained in human nature. I would mention as examples the need for some kind of companionship; the need for exhibiting energy, for bringing one's powers to bear upon surrounding conditions; the need for both cooperation with and emulation of one's fellows for mutual aid and combat alike; the need for some sort of aesthetic expression and satisfaction; the need to lead and to follow; etc.

Topic sentence: definition of needs

Type: physical
3 examples

Type: nonphysical

5 examples

—John Dewey, "Does Human Nature Change?" *The Rotarian,* February 1938.

Persuade   In the following paragraph, in order to persuade, the writer validates his opinion by citing specific instances which show that his generalization covers a widespread occurrence.

Reality

All literature tends to be concerned with the question of reality—I mean quite simply the old opposition between reality and appearance, between what really is and what merely seems. "Don't you *see?*" is the question we want to shout at Oedipus as he stands before us and before fate in the pride of his rationalism. And at the end of *Oedipus Rex* he demonstrates in a particularly direct way that he now sees what he did not see before. "Don't you *see*" we want to shout again at Lear and Gloucester, the two deceived, self-deceiving fathers: blindness again, resistance to the clear claims of reality, the seduction by mere appearance. The same with Othello—reality is right under your stupid nose, how *dare* you be such a gull? So with Molière's Orgon—my good man, my honest citizen, merely *look* at Tartuffe and you will know what's what. So with Milton's Eve—"Woman, watch out! Don't you see—anyone can see—that's a *snake!*"

Opinion

5 specific instances

—Lionel Trilling, *The Liberal Imagination*, Viking, 1950.

SELECTING MATERIALS ACCORDING TO METHOD

Many specific methods and materials may be used to develop the idea of the paragraph. Some of these are statistics, illustrations, examples, lists, definitions, points of comparison, and reasoning. Check the list on p. 46. Use any of these and others. The principle is to use enough definite material to make your idea clear to your readers or to persuade them of its validity. Formulate your central idea clearly. Then build your paragraph under it.

Examples   The following paragraph develops the idea mainly by examples. Pinpoint the topic sentence and count and evaluate the examples to see if you are persuaded of the validity of the opinion. Also note the phrase in the last sentence which connects it to the first sentence.

The Rise of Kindness

With the growth of wealth and the rising standard of comfort brought by the machine era, the quality of kindness and humanity spread throughout the civilized world. Only a few of the countless manifestations of its spread can be mentioned here—the gradual emancipation of women, who formerly were regarded as personal property or as slaves, almost entirely without rights, and subject to gross abuse and degradation; the increasingly considerate treatment of children, who even in the early capitalist period were treated as chattels devoid of feeling, and often beaten unmercifully in accordance with the Biblical injunction, "Spare the rod and spoil the child"; the gradual humanization of the treatment accorded criminals and insane persons; the emancipation of slaves; the humanization of religious doctrine, the change from the fire-and-brimstone appeal to that of love and mercy; and finally, the gradual development of a feeling of mercy for animals. The idea that animals can suffer, although not entirely new, is largely a product of the age of relative plenty which came with the machine.

—John Ise, *Economics*, Harper & Bros. 1946.

List of component parts or kinds   A common way to clarify is to divide an item into its component parts or to group a mass of items into classes. The following paragraph takes a large item, mind, and divides it into four layers. The writer further clarifies each part in turn by explanation and descriptive detail.

Layers of Mind

There are four historical layers underlying the minds of civilized men—the animal mind, the child mind, the savage mind, and the traditional civilized mind. We are all animals and never can cease to be; we were all children at our most impressionable age and can never get over the effects of that; our human ancestors have lived in savagery during practically the whole existence of the race, say five hundred thousand or a million years, and the primitive human mind is ever with us; finally we are all born into an elaborate civilization, the constant pressure of which we can by no means escape.

—James Harvey Robinson, *The Mind in the Making*, Harper & Bros., 1950.

Narration and anecdote   In support of exposition and argument, narration relates an incident from real life and uses it as example, evidence, or explanation of some idea or principle of life.

The following paragraph relates the incident first, leading up to the topic sentence in the last line: an ironic observation about the way men are. Notice the other methods of development through the descriptive details to bring the scene to life and the point of contrast with women to sharpen the ironic comment about men.

Miracles and Men

We stopped for half an hour the other afternoon in bright sunshine to watch the digging where the Murray Hill Hotel used to be. There were about forty of us kibitzers, every one a male. A huge Diesel shovel named Lorain was hacking the last few tons of dirt and rubble from the hole and dropping them deftly onto trucks. This was a large-scale operation—big, ten-wheel Mack trucks, plenty of mud and noise and movement. The shovel operator was conscious of his audience and played to it. Bathed in sunlight and virtuosity, he allowed his cigarette to drip lazily from his lips while he plucked his levers as cunningly as a chime-master. We men in the audience were frozen in admiration, in respect, in wonder. We studied and digested every trick of the intricate operation—the thrust, the hoist, the swing, the release—conscious of the power and the glory. To a man, we felt instructed, elevated, stimulated. To a man, we were at the controls, each one of us, learning the levers, nudging the rocks, checking the swing, clicking the jaws to coax the last dribble. The sun warmed us in our studies. Not a woman, of the many who passed, paused to watch and to absorb. Not one single female. There can be no question but that ninety-five percent of all the miracles in the world (as well as ninety-five percent of all the hell) are directly traceable to the male sex.

—*The New Yorker*, September 13, 1952,

Definition   Definition is used frequently, and usually with other methods, when the purpose is to clarify difficult or unfamiliar ideas. The main method of development in the following paragraph is definition. Find two other methods of development used to support the definition.

Flirtation

Flirtation is a slippery word, definable as much by your own attitude as by the dictionary. According to Webster it probably derives from the Old French *fleureter,* to move lightly from flower to flower," and means "to play at love." Playing at love, however, can mean almost anything you choose: from a slightly longer than necessary handshake to a kiss on the lips, from an intellectual conversation to a whispered invitation to lunch; from a meaningful glance across a crowded room to an outright proposition. Essentially it is sexual—not in fact, but in feeling. "Flirting," one wife stated, "is a way of saying, 'I'm a woman and you're a man; I know that you know it and you know that I know it.' "

—Norman M. Lobsenz, "The Innocent Game That Disrupts Marriage," *Redbook*, April 1967.

Cause and effect   Much of our thinking deals with tracing causes and effects. We ask "Why?" or "How?" or "What will be the outcome?" and then we trace the answer in one of several patterns. We may classify a list of causes, reasons, or effects. We may describe the causal connection between two events, or we may trace a whole series or chain of causes and effects. The following paragraph points out two causes for man's highest impulses of altruism. Pick out the two causes. Then find what other method of development is used to support the idea.

Causes of Altruism

Man's highest impulses would not exist if it were not for two simple biological facts—that his offspring are born helpless and must be protected and tended for years if they are to grow up, and that he is a gregarious animal. These facts make it biologically necessary for him to have well-developed altruistic instincts, which may and often do come into conflict with his egoistic instincts, but are in point of fact responsible for half of his attitude towards life. Neither a solitary creature like a cat or a hawk nor a creature with no biological responsibility towards its young, like a lizard or a fish, could possibly have developed such strong altruistic instincts as are found in man.

—Julian Huxley, "Variations on a Theme by Darwin," *Science in the Changing World*, Century Co., 1933.

Comparison and contrast   Comparison and contrast are usually used to clarify. Similarities or differences between two items are pointed out so that the reader can see one or both items more clearly. In the following paragraph, the political liberal is compared to a hunting dog, and then, on the basis of the analogy, the liberal is compared to two other political types.

Liberal and Conservative

The liberal holds that he is true to the republic when he is true to himself. (It may not be as cozy an attitude as it sounds.) He greets with enthusiasm the fact of the journey, as a dog greets a man's invitation to take a walk. And he acts in the dog's way, too, swinging wide, racing ahead, doubling back, covering many miles of territory that the man never traverses, all in the spirit of inquiry and the zest for truth. He leaves a crazy trail, but he ranges far beyond the genteel old party he walks with and he is usually in a better position to discover a skunk. The dog often influences the course the man takes, on his long walk; for sometimes a dog runs into something in nature so arresting that not even a man can quite ignore it, and the man deviates—a clear victim of the liberal intent in his dumb companion. When the two of them get home and flop down, it is the liberal—the wide-ranging dog—who is covered with burdocks and with information of a special sort on out-of-the-way places. Often ineffective in direct political action, he is the opposite of the professional revolutionary, for, unlike the latter, he never feels he knows where the truth lies, but is full of rich memories of places he has glimpsed it in. He is, on the whole, more optimistic than the revolutionary, or even than the Republican in a good year.

—*The New Yorker*, January 17, 1948.

Description   The purpose of description is to bring a scene to life, to make it seem as real as if you were there. Effective description has two features. It uses concrete details that appeal to the five senses. Then the details are selected and arranged to give a dominant impression or several features of a larger impression.

In the following paragraph, "Wallace," the writer uses concrete details to describe the physical appearance of a person and also to give a sense of his character. He does not tell everything that could be said about the person, but singles out "two most impressive things"—his mouth and his pockets. The details are sharply focused to give us a clear image. We get the sense of a self-contained, mischievous person interested in mechanics and gimmickry.

Wallace

The two most impressive things about him were his mouth and the pockets of his jacket. By looking at his mouth, one could tell whether he was plotting evil or had recently accomplished it. If he was bent upon malevolence, his lips were all puckered up, like those of a billiard player about to make a difficult shot. After the deed was done, the pucker was replaced by a delicate, unearthly smile. How a teacher who knew anything about boys could miss the fact that both expressions were masks of Satan I'm sure I don't know. Wallace's pockets were less interesting than his mouth, perhaps, but more spectacular in a way. The side pockets of his jacket bulged out over his pudgy haunches like burro hampers. They were filled with tools—screwdrivers, pliers, files, wrenches, wire cutters, nail sets, and I don't know what else. In addition to all this, one pocket always contained a rolled-up copy of *Popular Mechanics,* while from the top of the other protuded *Scientific American* or some other such magazine. His breast pocket contained, besides a large collection of fountain pens and mechanical pencils, a picket fence of drill bits, gimlets, kitchen knives, and other pointed instruments. When he walked, he clinked and jangled and pealed.

—Richard Rovere, "Wallace," *The New Yorker,* February 4, 1950.

EXERCISE 3-2
METHODS OF DEVELOPMENT

Find the topic sentence in each of these paragraphs. Analyze the various methods of development used to support the central idea. Determine whether the main purpose of the writer is to inform or to persuade.

A Happy Community

Different people have different conceptions of what makes a community good or bad, and it is difficult to find arguments by which to establish the preferability of one's conception. I cannot hope, therefore, to appeal to those whose tastes are very diffferent from my own, but I hope and believe that there is nothing very singular in my own tastes. For my part, I should judge a community to be in a good state if I found a great deal of instinctive happiness, a prevalence of feelings of friendship and affection rather than hatred and envy, a capacity for creating and enjoying beauty, and the intellectual curiosity which leads to the advancement and diffusion of knowledge. I should judge a community to be in bad state if I found much unhappiness from thwarted instinct, much hatred and envy, little sense of beauty, and little intellectual curiosity. As between these different elements of excellence or the reverse, I do not pretend to judge. Suppose, for the sake of argument, that intellectual curiosity and artistic capacity were found to be in some degree incompatible. I should find it difficult to say which ought to be preferred. But I should certainly think better of a community which contained something of both than of one which contained more of the one and none of the other. I do not, therefore, believe that there is any incompatibility among the four ingredients I have mentioned as constituting a good community; namely, happiness, friendship, enjoyment of beauty, and love of knowledge.

—Bertrand and Dora Russell, *Prospects of an Industrial Civilization,* Century Co., 1923.

Fraternities

Clubs, fraternities, nations—these are the beloved barriers in the way of a workable world, these will have to surrender some of their rights and some their ribs. A "fraternity" is the antithesis of *fraternity.* The first (that is, the order or organization) is predicated on the idea of exclusion; the second (that is, the abstract thing) is based on a feeling of total equality. Anyone who remembers back to his fraternity days at college recalls the enthusiasts in his group, the rabid members, both old and young, who were obsessed with the mystical charm of membership in their particular order. They were usually men who were incapable of genuine brotherhood or at least unaware of its implications. Fraternity begins when the exclusion formula is found to be distasteful. The effect of any organization of a social and brotherly nature is to strengthen rather than to diminish the lines which divide people into classes; the effect of states and nations is the same, and eventually these lines will have to be softened, these powers will have to be generalized. It is written on the wall that this is so. I'm not inventing it, I'm just copying it off the wall.

—E. B. White, *One Man's Meat,* V. Gollancz Ltd., 1943.

Gadget Man

Indeed, the bureaucratic-industrial civilization which has been victorious in Europe and North America has created a new type of man: he can be described as the *organization man,* as the *automation man,* and as *homo consumens.* He is, in addition, *homo mechanicus:* by this I mean a gadget man, deeply attracted by all that is mechanical, and inclined against that which is alive. It is true that man's biological and physiological equipment provides him with such strong sexual impulses that even *homo mechanicus* still has sexual desires and looks for women. But there is no doubt that the gadget man's interest in women is diminishing. A new Yorker cartoon pointed to this very amusingly; a salesgirl trying to sell a certain brand of perfume to a young female customer recommends it by remarking: "It smells like a new sports-car." Indeed, any observer of male behavior today will confirm that this cartoon is more than a clever joke. There are apparently a great number of men who are more interested in sports cars, television and radio sets, space travel, and any number of gadgets than they are in women, love, nature, food; who are more stimulated by the manipulation of nonorganic, mechanical things than by life.

—Erich Fromm, *The Heart of Man,* Harper & Row, 1964.

Poetry and Advertising

Poetry and advertising have much in common. They both make every possible use of rhyme and rhythm, of words chosen for their connotative rather than their denotative values, of ambiguities that strike the level of unconscious responses as well as the conscious. Furthermore, they both strive to give meaning and overtones to the innumerable data of everyday experience; they both attempt to make the objects of experience symbolic of something beyond themselves. A primrose by the river's brim ceases to be "nothing more" because the poet invests it with meanings; it comes to symbolize the insensitiveness of Peter Bell, the benevolence of God, or anything else he wants it to symbolize. The advertiser is concerned with the primrose only if it happens to be for sale. Once it is on the national market, the advertiser can increase its saleability by making it thrillingly reminiscent of gaiety, romance, and aristocratic elegance, or symbolic of solid, traditional American virtues, or suggestive of glowing health and youth, depending upon his whim. This is what the writer of advertising does with breakfast food, toothpaste, laxatives, whisky, perfume, toilet bowl cleaners. Indeed almost all advertising directed to the general public is the *poeticizing of consumer goods.*

—S. I. Hayakawa, *Poetry,* January 1946.

Nothing

We did sleep that night, but we woke up at six A.M. We lay in our beds and debated through the open doors whether to obey till, say, halfpast six. Then we bolted. I don't know who started it, but there was a rush. We all disobeyed; we raced to disobey and get first to the fireplace in the front room downstairs. And there they were, the gifts, all sorts of wonderful things, mixed-up piles of presents; only, as I disentangled the mess, I saw that my stocking was empty; it hung limp; not a thing in it; and under and around it—nothing. My sisters had knelt down, each by her pile of gifts; they were squealing with delight, till they looked up and saw me standing there in my nightgown and with nothing. They left their piles to come to me and look with me at my empty place. Nothing. They felt my stocking: nothing.

—Lincoln Steffens, *The Autobiography of Lincoln Steffens,* Harcourt, Brace, 1931.

EXERCISE 3-3
GATHERING DETAILS FOR BUILDING A PARAGRAPH

List details that you might draw from to develop each of the following topic sentences.

1. Many people drive recklessly.
2. People are capable of doing kind acts.
3. Cars could be designed for greater safety.
4. People act as if our sources of energy were endless.
5. College is harder than high school.
6. True patriotism is seldom understood.
7. You can't always trust first impressions.
8. Wit and humor are not the same thing.
9. A dormitory is a busy place at night.
10. Friendship needs to be defined.
11. Memory can be improved.
12. We are living in a computer society.
13. Students have strange ways of studying.
14. X television show is better than Y television show.
15. This is a dangerous age to live in.

Connective Devices

If your paragraph is to communicate effectively, then the relationships between the parts must be clear, smooth, and logical. If your readers cannot follow the direction of thought, of course you will lose them. There are two main ways to achieve a smooth flow of thought in your paragraphs: (a) a logical sequence of ideas and (b) the use of transitional devices such as key words, repetition, parallel structure, and transitional signals.

IDEAS IN ORDERLY ARRANGEMENT

There are several common ways to arrange the ideas and sentences of a paragraph in logical order. Depending on your subject and supporting material, you can move in (1) a time sequence or (2) a spatial sequence. You can move (3) toward a climax, from least important to most important; you can move (4) from general to particular or (5) from particular to general; or you can move (6) from the familiar to the unfamiliar. A paragraph may begin (7) with a general statement which is then supported by specific details, or, in reverse, it may begin (8) with a series of details and conclude with the generalizing or summarizing statement.

The following paragraph on "Learning in Animals" is built on an order of climax, moving from the least important idea to the most important: ant, earthworm, rat, cat, and higher apes. Notice the disjointed effect if the sentence on cats were to be placed second, between the ant and the earthworm.

Learning in Animals

An ant cannot purposefully try anything new, and any ant that accidentally did so would be murdered by his colleagues. It is the ant colony as a whole that slowly learns over the ages. In contrast, even an earthworm has enough flexibility of brain to enable it to be taught to turn toward the left or right for food. Though rats are not able to reason to any considerable degree, they can solve such problems as separating round objects from triangular ones when these have to do with health or appetite. Cats, with better brains, can be taught somewhat more, and young dogs a great deal. The higher apes can learn by insight as well as by trial and error.

—George R. Harrison, "How the Brain Works," *Atlantic Monthly*, September 1956.

Study the logical structure of this paragraph on "Business Jargon." The opening question, "Why," makes the reader look forward to the answer. First comes a statement of general reasons, then a narrowing down to a specific main reason: status. Then status is amplified to describe first the man with insecure status and then the man with secure status.

Business Jargon

Why do people who in private talk so pungently often write so pompously? There are many reasons: tradition, the demands of time, carelessness, the conservative influence of the secretary. Above all is the simple matter of status. Theorem: the less established the status of a person, the more his dependence on jargon. Examine the man who has just graduated from pecking out his own letters to declaiming them to a secretary and you are likely to have a man hopelessly intoxicated with the rhythm of businesese. Conversely, if you come across a blunt yes or no in a letter, you don't need to glance further to grasp that the author feels pretty firm in his chair.

—William H. Whyte, "The Language of Business," *Fortune*, November 1950.

TRANSITIONAL DEVICES

Transitional devices are more mechanical than the organic, logical structure of the thought pattern and can often be added during the final editing of the paragraph without much rewriting. The following paragraph illustrates several common transitional devices.

Repetition of key words and synonyms: adolescence—youth, boys and girls, young man; trouble—rebellion, fight.

Pronouns and demonstratives: us, their, he, this.

Restatement: treated as a child—still try to dominate—parent-child relationship continues; cause the amount of trouble—the fight is on.

Transitional signals: however, furthermore, however, in other words.

Youth and Rebellion

Among preliterate peoples adolescence frequently does not cause the amount of trouble it does with us. From an early age the boy is in almost constant association with his father and learns almost all his skills and attitudes from him. With us, however, an adolescent boy is educated more by other associations in the community than by his father. Furthermore, among many primitives, boys and girls at about the time of puberty are inducted into manhood and womanhood or at least take their first step toward that goal. Initiation rites and impressive ceremonies mark a definite change in their status, and they acquire new rights and freedom, though new responsibilities as well. In our own society, however, there is no social recognition of new status when adolescence comes on. The boy becomes a young man physiologically, but he is still treated as a child and does not attain his majority till he is twenty-one. He is like a child who has outgrown his clothes and toys but is not given any others. This is at the root of his rebellion, when it comes to such a pass. His parents still try to dominate him in all his behavior—in his choice of clothes, work, friends, recreation, and even bedtime. In other words, the parent-child relationship continues long after it should have changed to a parent-adult relationship. The youth resents this, and the fight is on.

—Ray E. Baber, *Marriage and the Family,* McGraw-Hill, 1939.

The following list supplies some words and phrases frequently used to provide continuity between parts of sentences and paragraphs.

Addition
and, also, moreover, next, first, second, furthermore, in addition, another

Cause and effect
then, consequently, therefore, thus, hence, then, accordingly

Comparison
likewise, similarly, in the same way

Contrast
but, however, nevertheless, on the other hand, yet, in contrast, on the contrary

Example and illustration
for example, for instance, that is

Concession
though, although, even though, of course

Summary or conclusion
in brief, in short, in conclusion, finally, in summary

EXERCISE 3-4
IDENTIFYING CONNECTIVE DEVICES

Find the connective devices in these paragraphs.

Impoverishment

To the description we have given so far, we must add the impoverishment of the individual in his relationship to the public community. In the first place, the individual finds himself with no meaningful work to do—his job is increasingly frustrating, artificial, and purposeless. In the second place, he finds himself powerless to take action that would have any meaningful impact on society, and on the social evils which are increasingly apparent. Thus, he is not only deprived of "private" experience, he is deprived of a man's role in society. Appearances cannot remove the fact of his impotency, or give him a sense of manhood in the public realm.

—Charles Reich, *The Greening of America*, Random House, 1970.

Democracy

In this antithesis there are, however, certain implications, always tacitly understood, which give a more precise meaning to the term democracy. Peisistratus, for example, was supported by a majority of the people, but his government was never regarded as a democracy for all that. Caesar's power derived from a popular mandate, conveyed through established republican forms, but this did not make his government any less a dictatorship. Napoleon called his government a democratic empire, but no one, least of all Napoleon himself, doubted that he had destroyed the last vestiges of the democratic republic. Since the Greeks first used the term, the essential test of democratic government has always been this: the source of political authority must be and remain in the people and not in the ruler. A democratic government has always meant one in which the citizens, or a sufficient number of them to represent more or less effectively the common will, freely act from time to time, and accordingly to established forms, to appoint or recall the magistrates and to enact or revoke the laws by which the community is governed. This I take to be the meaning which history has impressed upon the term democracy as a form of government.

—Carl Becker, *Modern Democracy*, Yale University Press, 1954.

EXERCISE 3-5
WRITING A COMPLETE PARAGRAPH

Formulate a topic sentence and develop it into a coherent paragraph. Keep in mind the standard principles of good paragraph writing:

1. Make clear the idea you want to clarify or confirm and write it as a definite topic sentence somewhere in the paragraph.

2. Determine which method or methods of development can be used best in supporting your idea.

3. Use enough details to put your idea across.

4. Make sure the ideas and the supporting material are closely related.

5. Use enough connective devices to make a clear, smooth flow of thought.

SUGGESTED TOPICS

How to study for an exam
Drug abuse
Campus types
Reducing crime
The worst / best thing about parents
Commuting to school
Qualities of a friend
An unusual / interesting scene
A likable / unlikable person
Defining alienation
What makes an athletic event interesting?
A traffic problem
Dangers to individualism
Television shows

4

The Sentence:
Clear and Forceful

The Basic Sentence: Grammar Review

In building sentences and in improving them, you must be able to see the parts of the sentences and their relationships. You must select, shape, fit, and juggle to make your sentences effectively say what you mean.

Checklist: Parts of Speech

The full sentence is made up of words functioning in various ways. According to their function in the sentence, words and groups of words are classified as one of the eight parts of speech:

[handwritten margin notes: Person/place/thing — Takes place of noun — Sentance must have]

Noun: A noun names something—*face, Richard.*
Pronoun: A pronoun is used in place of a noun—*he, it, they.*
Verb: A verb expresses time and either action or state of being— *helped, become.* *[handwritten: Fog is over]*
Adjective: An adjective modifies a noun or pronoun—*big, free.*
Adverb: An adverb modifies a verb, an adjective, another adverb, or a whole sentence—*very, quickly.*
Preposition: A preposition shows the relationship between a noun or pronoun and some other word in the sentence—*in, between.*
Conjunction: A conjunction connects words or groups of words— *and, but, or, nor, for, if, because, after, when, that.*
Interjection: An interjection is an expression of emotion. It is grammatically independent of the rest of the sentence—*Ouch!, Oh!*

Since it is function which determines parts of speech in a sentence, a word may be put in different classes according to how it is used.

The *light* is burned out. (noun)
He couldn't *light* his pipe. (verb)
He has a *light* touch. (adjective)
Jane has *light* blue yes. (adverb)

THE MINIMUM SENTENCE: ITS PURPOSE AND STRUCTURE

Who is he?
Of course they saw it.
Be careful.
Wow!

These are complete sentences. Each group of words is an independent unit of expression. Each is a basic unit of communication, is grammatically complete, and can stand alone. Though a sentence may contain words that are not clear until we check the sentences that come before or after, a sentence is a group of words that makes sense by itself.

1.   The four purposes of sentences   We put our communications into four kinds of sentences, according to what response we intend from the other person. We (1) make statements, (2) ask or answer questions, (3) request action, or (4) simply express emotion for the other person to share. These kinds of sentences are called *declarative, interrogative, imperative,* and *exclamatory.*

Glass breaks. (statement)
What is his name? John Smith. (question and answer)
Stop. (request action)
Ouch! (express emotion)

2.   The minimum structure   A minimum communication can be made with any one word, with a verb, or with a subject and a verb. Each of the four kinds of sentences has its typical structure.

   a.   *Declarative:* The *statement* sentence is the standard sentence in English. Most of our sentence rules are based on it. The complete statement sentence typically has two parts—a noun and a verb. A noun (or pronoun) names the subject, and the verb is the key word in making the statement about the subject.

subj   v
Glass breaks.   Glass dropped on stone usually breaks easily.

   b.   *Interrogative:* The *question* sentence (1) uses a question word, (2) inverts subject and verb, or (3) emphasizes the question mark. An answer is any set of words appropriate to the information asked for.

      ?
Who's there?   Me, Brenda Barnes.

      v   s
Are you hungry?   Of course.

↓
This book?   No, that one.

c. *Imperative:* The sentence to *request action* needs only a verb to specify the action. *gives, command*

v   v
Run.   Give me my change. *suprise*

d. *Exclamatory:* The sentence to *express emotion* uses (1) a stock exclamatory word, such as "What a . . . !" or "Such a . . . !" or (2) any set of words of emotional intent.

!   ↓   ↓
What a gal!   A louse in my bed!

There are variations from the usual patterns. Informal statements and questions, for example, often leave out parts of well-known expressions because the reader or listener can fill in the rest.

Going to the game? Not if I can help it.
Damned if you do, damned if you don't.
Final score, Giants 14–Vikings 7.
Now to the third point.

Such sentences are correct if the communication is complete enough to get the desired response.

Intention and typical structure must be distinguished, for the desired response of a given sentence may be different from its typical form. For instance, a declarative form may actually want action, and question forms may be exclamations.

Question form: What in the world are you doing here! (Could be *exclamatory* meaning "Surprise!")

Question form: Don't you think it's cold in here? (Could be imperative meaning "Close the window," or "Put your arm around me.")

It is part of communication to figure out intent and act accordingly.

───────

EXERCISE 4-1
SENTENCE PURPOSE AND STRUCTURE

Identify the probable purpose and basic structure of these sentences as declarative, interrogative, imperative, or exclamatory.

1. The continent was explored widely during the sixteenth century.
2. Wow! What a show!
3. Give me your answer in three days.
4. How many casualties have there been so far?
5. What if he will not change his mind?
6. What a strange attitude!
7. Who opposed the amendment?

8. Whoever opposed the amendment had good reasons.
9. First, read the directions carefully.
10. First, you must read the directions carefully.

THE SENTENCE AND ALL PARTS OF SPEECH

The usual sentence takes more than a single word or a subject and verb to express its intention and idea. *Nouns* and *pronouns* are used in sentences for other functions besides subjects, and a complicated sentence may take more than one *verb*. Whenever you need to name something, you use a noun or a pronoun. Whenever you need to assert time and action or state of being, you use a verb.

1. Noun used to name something.

The *guide* told us that we needed *courage* to climb the *mountain*.

2. Pronoun takes the place of a noun.

He sent *someone* to help *them*.
Jack sent a mechanic to help Joe and *his* friends.

3. Verb asserts action.

Whenever you *ask* her, she *helps* you if she *is* able.

Besides nouns, pronouns, and verbs, the usual sentence also takes *modifiers* and *connectives*. Modifiers are used to describe or modify the parts of the sentence, and connectives link the parts.

4. Modifiers The two classes of modifiers are adjectives and adverbs.

Glass breaks.
A *thin* glass breaks *easily*.
A *very thin* glass breaks *quite easily*.
Of course, a *very thin* glass breaks *quite easily*.

Adjective: An adjective is any word or word group which modifies a noun.

thin glass

Adverb: An adverb is any word or word group which modifies a verb, an adjective, an adverb, or a whole sentence.

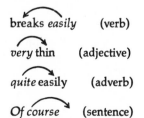

breaks *easily*   (verb)

very thin   (adjective)

quite easily   (adverb)

Of course   (sentence)

5. Connectives The two classes of connectives are prepositions and conjunctions.

A glass *or* a plate breaks easily *if* it is dropped *on* the floor.

Preposition. A preposition connects a noun or a pronoun to some part of the sentence in a subordinate relationship.

on the floor.

The preposition on connects *floor* to the verb *dropped.* The whole phrase *on the floor* functions subordinately as an *adverb.*

Common words often used as prepositions are *at, between, by, for, from, in, of, on, through, to, with.*

Conjunction. A conjunction is a word used to connect any words, phrases, or clauses. Coordinating conjunctions (*and, but, or, nor, for*) connect words of equal grammatical rank.

     noun   noun
a *glass* or a *plate*

Subordinating conjunctions (such as *when, where, if, because, since*) connect subordinating or dependent clauses to a main clause.

if it is dropped on the floor

The subordinating conjunction *it* connects the whole clause *if it is dropped on the floor* as an adverb modifying the verb *breaks.*

Certain pronouns (such as *who, whom, which,* and *that*) are also used to connect subordinate clauses to main clauses. When used to introduce subordinate clauses, these pronouns are called *relative pronouns.*

Jake is the man *who* drove the car.

The relative pronoun *who* connects the whole clause *who drove the car* as an adjective modifying *man.*

EXERCISE 4-2
PARTS OF SPEECH

Label the part of speech of each word in these sentences.

1. The attendant wrote my name on a sheet of paper.
2. The little boy whistled loudly when he walked past the window.
3. Did she vote for the school bonds or against them?
4. Give me one rood reason why we should support grafters and incompetent people in office.
5. Everyone suddenly stood up and left the auditorium.

THE FULL SENTENCE: EIGHT COMMON PATTERNS

Subjects, verbs, and complements are used to build the basic sentence.

The main complements are direct objects, indirect objects, predicate nouns, predicate adjectives, objective complement nouns, and objective complement adjectives. These are called complements because they complete a statement begun by the subject and verb. Eight sentence patterns are common in statement sentences.

1. Something does subject-verb

Subject: performs the action and is what we are talking about.

Verb: states the action and makes the statement about the subject.

s   v

The *grass grows.* (The grass does the growing.)

s   v

The *grass grows* fast in the spring.

In the spring, the *grass grows* fast.

2. Something does to something subject-verb-direct object.

Direct object: receives the action of the verb.

s v   do

Jim hit the *ball.* (The ball gets the action.)

s v   do

Sue earns her *living* in a factory.

s   v   do

The *group* thoughtfully *studied* the new *proposal.*

3. Something gives something to something Subject-verb-direct object-indirect object

Indirect object: receives the direct object.

s   v   io   do

The *cashier gave* the *woman* the *money.* (The woman gets the money.)

s v   io   do

He gave Tom and me a strange *look.*

4. The subject is done to subject-passive verb

Passive verb: A verb is in the passive voice if it acts upon the subject.

s v v

The *dog was hit* by a car. (The dog gets the action.)

s v

Active verb: A *car hit* the dog.

5. Something is something subject-linking verb-predicate noun

Linking verb: connects a noun, pronoun, or adjective to the subject.

Predicate noun: comes after a linking verb and is used to rename or identify the subject.

s v   pn

Tom became an *actor.*

s v   pn

The *sergeant had been* a professional *wrestler.*

s v   pn

This is the tallest *building.*

6. Something is described   subject-linking verb-predicate adjective

Predicate adjective: A predicate adjective follows the linking verb and describes the subject.

s   v   pa
Tom is clever.

s   v   pa
The *crowd was suspicious.*

s   v   pa
The *gambler felt good* about his winnings.

7. Something is changed to something else   subject-verb-direct object-objective complement noun.

Objective complement noun: renames the subject through the action of the verb.

s   v   do   ocn
The *collision made* the *car* a *junk heap.*

8. Something is given a different quality   subject-verb-direct object-objective complement adjective.

Objective complement adjective: describes the direct object through the action of the verb.

s   v   do   oca
The *collision made* the *car* very *ugly.*

Finding the subject

Five kinds of constructions sometime make the subject hard to locate.

1. *Compounds:* The subject may consist of two or more parts.

A *truck* and a *bus* had hit the train.

2. *Words coming between subject and verb.*

A list *of names* was pinned to the wall.

It is easy, though not correct, to assume that the noun (*names*) closest to the verb is the subject. But *of names* is a modifier of the true subject, *list.*

3. *Inversions:* The subject sometimes comes after the verb.

In the middle of the road stood the angry *man.*

In questions, the subject often follows part of the verb.

Did the *crew* have to abandon ship?

The introductory words *there* and *here* (*there is, there are, here is, here are*) cause the subject to follow the verb.

Here are the three *reasons* he gave.
There was *nothing* left for him.

4. *Word group used as subject.*

Whoever can do the job best will be hired.
Having too much money is not one of my handicaps.

5. *Commands and requests with no stated subject.*

Close the door, please. (The subject is *you* understood.)
Do your Christmas shopping early. (*You* understood.)

Finding the verb

Five kinds of constructions sometimes make the verb difficult to locate.

1. *Compounds.* Two or more separate verbs may be used with the same subject.

The snow *came* down softly and *covered* the ground.

2. *Words coming between parts of the verb phrase.* A verb phrase and a helper may be separated by a modifier.

They *did* not actually *see* us.

3. *Inversions.* In questions, part of the verb often comes before the subject.

Did you *hear* the news?

4. *Word groups used as one verb.*

Snow *is falling.*
Snow *has been falling.*
Snow *must have been falling.*

5. *Verbals or incomplete verb forms.* Verbals cannot make complete sentences. Carefully distinguish the verbal from the verb.

The man, *waving* his hand, stepped in front of the car. (verbal)
The man *was waving* his hand. (verb)

EXERCISE 4-3
FINDING THE SUBJECT AND THE VERB

Underline the simple subject (without modifiers or other related words). Circle the verb, verb phrase, or compound verb.

1. Three pretty girls were sitting on the bench.
2. He ran to the car and opened the door.
3. Only in early spring can one find violets.
4. The reason for her refusal was not known.
5. Some of the players forgot their lines.
6. Listening to the noise hour after hour grew tiresome.
7. He dived into the water and swam to the raft.

8. Both of us, Ralph and I, were accepted.
9. In such troubled times, could she have done any differently?
10. There were a knife and two guns in his car.
11. Out of the locker room burst the determined team.
12. Have any others had cause for complaint?
13. There proved to be only two items missing.
14. None of her reports was fully trusted.
15. The real meaning of the event, according to historians, was obscured by the newspapers.
16. All sources investigated were listed in the report.
17. Stopping for a little rest was sufficient.
18. The men and the mice should be separated.
19. Mary, having foreseen the disaster, had already called the police.
20. Laughing and shouting, we carried him off the field.

EXERCISE 4-4
FINDING OBJECTS, PREDICATE NOMINATIVES, AND PREDICATE ADJECTIVES

Identify the italicized words and write the appropriate abbreviations in the blanks to the right.

do	direct object	pa	predicate adjective
io	indirect object	ocn	objective complement noun
pn	predicate noun	oca	objective complement adjective
x	not a complement		

1. My parents will buy *me* a *car* in one year.
2. The captain was a *wrestler,* and he looked *strong.*
3. He *gave* my *suggestion* a good deal of thought.
4. The one *whom* I like best is a *teacher* of history.
5. Her story about the success of her *trip* was *encouraging.*
6. He *explained* each of the *rules* very slowly.
7. *Whom* did the *fraternity* nominate?
8. Father was *weary* of driving and wanted *to stop.*
9. She should have become a *junior* last *year.*
10. He asked us if *anybody* had seen his *dog.*
11. Only then did Mother agree to lend *us* the *car.*
12. There were *gallons* of hot coffee, which really tasted *good.*
13. The favored *contestants* were the *Eagles.*
14. She had been feeling *bad* since she told the *lie.*
15. He has played the *guitar* for only two weeks, but already he sounds *good.*
16. He painted the *fence white.*
17. We considered *her* rather *pretty.*
18. I was given a *firm handshake.*
19. We named the *group The Up Set.*
20. We called the *victim* a *hero.*

EXERCISE 4-5
FINDING SUBJECTS, VERBS, AND COMPLEMENTS

Draw vertical lines between the parts of these sentences.
Label each part, using the following abbreviations.

s   subject
v   verb
do   direct object
pn   predicate noun
pa   predicate adjective
io   indirect object
ocn object complement noun
oca object complement adj.

s   v   io   do

Example: We / gave / him / the wrong answer.

1. Jack is an idiot.
2. Tell me your name.
3. It's snowing.
4. The overshoes fit me.
5. The smudge was erased.
6. Don't tell that story!
7. The clerk marked the answer incorrect.
8. She could have been wrong.
9. She makes many mistakes.
10. Pat might have been killed.
11. He had a narrow escape.
12. The doctor gave him a lecture.
13. The doctor pronounced him uninjured.
14. The hospital released him.
15. She had been fortunate.
16. She had not been injured.
17. He had friends.
18. He had escaped.
19. She was leaving.
20. We considered her a thief.

WORD GROUPS AS UNITS: PHRASES AND CLAUSES

To build and revise sentences, you must recognize word groups used as units, such as *in the valley* and *when we were there.* You move or adjust the whole set of words as a single sentence part, such as adjective, noun, subject, and so on. The parts of the unit may also have functions within the unit.

1. Phrases

on a bench
the man on a bench
The man stood on a bench.

waving his hand
the man waving his hand
The man waving his hand stood on a bench.

A phrase is a group of related words, without subject and verb, used as a single part of speech. The two main kinds of phrases are *prepositional* phrases and *verbal* phrases. They may function as nouns, adjectives, or adverbs.

a. *Prepositional Phrases*

He is a man *of courage.* (adjective: modifies the noun *man*)
In the evening is the best time to study. (noun: used as a subject of *is*)
The play began *on time.* (adverb: modifies verb *began*)
He was inefficient *in his haste.* (adverb: modifies adjective *inefficient*)

b. *Verbal Phrases*
Gerund: A gerund is the *-ing* form of the verb used as a noun.

Swimming in the river was our favorite pastime. (subject)
We enjoyed *swimming in the river.* (direct object)
We rested before *starting home.* (object of preposition)

Participle: A participle is the *-ing* or *-ed* form of the verb and is used as an adjective.

The man, *carrying the box,* walked to the stage. (modifies *man*)
Having broken the arrow, he threw it away. (modifies *he*)

Infinitive: The infinitive is the *to* form of the verb, used as a noun, an adjective, or an adverb. To *to* is sometimes omitted.

To swim alone is dangerous. (noun: subject)
They wanted *to travel by boat.* (noun: direct object)
We were eager *to learn the rules.* (adverb: modifies *eager*)
We had many miles *to go before dark.* (adjective: modifies the noun *miles*)
Two boys helped *change the tire.* (infinitive with *to* omitted: object of verb *helped*)

EXERCISE 4-6
PHRASES

Identify the form, function, and part of speech of each phrase in these sentences.

1. Crouching in the doorway, the dog was ready to spring at the stranger.
2. Crouching in the doorway was a large black dog.

3. Then the wind struck, whipping the waves into whitecaps and battering the boats against one another.
4. The only person to object to the proposal was a little lady sitting in the back row.
5. The general hoped to conquer the city by nightfall.
6. Her riding the bicycle to school made people wonder about her.
7. The woman standing near the cash register looked insulted by the remark.
8. Over the fence was out.
9. The water came to within a foot of the porch.
10. Having been bitten once, he was skeptical of snakes.

2. Clauses

    s   v
People laughed.

     s   v
When they heard the news

 s   v   s   v
People laughed when they heard the news.

A subject-verb combination is called a *clause.* If the clause makes a grammatically self-contained statement, it is called an *independent clause* or a *main clause* and may be used as a complete sentence.

   s   v
Jake works in that store.

Some clauses are introduced by *subordinating conjunctions* or *relative pronouns* which indicate that the clauses are used not as sentences, but as nouns, adjectives, or adverbs. Such a clause is called a *subordinate clause* or a *dependent clause.*

      s   v
where Jake works

 s v   subc s   v
That is the store where Jake works.

Common subordinating conjunctions are *of, because, when, where, before, although,* and *that.* Common relative pronouns are *who, whom, which,* and *that.*

a. *Adjective Clause*
An adjective clause modifies a noun or pronoun.

This is the book *that caused a sensation.* (modifies the noun *book*)
Anybody *who objected* was asked to leave. (modifies the pronoun *anybody*)
He asked the first person *he met.* (modifies *person,* with the relative pronoun *that* or *whom* omitted)

b. *Adverb Clause*
An adverb clause modifies a verb, an adjective, or an adverb.

When the dam broke, the village was flooded. (modifies the verb *was flooded*)
She works more rapidly *than you do.* (modifies adverb *rapidly*)

c. *Noun Clause*

A noun clause may serve in most regular noun functions—subject, direct object, object of preposition, predicate noun.

> That is *when he left.* (predicate noun)
> *What this country needs* is lower taxes. (subject)
> She told me *whom she meant.* (direct object)
> His accusation, *that I was lying,* was unfair. (appositive)
> Give the job to *whomever applies first.* (object of preposition *to*)
> She believed *I was lying.* (direct object: subordinate conjunction *that* omitted)

EXERCISE 4-7
CLAUSES

Tell the part of speech of each dependent clause. If it is a noun, tell its function. If it is an adjective or an adverb, tell what it modifies.

1. This is the man who won the game for us.
2. That is the book we had to read.
3. Whenever I talked to him, he boosted my morale.
4. We were sorry that they were present to hear what she said.
5. Whatever you suggest is what we will do.
6. Send the book to whoever will read it.
7. The president fled the country after the army took over the palace.
8. We were amazed at what she told us.
9. They wanted to know whom we were talking about.
10. That was not a time when people were humane.

Fragments: Making Complete Statements

Which of these are complete sentences?

1. Who has the answer?
2. Jim never being quite sure of himself.
3. That bar has been wrecked three times.
4. Hey!

All are complete except number 2. A *complete sentence* is a word or group of words which forms an independent unit of expression, is grammatically complete, and can stand by itself. Though the total meaning of a sentence depends heavily on the sentences that come before or after it, a sentence is a group of words that makes sense by itself. Usually a complete sentence contains a subject-verb combination to make a statement or ask a question, or it contains a verb to request action.

A *sentence fragment* is a piece of a sentence punctuated as if it were a complete sentence.

> **Fragment:** He then stopped protesting and sat down. Finally realizing that the referee was right.

The second group of words, "Finally realizing that the referee was right," is incomplete. It cannot stand alone, but is a logical part of the first group.

How to correct pieces of sentences

1. *Correct Punctuation.* Tie the piece to a sentence. You can usually do this by changing a period to a comma or by removing a period.

> He then stopped protesting and sat down,
> finally realizing that the referee was right.

2. *Make the piece into a whole sentence.* Usually this change means adding a subject or a complete sentence verb. Especially watch for *-ing* words and *to* words trying to function as a sentence verb.

> He then stopped protesting and sat down.
> He finally realized that the referee was right.

Minor sentences   Subjects and verbs are not always necessary. The usual statement sentence has subject and verb, but many sentences, called minor sentences, express complete thoughts and can stand alone without subject and verb:

> **Answers to questions:**   How many chances can we expect to have? Only one.
> Marine geography as a career? An intriguing possibility.
> **Commands:**   (verb only) Stop.
> Look at his record.
> **Exclamations:**   Wow!
> What a hopeless future!
> **Idioms:**   Better late than never.
> And now to the final reason.
> **Colloquial expressions:**   A bad situation, that.

The best test of a sentence is that it conveys enough information to stand alone. The reader can respond to it. Minor sentences can be effective if the writer does not confuse them with sentence fragments, but uses them deliberately for special purposes of emphasis and brevity. But you should be wary of all idioms that don't make a complete sentence. Unless the group of words is a question, answer, imperative, or exclamation, it is better to give it a structure of subject and verb.

EXERCISE 4-8
IDENTIFYING FRAGMENTS

Identify each fragment and correct it in the most effective way.

1. You should study hard when you study. And do your playing only when your work is done.
2. My summer job turned out to be just what my father said it would be, A a thoroughly difficult but rewarding experience.   *NO VERB*
3. It doesn't take long to study for an exam. Unless, of course, one hasn't kept up with the assignments.

TOOK

4. Our flight from Dallas to Denver was fast, The whole trip taking only about three hours.

5. The northern part of the state contains oil wells and wheat fields. In the eastern part are pine forests. And to the west, deserts and mountains.

6. Where do we go from here? Only to where our past has prepared us to go.

7. Some people still believe alcohol is a stimulant. Although tests show that it relaxes the blood vessels.

8. His love of work was great. So great, in fact, that he could watch others do it by the hour.

9. Some students are just not suited for dormitory life. In which case it is better for them to live off campus.

10. Many students have criticized the student newspaper. Their chief complaint being that the news is dull.

11. I was trying to read *Anthony Adverse.* Which kept boring me to sleep.

12. After I had waited 35 minutes, Mary finally arrived. But better late than never.

13. In the morning she jumps out of bed as soon as the alarm rings. And then promptly goes back to bed.

14. To get an education we must study many things we don't like. Such as the important dates of the Renaissance.

15. He dropped out of school during the sixth week. The reason being that he wanted to work and buy a car.

Run-On Sentences: Separating Your Two Statements

What makes these sentences wrong?

Joe showed no spirit as halfback, he preferred to play end.
Coach Larson gave up on me, in fact, he told me I would never be a swimmer.
Failure may do a person good it may teach him humility.

These are wrong because each sentence contains two complete thoughts, and we do not know when the writer ends one thought and moves on to another. The statements just "run on" without adequate signals. A comma alone or an imagined pause does not let the reader know you have finished one thought unit and gone on to the next.

How to correct run-on sentences
There are three standard ways to separate two independent clauses or statements.

1. *Period and capital letter*

Joe showed no spirit as halfback. He preferred to play end.

2. *Semicolon*

Joe showed no spirit as halfback; he preferred to play end.

3. *Comma and coordinating conjunction (and, but, or, nor, for)*

Joe showed no spirit as halfback, for he preferred to play end.

Sometimes the best way to correct a run-on sentence is to change one of the independent statements to a dependent phrase or a clause.

Because Joe preferred to play end, he showed no spirit as halfback.

Contact clauses

Sometimes two independent clauses have such a close contact in idea that a comma is enough to separate them.

Acceptable:　It was not merely a government, it was a police force.
Acceptable:　Scholars study, students learn, wise men understand.
Acceptable:　Some people give up, others grin and bear it.

Such sentences are short and parallel in form. The second clause amplifies, opposes, or climaxes the first. Contact clauses can be useful and acceptable in informal writing, especially colloquial, but they must be used sparingly. They are almost always inappropriate in formal writing. Unless you have the experience to know what you are doing, you should avoid using contact clauses.

_____

EXERCISE 4-9
RUN-ON SENTENCES

Identify each run-on and correct it in the most effective way.

1. We packed our equipment, then we waited for the bus.
2. Mr. Larson was a good teacher, he was the best, in fact, that I have ever had.
3. Mr. Larson was a good teacher, in fact, he was the best that I have ever had.
4. He came, he saw, he conquered.
5. It was not by malicious intent, however, that we had insulted her.
6. We couldn't change the tire we didn't even have a jack.
7. I read the instructions and worked carefully, nevertheless, I couldn't make the parts fit.
8. While an adolescent lives at home, his parents will never let him grow up, they always think of him as a child.
9. Others merely boast, she achieves.
10. Nobody had invited her she had simply been overlooked.
11. "Is John here?" she asked, "I saw him come this way."
12. I was fortunate in my choice of a companion, although he talked slowly, he was quick-witted.
13. We are indebted to the Russians for some of our best music, moreover, Russians have written several of the world's great novels.
14. I jumped at his offer of a ride otherwise I would have had to walk home.
15. The weather was too rainy for horseback riding, we stayed in the cabin all day.

Coordination and Subordination: Weighing Your Ideas

Two related ideas of equal importance are *coordinate,* and you should write them in the same kind of sentence pattern. If the two related ideas are not of equal importance, the less important one is called *subordinate,* and you should write it in a less emphatic sentence pattern than the other. Put your most important idea in a main clause. Put the less important idea in a subordinate clause, a phrase, or a word.

With two related ideas, the idea of people being killed would usually be of greater importance.

Two people were killed.   Idea 1—more important
The roof fell.   Idea 2—less important

Main clause   Subordinate clause
Two people were killed when the roof fell.

Main clause   Subordinate phrase
Two people were killed by the falling roof.

With two related ideas like the following, you yourself have to determine whether you want them to be coordinate or subordinate. Write them as you want them to be.

I played the piano.
Mary sang.

        Main clause   Main clause
Coordinate: I played the piano, and Mary sang.

        Subordinate clause   Main clause
Subordinate: While I played the piano, Mary sang.

        Main clause   Subordinate clause
Subordinate: I played the piano while Mary sang.

        Main clause   Subordinate phrase
Subordinate: I played the piano for Mary's singing.

Weigh your ideas carefully, and give them proper rank.

Guides for weighing two or more related ideas

1. *The two ideas are of equal rank: join them.* Use two words, phrases or clauses. If you use two separate sentences, link them with a coordinating conjunction (*and, but, for, or, nor.*)

Tom won the first set and Ed, the second.
Tom won the first set, and Ed won the second set.

2. *One idea has lower rank: knock it down.*   Instead of a sentence or independent statement, make it a phrase, a word, or a dependent clause. Instead of *and* or *but,* use *because, although,* etc.

Ranked wrong: He was driving too fast to stop, and he crashed into the wall.

Reduced: Because he was driving too fast to stop, he crashed into the wall.

3. *Wrong idea claims rank: switch them.* Which of two ideas is more important depends, of course, upon you and your context. Just be sure the sentence comes out the way you think it. This sentence illustrates an up-side-down evaluation—lives are generally more valuable than planes.

Upside down: The plane skidded off the runway, killing ten people.

Switched: When the plane skidded off the runway, ten people were killed.

4. *Primer talk: change weight.* Short, simple sentences with the same subject-verb pattern usually suggest immature thinking. With a little weighing of ideas, groups of short sentences can be revised into one or two longer sentences. You get the same primer style if you string the short clauses together with *and*.

Primer style: Thirty dollars a week was not enough pay. I quit my job.

Weight changed: Because thirty dollars a week was not enough pay, I quit my job.

Primer style: Sam Baker stood there before us. He talked in a low voice. His voice was earnest. We felt in him sincerity and dedication. These qualities are not common to ordinary men.

Weight changed: As Sam Baker stood there before us talking in his low earnest voice, we felt in him a sincerity and dedication not common to ordinary men.

EXERCISE 4-10
COORDINATION AND SUBORDINATION

Rewrite these sentences, giving appropriate placement to more important and less important ideas.

1. I spent five years on a farm when I was a boy, and now I do not like the crowded city.
2. Russian is a very difficult language, but I decided to master it.
3. Scissor-tail flycatchers are quite common to this part of the country and they eat a lot of insects and are very helpful to the farmers and they are protected by state law.
4. I was waiting for a traffic light, when a car sped from behind me and struck a pedestrian.
5. The coach, who had been with the school for ten years, said he wanted to talk seriously with all the players at two o'clock that afternoon, and so we gathered at the edge of the playing field with its beautiful green grass.
6. The air over the city was tested, and chemists found that it was badly polluted.
7. The houses on either side of us were destroyed by the tornado, and our house was virtually untouched.

8. The police were trying to find the person who had stolen the car which had been parked in a parking lot which had been untended at the time.

9. I am not a woman-hater. I will discuss my reasons for disliking women drivers.

10. Ed glanced into the rear view mirror, noticing that a police car was following him with blinking red lights.

11. Mary went to see the doctor and the doctor found that she had pneumonia.

12. John was an impatient driver. There were seven cars ahead of him at the toll gate. Some of the drivers ahead of him were slow at paying their toll. John kept swearing under his breath and racing the engine.

13. Katherine Anne Porter was born in Indian Creek, Texas. She was a descendant of Daniel Boone. She spent her early life in Texas and Louisiana. She was educated in various convent schools in the South. She has lived in various parts of the world. She has lived in the South, in New York City, in Europe, in Mexico. Her experiences in these places are reflected in her fiction.

14. Somebody threw a large firecracker into the crowd, almost causing a stampede.

15. Colson spent four years collecting and processing statistics, but his conclusions were considered vague and almost worthless.

Inaccurate Connectives: Linking Your Thoughts

Some connectives have one very definite meaning—such as *and, but, where, when, that,* and *like.* Other connectives have several meanings— such as *so, as,* and *while.* Be sure to use the connective that indicates the exact relationship you want.

1. As

a. Do not use *as* for *whether* or *that*

Faulty: I do not know as I want to see the game.
Correct: I do not know that (whether) I want to see the game.

b. Do not use *as* when it could mean either time or cause. Use *when* or *because.*

Faulty: *As* the epidemic got worse, more doctors were called in.
Correct: *When* the epidemic got worse, more doctors were called in.
Correct: *Because* the epidemic got worse, more doctors were called in.

2. And

Use *but,* not *and,* when a contrast is intended.

Faulty: Five medical specialists had given up on Jackson, *and* Dr. Womack cured him.
Correct: Five medical specialists had given up on Jackson, *but* Dr. Womack cured him.

3. Where

Do not use *where* for *that*. *Where* means place. *That* (if not a relative pronoun) merely connects.

> **Faulty:** I read in the newspaper *where* a minister was indicted for theft.
> **Correct:** I read in the newspaper *that* a minister was indicted for theft.

4. Like

Do not use *like* for *as if* or *as though*. *Like* as a connective is a preposition except in colloquial English.

> **Faulty:** The driver acted *like* he did not know where he was going.
> **Correct:** The driver acted *as if* (or *as though*) he did not know where he was going.

5. While

a. Do not use *while* for *and* or *but*. *While* is a subordinating conjunction, not a coordinating conjunction.

> **Faulty:** Math is my favorite course, *while* English is second.
> **Correct:** Math is my favorite course, *and* English is second.

> **Faulty:** Math used to very difficult for me, *while* now it is quite easy.
> **Correct:** Math used to be very difficult for me, *but* now it is quite easy.

b. Do not use *while* when it can mean either time or concession. Use *when* or *although*.

> **Faulty:** *While* I had to face glaring headlights for several hours, my eyes did not get tired.
> **Correct:** *Although* I had to face glaring headlights for several hours, my eyes did not get tired.
> **Correct:** *When* I had to face glaring headlights for several hours, my eyes did not get tired.

EXERCISE 4-11
CONNECTIVES

Replace vague and inaccurate connectives.

1. It's best to buy tires of high quality as they are important to safety.
2. My roommate likes to study with the radio on, while I like to study in silence.
3. Many people buy a new car every year and their old one is hardly broken in.
4. As the siren was screaming, Alice pulled the car over to the curb.
5. Jim Bass said he didn't know as he liked being leader of such a sour crew.
6. When I walked into the room, they looked like they were seeing a ghost.
7. When the argument rose to a shout, I saw where I might as well leave.
8. Although he had known me for two years, he acted like he had never seen me before.

9. I used to have a good money-making job, while now I am a broke unemployed.
10. As the waters almost reached the top of the levee, people were evacuated from their homes.

Parallelism: Keeping Your Pattern

Parallelism is the use of the same kind of word patterns to express similar ideas. In this way, you link noun with noun, infinitive with infinitive, prepositional phrase with prepositional phrase, adjective phrase with adjective phrase, and so on.

To check on parallelism in sentences, make a diagram to show equal ideas and equal word patterns.

James is intelligent,
      pleasant, and
      reliable. (single-word adjectives)

James likes swimming,
      boating, and
      fishing. (single-word gerunds)

We learned that he had not been home Tuesday night, and
      that he refused to tell where he had been. (noun clauses)

We searched in the closets,
      in the dresser drawers, and even
      in the basement. (adverbial-prepositional phrases)

If ideas in a sentence are parallel or equal and they are not given parallel grammatical form, the sentence is usually clumsy and unclear. The following four cases show how parallelism is most commonly violated.

1. Parallel structure with coordinating conjunction The conjunctions *and, or, nor, for* and *but* are sure signs of parallel ideas. Make sure the parts connected are given the same grammatical forms.

> **Faulty:** The book was dull, long, and could not be easily understood.
> **Parallel:** The book was dull, long, and hard to understand.

> **Faulty:** Carol got off work by pretending to be sick and that she had to see a doctor.
> **Parallel:** Carol got off work by pretending that she was sick and that she had to see a doctor.

2. Faulty parallelism with *and who* or *and which* Do not use *and who* or *and which* unless it is linked to a preceding *who* or *which*.

> **Faulty:** Mike is a first-rate athlete and who is also an excellent student.
> **Parallel:** Mike is a first-rate athlete and an excellent student.

Parallel: Mike is a first-rate athlete and an excellent student.

Faulty: Back in the bushes by the pier was an old rowboat apparently belonging to nobody and which we decided to take over.
Parallel: Back in the bushes by the pier was an old rowboat which apparently belonged to nobody and which we decided to take over.

3. Correct position of correlatives The correlatives are *either-or, neither-nor, both-and, whether-or,* and *not only-but also.* Be sure you put the conjunctions in the right places to govern parallel grammatical constructions.

Faulty: Shakespeare is not only famous as a playwright, but also as a poet.
Parallel: Shakespeare is famous not only as a playwright
                                    but also as a poet.

Faulty: He was either talking too low or I was talking too loud.
Parallel: Either he was talking too low
or   I was talking too loud.

4. Repetition of sign words Repeat the sign word of each item of a pair or a series to make the parallelism clear. Common signs are prepositions, articles, related pronouns, subordinating conjunctions, "to" of the infinitive, and auxiliary verbs.

Faulty: The teacher told me that I spent far too much time daydreaming and I needed to study more.
Parallel: The teacher told me *that* I spent far too much time daydreaming and *that* I needed to study more.

EXERCISE 4–12
PARALLELISM

Revise these sentences to make parallelism effective.

1. Jack told us that he knew the way and the gang should follow him.
2. I took the summer job for both the interesting work and the high pay.
3. She was so eager to get a car that she worked all summer, spent nothing on pleasure, and even borrowing money.
4. My trip to New York gave me opportunity for visiting the tourist spots, seeing some plays, and in general to observe life in the big city.
5. I debated whether I should become a college teacher or to major in law.
6. By the third act the audience were showing signs of boredom, impatience, and some people were beginning to leave.
7. Our coach was a perfectionist himself and who expected perfection in others.
8. The quality of *Moby Dick* comes partly from the fact that it is a great adventure story and also because the fear of evil is universal.
9. That lawn seemed two miles in length and a mile wide.
10. He said that I was either mistaken, a fool, or he had been misinformed.

Shifts in Construction: Holding to Your Point of View

Once you choose the way you are going to say something, stick to your point of view unless you have a good reason to shift. Your readers or listeners are following the trail you have set. Don't lead them off. If you start out with one *person* as a subject of a first clause, you should not shift to another person in a second clause, unless there is good reason for the change. In the same way, avoid shifts in *subject or voice, person, tense, command and statement,* and *direct and indirect discourse.*

1. Subject or voice A shift from active to passive voice usually makes a change in subject. In a series, keep two subjects either both acting or both being acted upon.

> **Shift:** After I discovered a leak under the sink, the plumbing tools were got out. (Shift in subject: *I* to *tools.* Shift in voice: active *discovered* to passive *were got out*)
> **Consistent:** After *I discovered* a leak under the sink, *I got out* the plumbing tools.

> **Shift:** *He relocked* the box after its *contents had been* carefully *checked.*
> **Consistent:** The *box was relocked,* after its *contents had been* carefully *checked.*
> **Consistent:** *He relocked* the box after *he had* carefully *checked* its contents.

2. Person A common shift is from third person *(he, she, one, a person, they)* to second person *(you).* Another common shift is from singular *(a person, he, one)* to plural *(they).* Such shifts usually occur when the writer is not thinking of a particular person, but is stating some general truth about people in general.

> **Shift:** When *a person* does his best, even if *you* fail, you have the satisfaction of honest effort. (third to second)
> **Consistent:** When *a person* does his best, even if *he* fails, *he* has the satisfaction of honest effort.

> **Shift:** When any *person* feels *her* efforts are appreciated, *they* are likely to do a good job. (singular to plural)
> **Consistent:** When any *person* feels her efforts are appreciated, *she* is likely to do a good job.

3. Tense Especially watch for shifts between present and past.

> **Shift:** Macbeth *is delighted* when the witches tell him that no man born of woman will harm him, and then he *learned* that Macduff had an unnatural birth.
> **Consistent:** Macbeth *was delighted* when the witches told him that no man born of woman would harm him, and then he *learned* that Macduff had an unnatural birth.

> **Shift:** Then the whistle *blew,* but the ball *arches* through the air and *drops* through the basket.
> **Consistent:** Then the whistle *blew,* but the ball *arched* through the air and *dropped* through the basket.

4. Command and statement

Shift: First *skim* the chapter rapidly, and then *you can study* it thoroughly.
Consistent: First *skim* the chapter rapidly, and then *study* it thoroughly.
Consistent: First *you should skim* the chapter rapidly, and then *you can study* it thoroughly.

5. Direct and indirect discourse Especially watch for shifts between statement and question.

Shift: He asked *if I wanted* a taxi and *did I have* money to pay for it.
Consistent: He asked *if I wanted* a taxi and *if I had* money to pay for it.
Consistent: He asked, *"Do you want* a taxi and *do you have* money to pay for it?"*

EXERCISE 4-13
CONSISTENT CONSTRUCTION

Identify the kind of shift as voice and subject, person, tense, command and statement, or direct and indirect discourse. Revise to make the construction consistent.

1. Every individual has some characteristics all their own.
2. When she stepped off the plane and walked toward me, I almost think I am dreaming.
3. The art gallery exhibited a special collection of Italian paintings, and students were admitted free.
4. I found only one thing wrong with my new job. No matter how nice you were to the customers, they still complained.
5. Early in *Paradise Lost* Milton describes Satan as quite heroic, but later on the author made him repulsive.
6. I spend more study time on biology, but history is my favorite subject.
7. The teacher asked if we would finish one time and how good a job were we doing.
8. Decide just which subject to study first, and then you should concentrate all your thought upon it.
9. Jack investigated the inside of the old house, while the barn and grounds were checked by the rest of us.
10. The policeman asked whether I was trying to cause an accident or was there really an emergency.

Misplaced Modifiers: Parts Out of Place

We gave some milk to the stray cat that we had left over from breakfast.

What? Are we having cats for breakfast now? Adjectives and adverbs try to modify the word next to them. If you place your modifier so that a distracting word comes between the modifier and the word it modifies, the first reading may be either fuzzy or ludicrous. Here is a clear and logical version of the sentence about the cat.

> We gave some milk that we had left over from breakfast to the stray cat.

Correct misplaced modifiers by moving the confusing modifier so that it refers to one word or phrase and to one only. Sometimes the whole sentence must be reworked.

> **Confusing:** Mr. Wilson told me on Monday to practice more.
> **Clear:** Mr. Wilson told me to practice more on Monday.
> **Clear:** On Monday, Mr. Wilson told me to practice more.

> **Confusing:** My father warned me never to point a gun at anybody that was loaded.
> **Clear:** My father warned me never to point a loaded gun at anybody.

You should watch especially for the following kinds of misplaced modifiers.

1. Single words in the wrong place Such words as *almost, also, even, just, nearly,* and *only* should usually come just before the word modified.

> **Misplaced:** It was the worst food I have nearly ever eaten.
> **Clear:** It was nearly the worst food I have ever eaten.

2. Phrases and clauses in the wrong place

> **Misplaced:** We put up posters about the dance all around town.
> **Clear:** All round town, we put up posters about the dance.
> **Misplaced:** After the dance we served refreshments to the guests on paper plates.
> **Clear:** After the dance, we served refreshments on paper plates to the guests.

> **Misplaced:** The landlord told us on the following Tuesday we would have to move.
> **Clear:** On the following Tuesday, the landlord told us we would have to move.
> **Clear:** The landlord told us we would have to move on the following Tuesday.

3. Split infinitives Usually parts of an infinitive should not be split. It is better, though, to split an infinitive than to be artificial.

> **Awkward split:** He determined to more than ever study mathematics.
> **Improved:** He determined to study mathematics more than ever.
> **Justifiable split:** He determined to more than double his study time.
> **Justifiable split:** They asked us to please be quiet.

4. Clumsy separation of main sentence parts English word order is very flexible, but a writer should not jolt the reader with split constructions which are clumsy and pointless. Guard especially against awkward splitting of subject and verb, verb phrases, and verb and complement.

Awkward: Borrowing frequently leads to loss of friendship.
Improved: Frequently, borrowing leads to loss of friendship.
Improved: Frequent borrowing leads to loss of friendship.

Awkward: He hit with one mighty swing at a fast ball a home run.
Improved: With one mighty swing at a fast ball, he hit a home run.

EXERCISE 4-14
MISPLACED MODIFIERS

Revise these sentences to correct misplaced parts.

1. Because he had almost answered all the questions, he got a good grade on the test.
2. The next patient we visited was a little girl lying on a cot with two broken legs.
3. The investigators only wanted to find out how the people lived, not to tell them how to live.
4. She wore a ring on her left hand with a large diamond in it.
5. The book about the honey bees which James lent me was very interesting.
6. She asked me on Tuesday to call her.
7. He bought a guitar at a pawn shop that cost ten dollars.
8. He bought without haggling at all over the price the car.
9. The woman who had been yelling quietly sat down.
10. Mother warned me not to marry Tom very seriously.

Dangling Modifiers: Parts Left Hanging

A *dangling modifier* is a phrase or clause which is not attached clearly to some word in the sentence. It seems to modify a word to which it is not logically related, while the word it should modify is not even in the sentence.

Walking through the park, the *flowers* were beautiful.

Logically, the opening phrase needs a word like "we" or somebody to do the walking.

Walking through the park, we thought the flowers were beautiful.

A modifier must usually be attached to some word or words in the sentence. If the word it should modify is not even in the sentence, the part is left hanging and tries to attach itself to a word to which it is not logically related. Watch for two main locations for dangling modifiers.

   1. Dangling modifier at the beginning of the sentence   Most dangling modifiers are phrases which come at the beginning of the sentence and which should connect to the subject but do not do so. Most of these are *to* words or *-ing* words, or verbals. Verbals imply action and to be clear must point to a word that names the doer of the action.

Swimming rapidly,   ✗

Check the word just after the introductory phrase. The reader expects the word in the X spot to be doing the "swimming." If the wrong word is there, the reader is confused.

Swimming rapidly, the river . . .

We do not expect the river itself to be swimming. Obviously something else is meant. There are two easy ways to correct such dangling parts at the beginning of the sentence.

1. *Put in a noun or a pronoun for the phrase to tie to.*

Swimming rapidly, we . . .

2. *Change the dangling phrase to a clause with subject and verb.*

Because we swam rapidly, the river . . .

2. Dangling modifiers at the end of the sentence Check phrases indicating cause or result coming at the end of the sentence and introduced by such words as *caused by, resulting in, thereby,* and *thus.* If these phrases have no noun or pronoun to be the specific cause or result suggested, they are best corrected by rewriting the entire sentence. Ask the question, what caused? and answer it with a specific word. If the specific word that fits is not in the sentence, rewrite.

Dangling: John worked fast and hard, causing him to make mistakes.
Clear: Because John worked fast and hard, he made mistakes.

Dangling: Playing the guitar is his passion, thereby not getting enough outside activity.
Clear: Because playing the guitar is his passion, he does not get enough outside activity.

EXERCISE 4-15
DANGLING MODIFIERS

Revise these sentences to eliminate dangling modifiers.

1. Looking out the window, the lawn was a vast green plain.
2. To be a good actor, a sharp memory is necessary.
3. Having read Porter's *Collected Stories,* my love of fiction increased very much.
4. By working at the concession stand, all the drinks were free.
5. At last having proved my driving ability, my parents allowed me to own a car.
6. A good light is essential to study efficiently.
7. The rain having slackened, we decided to run for the car.
8. Before leaving the house, my room had to be cleared.
9. Her nerves were shaking, resulting from the accident.
10. Wearing my new suit and necktie, Mother took me to the employment office.

Reference of Pronouns: Fuzzy Pronouns

Pronouns usually take their meaning from nouns which have preceded them. Thus a pronoun—such as *he, his, it, they, which,* and *that*—has meaning only when it clearly refers to a specific noun (its antecedent). The following sentence is loaded with the kinds of vague reference that make communication fuzzy:

> John told his father that he was driving too fast when he passed the police car in heavy traffic, which annoyed them.

The pronouns *he, which,* and *them* are vague. To get rid of the fuzzy reference, make every pronoun clearly point to a single noun, not a near-noun or two nouns.

> John admitted to his father that the police were annoyed because he was driving too fast when he passed the police car in heavy traffic.

Or, depending upon your meaning:

> John told his father, "You annoyed the police because you were driving too fast when you passed the police car in heavy traffic."

Five types of construction most commonly cause vague reference:

1.   Two words as possible antecedents   If there are two possible antecedents for a pronoun, recast the sentence to leave one clear antecedent.

> **Ambiguous:**   *Mary* told *Ann* that *she* had made a mistake. (Is *she* Mary or Ann?)
> **Clear:**   Mary told Ann, "You have made a mistake."
> **Clear:**   Mary told Ann, "I have made a mistake."
> **Clear:**   Mary admitted to Ann that she had made a mistake.
> **Clear:**   Mary accused Ann of making a mistake.

2.   An almost-noun   The antecedent should be the exact form of the noun for which the pronoun is a substitute. Modifiers, possessives, or implied nouns are fuzzy.

> **Vague:**   Before he could repair his *rabbit* pens, some of them got away. (modifier)
> **Clear:**   Before he could repair his rabbit pens, some of the rabbits got away.

> **Vague:**   Toward the end of *King Lear's* life, he realized how blind he had been. (possessive)
> **Clear:**   Toward the end of King Lear's life, King Lear realized how blind he had been.

> **Vague:**   His father was a *lawyer,* which is a profession I have always admired. (implied noun)
> **Clear:**   His father was in law, which is a profession I have always admired.

3.   An idea or a group of words as antecedent   The pronouns *which, that, this,* and *it* are often used vaguely to refer to an idea. Give them a specific single noun word or compound to refer to.

Vague: I did not buy a ticket, *which* was considered a disloyalty to the school.
Clear: My not buying a ticket was considered a disloyalty to the school.

Vague: The play ended a little before eleven; this gave us plenty of time for dinner afterwards.
Clear: The play ended a little before eleven, and so we had plenty of time for dinner afterwards.

4. Personal pronouns in a general sense *You, they,* and *it* are usually vague and illogical when they stand for people and things in general rather than for a specific noun.

Vague: At the state hospital, *they* treat the patients courteously.
Clear: At the state hospital, the doctors treat the patients courteously.

Vague: I like courses in economics because they teach *you* how to use money wisely.
Clear: I like courses in economics because they teach a person (or *me*) how to use money wisely.

Indefinite "it" and "you": Colloquial speech and writing allow *you* to mean "people in general."

In pioneer days, you had to be strong to survive.

The word *it* can be used in idiomatic expressions of time, weather, and distance (It is raining. It is fifty miles to Chicago.) and as an introductory subject (It is too late to turn back.).

5. Far-off antecedent If the antecedent is too far back in the sentence or paragraph, repeat the noun or rewrite the sentence.

Vague: The little pup chased the birds from the yard and then trotted back and curled up by the other dogs to sleep, but immediately *they* came back.
Clear: The little pup chased the birds from the yard and then trotted back and curled up by the other dogs to sleep, but immediately the birds came back.

EXERCISE 4-16
REFERENCE OF PRONOUNS

Eliminate vague reference in these two groups of sentences.

1. Because the gas station attendant was not paying attention, some of it overflowed onto his shoes.
2. In the southern European countries, they are likely to be overly emotional.
3. Even though we trimmed the tree very carefully, Mother did not appreciate it.
4. Janet worked fast and efficiently, and that pleased her boss.
5. In Emerson's *Self-Reliance,* he says that a person should trust himself.
6. He was an excellent football player in college, but he did not plan to make it his career.
7. A medical student may concentrate too exclusively on professional courses, which leaves him generally uneducated.

8. Bill told his father that he had dented the fender of the car.
9. She made promises to her parents that she would study hard and make good grades, but it was spring and studying was dull and so they were soon forgotten.
10. There was one big question: What was the woman's name who had visited us yesterday?

1. Diane found that in France they did not understand her very well.
2. The teacher cancelled the exam, which was just what I wanted.
3. She clenched the arms of the chair until they turned red.
4. Richard wanted to be a painter, although he knew he would hardly make a living at it.
5. Sam told his father that his voice was getting hoarse.
6. In Shakespeare's *Macbeth,* he tells of the evils of ambition.
7. The dog leaped into the chicken yard and began to chase them.
8. A liar lives a risky life, for you never can tell when a lie will catch up with you.
9. When I looked through the leaves and saw the black shapes of the bass in the water, I began to creep through the bushes to the edge of the stream, being careful not to make a sound or an obvious movement, for they are easily scared.
10. *Of Human Destiny* is a book everyone should read, for you can derive much good from it.

Omissions: Fill in the Gaps

Be careful not to omit words necessary to make your sentences clear and logical. Omission of necessary words usually occurs because you are thinking ahead of your writing or because you are imitating speech patterns. Written sentences must be more precise and complete than spoken sentences, so you must carefully proofread for omission of necessary words. Be especially careful not to omit the second term in a compound construction, which needs two key meaning-words or two function words. Here are the kinds of constructions in which necessary words are likely to be omitted.

1. Verbs Check to see if two verbs for the same subject require a different tense or form.

> **Omission:** All the items *were* inventoried and a report made. (change in subject)
> **Correct:** All the items *were* inventoried and a report *was* made.

> **Omission:** An honest man always *has* and always *will* be hard to find. (change in tense form)
> **Correct:** An honest man always has *been* and always will *be* hard to find.

2. Subjects Check to see if two verbs require different subject words. Do not omit a necessary subject in a sentence with two verbs.

> **Omission:** The cost of my trip to Europe was $1,200 but contributed much to my knowledge of other peoples.

Clear: The cost of my trip to Europe was $1,200, but the trip contributed much to my knowledge of other peoples.

3.   Prepositions in idioms   In parallel phrases do not omit one of the necessary prepositions. Certain adjectives and verbs are normally followed by certain prepositions. For example, idiom calls for

interested *in*	devoted *to*
object *to*	aware *of*
coincide *with*	disturbed *by*

Omission: He was either unaware or undisturbed by the hammering.
Correct: He was either unaware *of* or undisturbed *by* the hammering.

In idiomatic phrases of time, the preposition may be omitted if the sentence is not awkward.

Correct: He left that winter for South America.

Omission: Weekends the campus is deserted.
Correct: On weekends the campus is deserted.

4.   Article or determiner in a compound   Repeat the article or determiner (such as *the, an, my*) to show that two words joined by *and* refer to two things, not one.

One person: My roommate and best friend helped drill me for the exam.
Two persons: My roommate and my best friend helped drill me for the exam.
Clearly two persons: My aunt and uncle visited me at camp.

5.   That conjunction   The conjunction *that* should not be omitted from a dependent clause if there is danger of misreading the sentence.

Omission: He suggested the answer would be hard to find.
Clear: He suggested *that* the answer would be hard to find.

6.   Terms of comparison   To make comparisons clear, complete, and equal, don't omit words necessary to the comparison. Check to make sure these items are present:

1.   The two items compared: *Mary—Sue*
2.   The aspect compared: *tallness*
3.   The function words or parts necessary to state the comparison: *as, than, -er*

term 1   *aspect funct*   *term 2*
Mary is   tall*er than*   *Sue*

        funct   *funct*
Mary is   *as*   tall   *as*   Sue.

        funct   *funct*
Mary is   *as* tall *as,*   if not tall*er than,* Sue.

Items often omitted are one of the terms to be compared or one of the function words. The following examples show common kinds of omissions:

Term omitted: The smog in Los Angeles is greater than New York City.
Complete: The smog in Los Angeles is greater than that in New York City.

Aspect omitted: He likes golf better than his wife.
Complete: He likes golf better than he likes his wife.
Complete: He likes golf better than his wife does.

Second term omitted: Jack is one of the strongest, if not the strongest man, I know.
Complete: Jack is one of the strongest men, if not the strongest man, I know.

Function word omitted: He is as smart, if not smarter than, his brother.
Complete: He is as smart as, if not smarter than, his brother.

EXERCISE 4-17
OMITTED WORDS

Insert necessary words omitted from these sentences.

1. My grade in math at mid-term was D and stood little chance of improving it.
2. In life, friends are scarce and one very good friend very scarce.
3. The election's outcome was prophesied the same on the radio, the television, and the newspaper.
4. I believed the story, if not explained, would be accepted as true.
5. A new den and library were too much to add to the house at that time.
6. The attendance at the district rally was larger than last year.
7. Mr. Benton paid me more than Mary.
8. *Zorba the Greek* is as interesting, if not more interesting than, any book I have read.
9. Our new governor seems much more capable.
10. *The Bead Game* is one of the hardest if not the hardest book I have tried to read.

Emphasis: The Final Force

Emphasis is important in two ways. The sentences must have enough force to hold your readers' interest, and the important ideas must be kept foremost in their minds.

Emphasis is a result of many things: (1) clear thinking about worthwhile ideas; (2) correct and clear sentence structure; (3) vivid and accurate word choice; (4) careful use of subordination, placement of modifiers, reference of pronouns, parallelism, and so on.

Beyond these principles, emphasis is achieved by the following devices:

1. Beginning and end as key positions
2. Order of climax
3. Periodic sentences

4. Delayed subject
5. Unusual word order
6. Active voice
7. Repetition of key words

BEGINNING AND ENDING AS KEY POSITIONS

End your sentence with the most important idea. Strongest in our minds is what we have read last. Lead off with your next most important idea. Bury the minor, dull, but necessary ideas in the middle.

Weak ending: When the flood waters rose, over 3,000 people were left homeless, it was calculated.
Emphatic ending: When the flood waters rose, over 3,000 people, it was calculated, were left homeless.

Weak beginning: In my opinion, apathetic voters are the basic cause of corrupt politicians.
Emphatic beginning: Apathetic voters are, in my opinion, the basic cause of corrupt politicians.

EXERCISE 4-18
EMPHATIC POSITION

Revise the following sentences by putting important ideas in emphatic position.

1. According to doctors, lung cancer is caused by smoking, to some extent.
2. Our country is in for a period of social strife, if I am reading the signs correctly.
3. Practice is necessary for one to achieve perfection, generally.
4. As his lawyer saw it, the trial was prejudiced against John from the very beginning.
5. On the other hand, the new high-yield rice introduced in India will reduce famine, specialists believe.

ORDER OF CLIMAX

Three or more items in a series should be arranged in emphatic order:

The country's main concerns are hunger, sickness, and death.

While some items usually take a logical order, such as death over hunger, you may choose your own rising order of importance according to context and purpose. For instance, you may wish to stress food problems:

The country's main concerns are sickness, death, and, most immediately, hunger.

Final position is most emphatic. Make sure you put the items in the order of importance called for by your context.

Anticlimactic: The tornado in our area killed nine people, injured twenty people, and destroyed two houses.

Emphatic: The tornado in our area destroyed two houses, injured twenty people, and killed nine people.

EXERCISE 4-19
ORDER OF CLIMAX

Revise the following sentences to put the ideas in order of climax.

1. According to the police record, Harry Satin had been suspected of being a dope pusher, of robbing parking meters, and of running around with a juvenile hoodlum gang.
2. Jim Haggard was president of the bank, chairman of the hospital board, and member of the Rotary Club.
3. Then her uncle died and left her a string of apartment buildings, an antique watch, and three war medals.
4. The dog raced through the house overturning the Christmas tree, breaking Mother's precious hall mirror, and scattering gifts all over the room.
5. The news of my winning the award made me want to shout for joy, to dance, and to laugh.

PERIODIC SENTENCES

The *periodic sentence* withholds its main or completing idea until the very end. A *loose sentence* states the full idea early and then adds qualifiers and other details, often parenthetically. With a loose sentence, readers' attention can lag after they read the main idea. But a periodic sentence creates suspense and demands attention because, to get the meaning, the readers cannot stop until they get to the period.

Loose and unemphatic: I entered the tournament and, of all wonders, I won first place, going against the advice of my friends, the cautions of my coach, and in some ways my own best judgment.

Periodic and emphatic: Against the advice of my friends, the cautions of my coach, and in some ways my own best judgment, I entered the tournament, and, of all wonders, I won first place.

Not all sentences should be made into periodic sentences since it is often most effective to put the central idea first.

Loose and effective: She stopped the flow of blood with a piece of cloth torn from the hem of her dress.

EXERCISE 4-20
PERIODIC SENTENCES

Revise whichever sentences can be made more emphatic as periodic.

1. I stepped to the plate and hit a home run in the last half of the ninth inning with two outs and the score tied.
2. We finally won the game after three hazardous, breathtaking extra innings.
3. We will never have peace on earth until man sees not only that he must love others but that others need to be loved.
4. The silence was so absolute it was eloquent, when we paused breathlessly to let the mind hear.
5. We will have better government only when the people take it upon themselves to vote with intelligence and with concern for the total society.

DELAYED SUBJECT

The subject is delayed in the periodic sentence simply by putting phrases in a certain order. Verbal devices like the expletives *it* and *there, what* clauses, and general synonyms also hold suspense by pointing to the subject to come later. These introductory words are like warning signs to alert the reader: "Important idea just ahead."

> **Standard:**   An angry crowd was gathering at the corner.
> **Delayed:**   There was an angry crowd gathering at the street corner.

> **Standard:**   Thoughts of the starving children in Burma disturbed me most.
> **Delayed main idea:**   What disturbed me most was thoughts of the starving children in Burma.

> **Standard:**   I speak of freedom of speech and expression, freedom of every person to worship God in his own way, freedom from want, freedom from fear.
> **General synonym:**   I speak of four freedoms—freedom of speech and expression, freedom of every person to worship God in his own way, freedom from want, freedom from fear.

EXERCISE 4-21
DELAYED SUBJECT

Put in more emphatic order by delaying the subject with verbal devices.

1. Famine, over-population, and political corruption are the most serious problems in the country.
2. The job can be done in more than one way.
3. The emptiness of the old house made me nervous.
4. To observe one person being cruel to another is never very pleasant.
5. I have always had difficulty feeling at ease with strangers.

UNUSUAL WORD ORDER

Any word gains emphasis when it varies from the expected word order, such as *subject-verb-complement.*

> **Normal:** I would never put up with such an insult.
> **Out of order:** Never would I put up with such an insult.

> **Normal:** The gun went crack and the hawk crumpled out of the sky.
> **Out of order:** Crack went the gun and the hawk crumpled out of the sky.

Unusual word order must be used sparingly. As such a forceful means for gaining emphasis, it can easily become artificial and affected. We could well advise, "Sparingly must unusual word order be used."

EXERCISE 4-22
UNUSUAL WORD ORDER

Use unusual order in these sentences to gain emphasis.

1. The rafter went crack and the roof began to sag.
2. I dared not risk such a dangerous move.
3. He would never write such a story in a million years.
4. We could hardly expect honesty and integrity from a man with his past.
5. All the glory of that once great empire is gone.

ACTIVE VOICE

Because the active voice expresses the direct action of the subject, it is more emphatic. As a rule, use the active voice. Use passive only when you can clearly justify it.

> **Weak passive:** Ten dollars was given to me by my father.
> **Strong active:** My father gave me ten dollars.

> **Weak passive:** As the top of the mountain is reached, the whole valley is spread out before you.
> **Strong active:** As you reach the top of the mountain, you see the whole valley spread out before you.

Some passive constructions are preferred to the active. If the subject is not known or if the receiver of the action is more important than the action, use passive voice.

> **Strong passive:** The new recreation hall was finished in September.
> **Strong passive:** The Christmas tree was decorated entirely in blue.
> **Strong passive:** Cynthia Barnes was arrested, tried, and convicted of the crime of burglary.

EXERCISE 4-23
ACTIVE VOICE

Replace the weak passive voice by the active.

1. The swollen river was crossed carefully by the wagon train.
2. As the curtain was brought down on the play, the actors were loudly applauded by the audience.
3. *To the Lighthouse* was first published in 1927.
4. Considerable nervousness was felt by Hal when he was stopped by the policeman.
5. A thin line of black paint is put along the edge of the plate to indicate where the motion block is to be attached.

REPETITION OF KEY WORDS

Repetition of sentence patterns for effectiveness has been discussed under *Parallelism.* Key words can also be repeated to give force to main ideas.

Liberty, I am told, is a divine thing. Liberty when it becomes the "Liberty to die by starvation" is not so divine!

—Thomas Carlyle

. . . that government of the people, by the people, and for the people, shall not perish from the earth.

—Abraham Lincoln

Repitition must be confined to key words or sentence patterns and must be carefully used to gain emphasis. Careless and needless repetition of words leads to dull, flat writing.

Wordy: When *one* studies the *poem* carefully, *one* will find that the many allusions in the *poem* really carry the meaning of the *poem* to a level deeper than *one* first found in the *poem.*

EXERCISE 4-24
REPETITION OF KEY WORDS

Analyze the following passages for emphatic repetition.

1. It is true that you may fool all the people some of the time; you can even fool some of the people all the time; but you can't fool all of the people all the time.

—Abraham Lincoln

2. The governor and the legislators are corrupt. Their hired servants and underlings are corrupt. But worst of all, the voters who allow them in office are most corrupt.

—William Kinser

3.   And the entire object of true education is to make people not merely *do* the right things, but *enjoy* the right things:—not merely be industrious, but to love industry—not merely learned, but to love knowledge—not merely pure, but to love purity—not merely just, but to hunger and thirst after justice.

—John Ruskin

4.   That year the grasshoppers came. They ate the vegetables—vegetable, leaf, and stem. They ate the grass and shrubbery. They ate the leaves off the trees. And when there were no leaves left, they ate the bark. In three days the farm was stripped.

—Karen Matthews

5.   Words, and more words, and nothing but words, had been all the fruit of all the toil of all the most renowned sages of sixty generations.

—Thomas Macauley

5

The Word:
Precise, Direct, Alive

Exactness

Check the dictionary for meanings of words that you are not sure about. Almost all words have two kinds of meanings: *denotation* and *connotation*.

DENOTATION

The denotation of a word is its basic dictionary definition. It identifies an idea, an object, or a quality. It is the word's core of meaning and is the first you must consider.

The basic dictionary denotation of *mother* is "female parent." *To be drunk* is "to have one's faculties impaired by an excess of alcoholic liquor." *War* is "a major armed conflict between nations or between organized parties within a state." To the extent that a word refers to the same thing for all people concerned, the meaning is denotative. Some words have only one denotative meaning with no other suggestive force or shade of meaning, such as *magnesium, diatom, parallax, diesel.* But most words have different shades of meaning that different people associate with the word because of their particular experience with it.

CONNOTATION

The connotation of a word is the suggestions, associations, and emotional responses of the word. Connotations are somewhat different for everyone. But many words have fairly standardized connotations. Thus, *mother* usually means more than the dictionary's denotation of "female parent." The word often connotes emotional warmth, security, and comfort. The word *drunk* may connote immorality, degeneracy, happy irresponsibility, unhappy irresponsibility, or pleasure, depending on the context and the attitudes one has toward the experience described by the word *drunk.* And *war* would have different emotional meanings for one who has been maimed by war, for a family who have fled for shelter when the bombs fell, for one who is getting wealthy because of war. The connotation of a word may not only indicate a special shade of meaning different from a near-synonym (such as *drunk* or *plastered*), but it may also suggest attitudes, such as approval or disapproval, ludicrous or serious.

> The poor child needs somebody to *mother* him.
> (approval: to care for; give affection, comfort, and security)

> Johnny is spoiled because you've been *mothering* him.
> (disapproval: overprotecting, catering to)

The adjectives *thin, skinny,* and *slender,* all have the same denotation, in referring to below-average weight for one's height. But you may please someone if you call them *slender,* displease them if you call them *skinny.*

USING WORDS EXACTLY

In using words with exact meaning, you must check both the denotation and the connotation.

a. *Does the word have the meaning you give it?* Check the various definitions in the dictionary to see if the word has the meaning you are trying to give it. Are you confusing it with another word? For instance, the word *infer* is occasionally misused as if it had the same meaning as *imply.*

> **Incorrect:** He *inferred* by his grin that he was not telling the truth.
> **Exact:** He *implied* by his grin that he was not telling the truth.
> **Exact:** I *inferred* from his grin that he was not telling the truth.

b. *Is the meaning of the word the meaning you want?* Check both the dictionary and your knowledge of human experience to see if the word has the proper shade of meaning to express your thought. Do you want to suggest approval or disapproval?

> **Inexact attitude:** It certainly was an exhilarating experience to hear Yehudi Menuhin play the Mendelssohn concerto on his *fiddle.*
> **Exact:** It certainly was an exhilarating experience to hear Yehudi Menuhin play the Mendelssohn concerto on his *violin.*

EXERCISE 5-1
USING WORDS CORRECTLY

Use each of the following words in a sentence to indicate its correct meaning.

1.	healthful	2.	healthy
3.	enervate	4.	invigorate
5.	practical	6.	practicable
7.	disinterested	8.	uninterested
9.	immigrant	10.	emigrant
11.	flaunt	12.	flout
13.	climactic	14.	climatic
15.	borne	16.	born
17.	historic	18.	historical
19.	opaque	20.	translucent

EXERCISE 5-2
EXPLAINING DIFFERENCES IN MEANING

Explain the differences in meaning among the following groups of words.

1. fat, plump, obese, heavy, stout
2. lady, woman, dame, wench, girl
3. drunk, inebriated, plastered, intoxicated, stoned, potted
4. dead, defunct, expired, deceased
5. persistent, strong-willed, firm, stubborn, obstinate, pig-headed
6. renown, fame, notoriety
7. house, home, residence, dwelling, domicile, pad

EXERCISE 5-3
EVALUATING MEANINGS OF A WORD

Evaluate the word "old-fashioned" in the following sentences to see what meanings it has besides its denotation of referring to past time.

1. The dress she was wearing was rather old-fashioned.
2. She is decorating her living room in old-fashioned American.
3. That idea is a little old-fashioned, isn't it?
4. I'm just a simple, old-fashioned girl.
5. I believe in the old-fashioned philosophy of no work, no eat.
6. Stop in for some old-fashioned cooking.

Concrete and Specific

All words can be classed as concrete or abstract and as specific or general.

CONCRETE AND ABSTRACT

Words that name the ideas and qualities of things are *abstract*. What they refer to cannot be perceived through the five senses of touch, taste, sight, hearing, and smell. Some abstract words are *courage, beauty, goodness, honor, color, education.*

Concrete words are sensory words. What they refer to can be perceived through the five senses. Some concrete words are *book, animal, tree, building, sound.*   [handwritten: VISIBLE CAN SEE ↑ feel & Touch]

SPECIFIC AND GENERAL

A *general* term names a class or a group and stands for broad characteristics or things. A *specific* term names a member of a group and stands for more definite, precise things or characteristics. *Flower* is a general word; *rose* is a specific word. Context may make a word more or less specific in relation to another word. Thus, flower is more specific than *plant, rose* is more specific than *flower, red rambler rose* is more specific than *rose.*

GENERAL	SPECIFIC	MORE SPECIFIC
animal	mammal	man
reading matter	novel	*Wuthering Heights*
vehicle	automobile	Chevrolet
food	appetizer	shrimp cocktail

Abstract words tend to be general. Concrete words tend to be specific. A word is either abstract or concrete. It will be more or less specific depending on the context.   [handwritten: CANT SEE IT (FAR OFF)]

life	abstract
living thing	concrete and general
animal	concrete and general
dog	concrete and general
collie	concrete and more specific
my collie, Jiggs	concrete and most specific

The value of general and abstract words is that they allow us to summarize a broad range of experience, to express large concepts and theories.

General and abstract: Man is capable of cruelty.
Man is capable of generosity.   [handwritten: MUST BE SPECIFIC]

The value of concrete and specific words is that they illustrate and support general statements.

Concrete and specific: Mr. Jenkins whipped his eight-year-old-son with a belt so viciously that a doctor had to treat the welts on the boy's back.

Mrs. Jackson gave that poor family her last dollar.

Too many abstract and general terms are bound to make writing and speaking vague and dull. You must use abstractions and generalizations to make statements of significance. Then you must pin down your generalizations to tangible experience by means of specific and concrete words. It is concrete and specific details which make the idea meaningful and which allow the reader or listener to grasp it.

Vague generalization: Jane Campbell has courage.

Meaningful concrete and specific experience: Although not a good swimmer, Jane Campbell jumped into the rushing water and pulled Johnny to safety.

EXERCISE 5-4
MAKING GENERAL WORDS SPECIFIC

Make a list of more specific words for the following general terms. For instance, for *say,* you could list *mumble, mutter, whisper, shout, yell, state, utter, drawl.*

1. look
2. sit
3. ask
4. walk
5. good

6. bad
7. entertainment
8. person
9. vegetation
10. land

EXERCISE 5-5
MAKING ABSTRACT TERMS CONCRETE

List enough specific, concrete details to make each of the following abstractions meaningful and tangible.

1. democractic
2. virtue
3. beautiful
4. brotherly love
5. peace

6. American way of life
7. unselfish
8. charity
9. happiness
10. reality

EXERCISE 5-6
MAKING THE GENERAL MORE SPECIFIC

Rewrite the following sentences, making general words more specific.

1. A man was looking into a store window.
2. I did a lot of things during my vacation.
3. Several aspects of the room made it unattractive.
4. The injury that our best player had suffered was serious enough to keep him out much of the season.
5. After eating, we had some really good entertainment.
6. One member of the group was irresponsible about some of her duties.
7. During the last part of the trip, we encountered several difficulties.
8. Many items around the place needed to be repaired before the people could move in.
9. It's an interesting book.
10. The actions of the people represented both a test of strength and an effort to gain prestige for the cause.

Freshness   *ALIVE*

Use fresh expressions, not trite expressions. A trite expression is also called a *cliché*, a *stereotyped expression*, or a *hackneyed phrase*. It is one that has become worn out by overuse, such as *straight from the shoulder, burn the midnight oil, last but not least.*

Individual words themselves do not become trite. Words like *go, eat, road, wise, pay, nose* can constantly be fresh. It is the phrase, perhaps once vivid and fresh, that has become commonplace and meaningless through overuse and lack of original thought. Consider the following sentence:

Jack Elman earns his *bread and butter* by the *sweat of his brow.*

We are not convinced of the genuineness of Jack Elman's industry or difficulty. Because of trite thinking the wording is trite and the experience is empty. The following simple sentence, although not worthy of Shakespearean tragedy, is worthy of our sympathy.

Jack Elman works fifty hours a week at hard labor in a factory.   *SAYS MORE*

Checklist: Trite Expressions

You can hardly avoid trite expressions entirely. But you can take two helpful steps. First, you can do your own fresh, original thinking and use the best words to describe your actual thoughts. And, second, you can become aware of clichés and try to avoid them.

Here is a list of trite expressions. There are thousands more.

abreast of the times	blissfully ignorant	crack of dawn
acid test	blushing bride	depths of despair
after all is said and done	bolt from the blue	dire necessity
agony of suspense	bored to death	dire straits
agree to disagree	bow to the inevitable	doomed to disappointment
all nature seemed clothed in	breathless silence	drastic action
all work and no play	brilliant performance	dull, sickening thud
among those present	bring order out of chaos	each and every
an uphill climb	budding genius	easier said than done
artistic temperament	burn the midnight oil	equal to the occasion
as luck would have it	busy as a bee	familiar landmark
at a loss for words	by leaps and bounds	few and far between
at cross purposes	by the sweat of his brow	filthy lucre
at one fell swoop	call it quits	financially embarrassed
beat a hasty retreat	caught like rats in a trap	finger of suspicion
better half	center of attraction	for better or worse
better late than never	cold as ice	goes without saying
bitter end	conspicuous by his absence	good personality
black as ink	cool as a cucumber	green as grass
blazing inferno		green with envy
blighted romance		heartfelt thanks

holy matrimony
ignorance is bliss
in conclusion
in all its glory
in the last analysis
in the final analysis
in this day and age
it stands to reason
last but not least
long arm of the law
long-felt need
make hay while the
  sun shines
memorable occasion
method in his
  madness
mine of information
mother nature
neat as a pin
needless to say
never put off till
  tomorrow what
  you can do today
nick of time
nip and tuck
nip in the bud
none the worse for
  wear

on the ball
on the beam
partake of
  refreshments
picture of health
point with pride
poor but honest
proud possessor of
psychological
  moment
put in an appearance
powers that be
quick as a flash
reign supreme
rich and varied
  experience
ripe old age
rotten to the core
sadder but wiser
slowly but surely
smell a rat
snail's pace
sober as a judge
square meal
steady as a rock
straight from the
  shoulder
sumptuous repast

tall, dark, and
  handsome
this day and age
tide of battle
tiny tots
tired but happy
to the bitter end
too funny for words
traffic snarled
truth is stranger than
  fiction
undercurrent of
  excitement
untiring efforts
variety is the spice of
  life
venture a suggestion
view with alarm
wend our way
wheel of fortune
white as snow
without further ado
words fail to describe
work like a horse
work like a Trojan
wreak havoc

EXERCISE 5-7
AVOIDING CLICHÉS

Write sentences using fresh substitutes for ten of the clichés in the preceding list. Use brackets to enclose the cliché you are replacing.

EXERCISE 5-8
CLICHÉS

Make a list of twenty clichés other than those in the preceding list.

Naturalness *Be Yourself*

Good writing, especially exposition, should be natural, simple, and straightforward. The reader is likely to lose faith in your sincerity if you use pretentious, artificial diction. Such writing tends to emphasize words rather than ideas—usually not even interesting words, but vague, fuzzy, and abstract words. There are three main kinds of unnatural diction (word choice): *jargon, fine writing,* and *unidiomatic phrases.*

JARGON

In its best sense, jargon is the technical or specialized vocabulary of a particular group, trade, or profession, such as medical jargon, educational jargon, prison jargon, musician's jargon. Such use of language is shoptalk and is quite appropriate among members of the in-group. But it is out of place with a general audience since many of the words are meaningless to them. One member of a group may say to another, "Jack's topkick just gummed his mini. I think that's fish." But if you want to communicate to somebody outside the group, you probably should say something like, "Jack's father has taken away his driving privileges. I don't think it's fair." If you want to communicate, you must use the language known by your audience.

Jargon at its worst is an imitation of a specialized vocabulary. It uses long, abstract words, elaborately constructed sentences, circumlocutions, and technical language for its own sake. The cure for most jargon is clear, direct thought and simple, straightforward language.

> **Jargon:** Inasmuch as the teacher is now aware of the parental causes relative to the child's lack of motivation of study habits, she can cooperate in taking the necessary steps to remedy the situation.
> **Natural:** Now that the teacher knows the child's poor study habits are caused by his parents, she can help the child improve.

> **Jargon:** It is my considered opinion that by examining Wilson's thought processes we shall be in a position to determine the real validity of his hypotheses and conclusions concerning the Jacksboro case.
> **Natural:** I think we should examine Wilson's theories about the Jacksboro case to see how true they are.

FINE WRITING

Fine writing (or *poetic diction)* is writing which is too ornate for its subject. The fine writer uses poetic or lofty words when the simple, direct expression is appropriate.

> **Fine writing:** I uttered a cry of alarm when my sanctuary of study was peremptorily invaded by a band of inebriated cronies.
> **Natural:** I yelled out when a bunch of my drunken friends burst into my room.

The following lists illustrate fine writing.

FINE	NATURAL
domicile	home
king of birds	eagle
halls of learning	university

state of connubial bliss	marriage
beauteous	beautiful
imposing edifice	large house
homo sapiens	man
member of the fairer sex	woman
canine friend	dog
torrential downpour	heavy rain

EXERCISE 5-9
NATURAL DICTION

Rewrite the following sentences in simple, straightforward diction.

1. We may find it necessary to communicate with him tomorrow relative to the change in plans and ascertain what alternate arrangement he may consider feasible.
2. The last rays of the sun were sinking behind the western horizon, when I returned wearily to my domicile after my futile search for the denizens of the deep.
3. They did not find it practicable to make the journey to our place of residence because of the inclement weather conditions.
4. They were holding an intense verbal contention as to whether canines or felines are the most desirable members of the animal kingdom.
5. We must be cognizant of the fact that although a substantial segment of the population occupies areas comprising numerous agricultural units, yet this same segment suffers a deficiency in units of nutritional intake.

IDIOMATIC EXPRESSIONS

Idioms are special word groups which have a total meaning not obviously suggested by the parts. The following idioms are ridiculous or nonsensical if analyzed literally:

to board a train
look up an old friend
catch his eye
takes after her mother
strike a bargain

Prepositions especially get attached to certain words and natural usage demands accustomed combinations. We say "full of joy" not "full with joy," and "filled with joy" not "filled of joy." The following checklist contains a few of the most common idioms.

Checklist: Idiomatic Expressions

abstain from	account to (a person)
accede to (a wish)	accountable for (one's actions)
accommodate (oneself) to (circumstances)	acquaint (oneself or others) with (the facts)
account for (a mistake)	acquiesce in

agree

addicted to (a habit, a drug)
adhere to (principles)
agree with (a person)
authority for (an assertion)
authority on (a subject)
authority over (a subordinate)
averse to (doing something)
capable of (doing something)
capacity of (a container)
characteristic of (a person, special object, or pattern)
desire for (an object)
desirous of (doing something)
desist from (doing something)
dissent from (some opinion)
empty of (some feeling)
envious of (a person)
foreign to (one's nature)
guard against (threat)
infer from
inseparable from
interest in
jealous of (a person or thing)
join in, to, with

obedient to (one's superiors)
part from (one's friends)
peculiar to
preparatory to
prerequisite to (something)
prior to (before)
prohibit from (doing something)
protest against (a situation or assertion)
reason with (someone)
repugnant to (someone)
responsible for (something)
responsible to (someone)
reward for (an act)
separate from (another thing)
substitute for
superior to
sympathize with (someone)
tamper with (a thing)
unmindful of (a situation)
variance with (another)
vary from, in, with
vie with (a person)
worthy of (consideration)

EXERCISE 5-10
USE OF IDIOM

Correct the unidiomatic use of prepositions.

1. We were quite desirous to arrive before sunset.
2. Ever since Peggy became angry at me, she has refused to talk to me.
3. He would not admit to making the mistake, and his father would not absolve him of the responsibility.
4. The usual voter seems oblivious to the skills of the candidates.
5. His aims were identical to mine.
6. Your aims are different than mine.
7. The jury acquitted him from the crime of arson.
8. Three people refuse to conform with the rule against smoking.
9. Everybody complied to his request to talk softly.
10. I am incompatible to her theories of anarchy.

Brevity

An effective writer makes every word count and ruthlessly states ideas in the fewest words possible. Wordiness has several names.

It is called *deadwood* if the sentence has words that aren't working. In the sentence, *The rain which fell yesterday is turning to ice,* the words *which* and *fell* are deadwood. *Yesterday's rain is turning to ice* has brevity.

Wordiness is called *circumlocution* (talking around) if the sentences take the long way around, using several words instead of a single direct one. *In this day and age* means *today; to give advice* means *advise; became the owner of* means *bought* or *received.*

Wordiness is called *tautology* or *redundancy* if it unnecessarily repeats the same idea in different words. These phrases state the same idea twice:

red in color	a true fact
advanced forward	modern youth of today
tall in height	audible to the ear

State your idea directly in the fewest words possible. Constructions which tend to be wordy can usually be traced to one of these causes:

1. Unnecessary words   Delete all words that are not working.

> **Wordy:**   Most of the new styles in this day and age pass quickly.
> **Concise:**   Most new styles pass quickly.

2. Repetition of ideas   Unless for emphasis, state the idea only once.

> **Wordy:**   Sally likes long fictional literature. Reading novels is a real pleasure for her.
> **Concise:**   Sally likes reading novels.

3. Dependent clauses and phrases   Reduce to a phrase or a word.

> **Wordy:**   John Colee, who has been my friend all my life, wanted me to join the army with him.
> **Concise:**   John Colee, my lifelong friend, wanted me to join the army with him.

4. Expletives   Use the true subject instead of *it is* and *there is* when they serve no emphatic purpose in the sentence.

> **Wordy:**   It was on the first day that I ran out of money.
> **Concise:**   On the first day I ran out of money.

5. Excessive adjectives and adverbs   Use specific verbs, nouns, and modifiers instead of a general combination with adjectives and adverbs. *Run quickly* means *speed* or *rush. Turned red with embarrassment* means *blush. A person under twenty-one* is a *minor. A worker in the factory* is a *factory worker. Extremely tired* is *weary* or *fatigued.*

6. Series of short sentences   A series of short sentences may use a wordy repetition of subjects and verbs.

> **Wordy:**   I studied history in the afternoon. Then in the evening I studied English. After that, I treated myself to a movie.
> **Concise:**   After studying history in the afternoon and English in the evening, I treated myself to a movie.

EXERCISE 5-11
BREVITY

Make the following sentences concise.

1. This is the time when we should be examining our basic values.
2. There are many people who are motivated by love of others.
3. It was the most impressive performance I had ever seen before in my life.
4. After she graduated from high school, Pat Larson entered the university where she majored in law.
5. We asked Mr. Wilson to give us advice because of the fact that he is such a wise man.
6. I have observed that often people who are large in size are pleasant in disposition.
7. The group of police sent at the time to be on guard at the railroad terminal had been able to intercept and detain two of the men thought to be suspected of participation in the First National Bank robbery in which money was stolen from the bank.
8. He hopes his sermons will reinstate in the minds of the people the primary and fundamental purpose of a religious belief and way of life.
9. The most consequential of the causes operating to facilitate gastric disorder was respiratory insufficiency induced by an inadequacy of oxygen for sustaining normal inhalation in the smoke-filled atmosphere of the room.
10. It is now time when something must be done about the cafeteria facilities that are being offered at the University. I am confident that the whole student body joins me in a request for higher quality and less expensive food.

6

The Thought:
Logical and Convincing

The Rules of Evidence: Inductive Reasoning

The thought process of examining evidence and forming a general rule to account for the separate pieces of evidence is called *inductive reasoning.* One begins with particulars and ends with a *generalization.* Note the following example.

> **Evidence:** The ripe watermelon I tasted last week was sweet and juicy. This ripe watermelon I have here is sweet and juicy. All the ripe watermelons I have checked before, some 30 to 40, have been sweet and juicy.
>
> **Conclusion:** Therefore, I can state it as a general principle that ripe watermelons are sweet and juicy.

A generalization asserts that on the basis of evidence about some things in a class, something is true of all or some or many of the class.

A special kind of generalization is the *hypothesis.* A hypothesis is a conclusion or explanation to account for a number of related facts about a specific individual, event, or condition (as in a criminal trial).

> John and Mary were observed frequently in each other's company until last Saturday.
> Since last Saturday they have not been seen together.
> John is reported to have been very glum and irritable since last Saturday.
> Until last Saturday, Mary wore an engagement ring on her finger, but it has not been seen there since.
> When someone mentioned John's name to Mary yesterday, she quickly changed the subject.
> *Therefore:* John and Mary had a serious quarrel last Saturday.

There are four main rules of evidence:

CONSIDER THE EVIDENCE

You must actually look at the evidence itself. You must not begin with a ready-made conclusion or opinion and then select evidence and force it to fit. Start with the evidence and then follow it to wherever it leads, guided by all the experience you have ever had with similar evidence.

To be reliable, a generalization must be based on a large number of verifiable and relevant facts, carefully interpreted. To be creditable, the evidence supporting a generalization must be (1) known or available, (2) sufficient, (3) relevant, and (4) representative.

The following examples illustrate misuse of these principles:

1. Facts completely lacking or unknown

UFO's are ships from outer space.
Ten out of fifteen businessmen use Rol-aids.

2. Insufficient evidence   A hasty interpreter concluded from the following evidence in the newspaper that crime and violence are taking over the city:

Last week the Carpenter murder case dominated the newspaper. Today the front page describes a murder and two car accidents. The inside pages report on three thefts, two muggings, a cafe brawl, and a non-casualty skirmish between policemen and strikers. The newspaper contains 20 pages.

The interpreter did not consider such other relevant evidence as the 500,000 population of the city; the several other stories in the same paper describing happy social gatherings, entertainments, and charity drives; the abundance of evidence about city life from sources other than the newspaper.

3. Irrelevant evidence   Beware of pleasant and otherwise interesting facts, examples, and associates that do not logically apply to the issue at hand.

Jim Carson is certainly the best candidate for Governor. He has been endorsed by Shirley Wyll, the popular movie star.

Shirley Wyll as a voter certainly has the value of her vote, but the evidence here of Carson's suitability is Wyll's prestige as a movie star. The relevant point is this: what are her qualifications as an expert in politics? Does a movie star endorsement make for a good governor?

4. Nonrepresentative evidence   Such evidence is generally used to support a hypothesis or a generalization already formed.

A study of 2,800 Chicago citizens who had recent heart attacks showed that 70 percent of them were ten to fifteen pounds overweight. Obviously, obesity is a cause of heart disease. (70 percent of *all* Chicago citizens might be overweight.)

There is special danger in the decimal point—like 95.3 percent of all doctors interviewed—because figures seem like hard facts. To make reliable generalizations from statistical data, you must carefully process the kinds and sources of the information. You must check kinds of samplings, number of samplings, breadth and relevance of coverage, and so on. Test this one.

A businessman accused of paying starvation wages replies that the average income of those working in his business is $8,500.

The statistics:		
	1 proprietor	$48,000
	1 office worker	5,000
	8 shop workers/ $4,000 ea.	32,000
		$85,000
		(av. = $8,500)

TAKE THE SIMPLEST INTERPRETATION

Don't accept the complex interpretation until simpler ones will not fit. The simplest conclusion that accounts for all the evidence is probably the best. (This principle is also called the Law of Occam's Razor.) The simplest is likely the best because it is most like the interpretation that has before explained similar evidence. The odds favor it.

If, during a heavy rainstorm, you hear sharp clicks as if something were striking the window glass, they are probably caused by hail, not by somebody shooting buckshot. If all the lights suddenly go out in your house, one complex interpretation would be that an aircraft from outer space is hovering over your house and the magnetic field generated by the craft has set up a counterfield to blank out your house current. A simpler explanation, and most likely to be valid, is that an electrical overload has flipped the main fuse in the switch box.

CONSIDER ALL LIKELY ALTERNATIVES

Start with the simplest interpretation, but do not fix on it and refuse to consider others. All likely conclusions must be considered, for the best judgment requires comparison. Look at the following piece of evidence and the interpretation drawn from it.

Mr. Jones has been taking the bus to work this week and his new Oldsmobile is not in his garage. Either he has sold his car or the loan company has foreclosed on him.

The two alternatives of selling and foreclosure are both simple and both common to usual experience. However, still another alternative to consider is that the car is in the repair shop having some major tune-up or adjustment made. There is no solid evidence for either selling or foreclosure, and with a new car the third hypothesis seems most reasonable.

BEWARE OF ABSOLUTES

Don't claim more than the evidence allows. A generalization is a general rule and not an absolute. Don't let your statement say *all* when the evidence allows only for *some.* Instead of hundred-percenters like *all, never, always,* maybe you should use more exact terms like *many, sometimes, often,* and *probably.*

> **Absolute generalization:** The Scandinavians are exceptionally talented people.
> **The evidence:** 1. Rölvaag's novel *Giants in the Earth*
> 2. Lagerkvist's novel *The Dwarf*
> 3. Music of Sibelius and Grieg
> 4. Sculpture of Thorwaldsen
> **Qualified conclusion:** A number of Scandinavians have produced outstanding work in music, literature, and sculpture.

The Rules of Connection: Deductive Reasoning

Deductive reasoning is a companion to inductive reasoning. Deduction works with the generalizations arrived at by induction. When you use sound deductive reasoning, you put two related ideas together and draw a third idea or conclusion from the connection between the first two.

Very simply, the deductive process can be stated as a formula: 1+2=3

> **Idea 1:** Most men like to look at pretty girls.
> **Idea 2:** Mary is a pretty girl.
> **Idea 3:** Therefore, most men like to look at Mary.

VALID THOUGHT PROCESSES

To be valid, the thought process must follow two principles:

1. The ideas must be true An idea is true if the facts that support it are known, sufficient, relevant, and representative. Check the implications of the following typical propaganda:

> You should vote for Jack Stack for governor. He's been a successful businessman in our city for twenty years.

The logical formula would run like this:

> All successful businessmen make good governors.
> Jack Stack is a successful businessman.
> Therefore, Jack Stack will make a good governor.

We would need a lot of evidence to accept as true the generalization that all successful businessmen make good governors.

You find a similar lack of sound thinking in this statement.

> Sure she can vote; she s an American citizen. (But one also has to be 18 years old, registered, etc.)

2. The ideas must have a relevant connection Two ideas may be offered as having a strong logical connection when they have at most a weak connection or no connection at all. In an advertisement in which a baseball hero is used to sell razor blades, the apparent thought process we are asked to accept could be reduced to these straightforward terms:

Idea 1:   Slugger Joe has the highest RBI in the American League.
Idea 2:   Slugger Joe shaves with Gillette blades.
Idea 3 (Conclusion):   Therefore, all men should shave with Gillette blades.

Ideas 1 and 2 may be accurate in themselves, but the thinker has not established a valid connection between these items:

Joe's hitting ability and shaving needs.
Joe's shaving needs and other men's shaving needs.
Joe's hitting ability and other men's shaving needs.
Gillette blades and all of the first three ideas.

Besides having weak connection or no connection, the ideas themselves may be misleading. For instance, although Joe may use Simon's blades, he may not like them, he may have used them only for the ad in question, and he may also use 15 other brands.

KINDS OF TWISTED THINKING

Here are some common kinds of twisted thinking in which the thinker fails to establish a strong connection between valid ideas and so does not draw a valid deductive conclusion:

1.   Proof by repetition   Also called *begging the question* and *reasoning in a circle.* A synonym or repetition of the statement is offered as proof of that statement. The thing itself is offered as its own proof.

His handwriting is hard to read because it is illegible.
It is the beer beer drinkers drink.

2.   Proof by false connection   Also called *post hoc, propter hoc.* The event that happened first is presumed to be the cause and the event that follows, the result. Time sequence is confused with causal sequence.

All of these improvements in the economy and so on occurred *because* I have been your Senator.

3.   Proof by no connection   Also called *non sequitur* (it does not follow). A hasty or thinly connected inference is presented as a logical conclusion.

This is the best book I have read this year and should win the Pulitzer Prize (valid only if the reader is one of the judges for the Pulitzer).
Why was the elephant wearing pink tennis shoes? Because . . .

4.   Proof by comparison   Also called *false analogy.* One or a few similarities between two things (persons, ideas, events) used to try to make the point that the two are entirely similar.

Don't change horses in the middle of a stream; don't change presidents during a crisis.

5. Proof by oversimplification   Also called *false dilemma, open-and-shut case, all-or-nothing fallacy, two-valued orientation, capsule thinking,* and *tabloid thinking.* Hasty or shallow thinking can leap over a very complex thought situation and come to large conclusions that are not contained in the basic generalizations and their connection. Oversimplification usually either eliminates in-between relationships or degrees or claims absolute coverage for small premises.

Truth is sometimes an either/or sort of thing. A light is either on or it is off. You either went to St. Louis or you did not. You either passed the exam or you did not. But most things that we argue about are not so clear-cut. People, governments, actions are seldom either all good or all bad. It is a fallacy to argue as if there are only two possibilities when the evidence justifies several possibilities.

> America—love it or leave it.
> Whenever you find corruption in government, the people ought to vote another party into power.
> This is the real issue: shall we put government into business, or shall we let initiative be free to create real wealth?

Look for the fallacy of oversimplification in your own writing and in others' when you come across phrases like these:

> the simple, unvarnished truth
> it all boils down to this
> the issue is plain and clear
> in a nutshell
> good or bad
> victory or defeat
> militarism or pacifism
> foreign aid or isolationism
> true or false
> right or wrong
> on balance

6. Proof by distraction   This fallacy is the complete breakdown of the principle of logical connection. The thinker either does not connect the two premises or does not make the conclusion grow out of the premises. The thinker either deviates from the subject or throws such obstacles in the way that the real issue is lost track of. There are many ways to evade the issue. Some of the common ones are called *neglected aspect, ignoring the question, red herring, card-stacking, slanting, wrenching from context, obfuscation, equivocation, ambiguity,* and *tu toque* (you're another).

> **Wrenching from context:**   When Mr. Bond (who is married) was in New York last month, he was seen having dinner with a showgirl . . . (context: . . . and her husband and their two children.)
> **Equivocation** (shifting of terms):   Look! Band-Aids in color! (But do they medicate?)
> **Tu toque** (you too, or you're another):   *Charge:* "You were cheating on that exam." *Defense:* "Well, others were, too." (The issue, though, is the cheating of "you.")

7. Proof by non-sense By nonsense here is meant no actual verifiable meaning or sense, although a statement may *seem* to have meaning. In looking for substantial meaning, keep in mind that it takes two things to express responsible, substantial meaning. (1) The words used must have definite meaning, and (2) a statement sentence must be used. Groups of words without these two features can only seem to have meaning.

Here are some common kinds of outright nonsense:

a. *Unfinished comparisons* Add your own finish to unfinished comparisons to see what non-sense they actually can be.

Now in Ungentine TWO TIMES the pain-relieving medication for FASTER PAIN RELIEF.

1. "TWO TIMES" the medication held by a container half the size of this one.
2. "Faster" . . . than you would get with a bed of spikes.

b. *Nonreferent abstractions* These are abstractions that do not refer to any tangible things in experience. Special device words, usually capitalized and often hyphenated, are concocted by the claims and so have only their meaning—they are just *like* similar words. The *apparent* idea is not actual. To say "Swing-Out Shelves" is not the same as to say "shelves that swing out," which many refrigerators have.

Nonsense: Only Hotpoint Refrigerator-Freezers bring all these . . . Swing-Out Shelves . . . Reserve Cold Power and Frost-Away Automatic defrosting.

Reduced to sense: The Hotpoint company makes a refrigerator just like many other brands, with shelves that swing out, capable of temperatures colder than needed, and automatic defrosting. But only Hotpoint calls these features by these special names.

c. *No-statement claims* These are claims that are apparent rather than actual. The group of words may seem to make a statement or a claim that the speaker should stand behind, but actually makes no such claim.

Spray Contact nasal mist *to* stop nasal congestion.

This is almost complete non-sense. The word "to" indicates purpose, not effect. The words are a phrase, not a statement, and it normally takes a statement to make a claim. And, of course, the stuff may have no curative effect at all on the cold itself, since it is only for the congestion, not the cold. A blast of air could have the same effect.

d. *Contradictions* Two ideas, one of which cancels out the other, since both cannot be true.

I never watch TV, but last night I was looking at this show, and . . .
I'd like to lend you $10, but . . .

Emotional Appeals

Some thoughts and actions should spring from emotions. Others should come from sound sense and logic. If your action, decision, or conclusion is to be logical, then you want the thought process to be logical and based on analysis and fact, rather than emotional and based on prejudiced interpretation. Here are common emotional appeals that deviate from a sensible thinking process. To find sense behind the nonsense, ask, "Just what is the real issue?"

1. Personal appeals These exploit our being individual human beings. These appeals work to discredit or praise the person connected with the issue, rather than dealing with the issue or idea itself. Common nicknames for the process are *name-calling* and *appeals to pity.* Formal logic calls it *ad hominem,* or "appeal to the man." These seek to praise or discredit the character, motives, family, associations, and so on of a person. The person is an atheist, leftist, hawk, dove, pig, Commie, racist, or a family man, girl scout, Christian, good guy.

> "There sits the defendant. He is a good neighbor, a considerate husband, a kind father. He has never been accused of a crime. He is an elder in the local church. Surely you do not think for a moment that such a man could commit murder." (But the one issue is: *Did* he commit the murder?)

2. Popular appeals These exploit our urge to belong to groups. These appeals are based largely on a popular custom, belief, notion, figure, or symbol. Common nicknames for these appeals are *bandwagon, everybody's doing it,* and *appeal to the crowd.* Such appeals may refer to the flag, the church, mother, Uncle Sam, the gang, and so on.

> Joe Blow is a grass-roots candidate.
> I'd rather fight than switch.
> Four Roses for men of distinction.
> Mrs. Blount, a Kansas City housewife, says, "Use Tide in your washer."

3. Prejudiced associations These exploit the whole core of our emotional nature—desires, needs, urges, longings, and unfulfillments. The list is long.

Check this list for emotional associations, pleasant or unpleasant, that come to your mind. Note how often logical thought turns off and emotion turns on.

sex	free prizes
ego	the free world
rich people	anybody over 30
establishment	anybody under 20
fuzz	black
pig	white

commie	Formula X-20 with Celustan (or any scientific label)
health	computerize
money	modern
silent majority	un-American
hard-hat	hippie
middle class	country club

EXERCISE 6-1
GENERALIZATION AND EVIDENCE

Evaluate these pieces of evidence, determine which generalizations, if any, are reliable, and circle their letters.

1. During the month of July, about 10,000 people were interviewed on their way into Athletic Stadium, and 8,581 said they opposed the Athletics moving to another city. This evidence shows that
   a. the city enthusiastically supports the ball club;
   b. about 85.8 percent of the people of the city are opposed to the Athletics moving to another city;
   c. people who go to see the Athletics play like to see the Athletics play.

2. What's Breck Fresh Hair got? The only instant hair cleaner so fresh-air fragrant it leaves your hair smelling blue-sky clean. (Sniffing's believing!) Get Breck Fresh Hair—and keep the clean going! This evidence shows that
   a. Breck Fresh Hair will indeed clean hair;
   b. if you wash your hair with the substance in question, you will be clean, pure, and authentic;
   c. there is a shampoo called Breck Fresh Hair;
   d. you should buy and use Breck Fresh Hair.

3. A Dodge won the Annual Marathon Race from Los Angeles to La Paz. Dodge cars are commonly used by the state highway patrol in my state. Fifteen garagemen in the town selected at random report that Dodge cars need less repair than four other common brands. This evidence shows that
   a. Dodge cars are the most durable cars;
   b. many Dodge cars are rugged cars;
   c. you should buy a Dodge car.

4. LEARN SHORTHAND IN SIX WEEKS
   . . . AND LAND A GLAMOR JOB WITH A TOP FIRM
   This evidence shows that
   a. after studying shorthand for six weeks, a person can get a glamorous job with a top company;
   b. all that it takes to find a glamorous job is a little shorthand;
   c. one can take a course in shorthand that probably lasts six weeks.

5. Of hundreds of references to college students in the *Washington Post* between June and September 1972, a majority of students mentioned were

involved in car accidents that were partly caused by carelessness on their part. This evidence shows that

a. most college students are reckless drivers who become involved in car accidents;

b. car accidents are the most newsworthy item about college students during the summer;

c. most car accidents are caused by careless young people.

EXERCISE 6-2
HYPOTHESIS AND EVIDENCE

Which hypothesis best accounts for the evidence?

1. Evidence: This light doesn't go on, but the bulb is all right.

Hyp. A: Two of the workmen at the power plant got into an argument and accidentally threw a switch that cut off the electric power from this neighborhood.
Hyp. B: The plug is loose in the wall-outlet.

2. Evidence: Three people assert that they saw Mr. X fire a gun at Mr. Y at 1:00 A.M. in the garden behind Shilly's roadhouse. Mr. X claims he went home at 12:00, but none of the employees recalls seeing him leave or seeing him present after twelve.

Hyp. A: Mr. X fired the gun at Mr. Y.
Hyp. B: Mr. X was home in bed, but the three witnesses invented the story in order to give Mr. X some bad publicity to lessen his chances of winning the forthcoming election against Mr. Y.

3. Evidence: Three people assert that they saw Mr. X fire a gun at Mr. Y. at 1:00 A.M. in the garden behind Shilly's roadhouse. Mr. X claims he went home at 12:00, but none of the employees recalls seeing him leave or seeing him present after twelve. The night was very dark. The three witnesses are well-known gamblers from out of town who are contributing to Mr. Y's campaign because Mr. Y is strongly in favor of legalized gambling in his state. A policeman says he saw Mr. X entering his apartment in town at ten minutes to one.

Hyp. A: Mr. X fired the gun at Mr. Y.
Hyp. B: Mr. X was home in bed, but the three witnesses invented the story in order to give Mr. X some bad publicity to lessen his chances of winning the forthcoming election against Mr. Y.

EXERCISE 6-3
RELIABILITY OF EVIDENCE

Evaluate the reliability of the generalizations drawn from the evidence given.

1. Nine out of ten people interviewed said they preferred Marlboro cigarettes. Marlboro is the favorite of American smokers.

2. Though she has made some mistakes, her record as a political prognosticator has been very good. At least three-quarters of her predictions have been borne out by subsequent events. I should think she would be a reasonable guide to follow in the future.

3. It is quite certain that Cutler wrote the letter. It is in his handwriting, on his personal stationery, and his fingerprints and no one else's are on it. Moreover, two reliable witnesses have testified under oath that they saw him writing it at his desk.

4. I have looked everywhere for my watch. It is not in any of my clothes or in any likely place around the house. I have checked with the lost and found departments of the stores and buses I have been in during the week. I have even looked around outside the house. The only thing I can think of is that it has been stolen.

5. Joe Barcerini, who arrived five months ago from Italy, is sure to make a poor record in all his exams in college. He has already received five low grades on examinations.

EXERCISE 6-4
EVALUATION OF THINKING

1. There have been fewer strikes since Joe Smith has been your senator. You can see that he is the man who can keep peace between capital and labor.

2. Senator Smith said, "I am confident we are going to have peace. If the people want peace, there is no reason why we cannot have peace."

3. Absence makes the heart grow fonder.

4. Well, it all boils down to this. Either the delinquent nations pay up immediately, or we should pull out of the United Nations. It is time we stopped footing the bill for the entire world.

5. It's time we stopped throwing our money away on foreign aid. We have problems of our own: unemployment, race relations, education, juvenile delinquency, and we'd better be spending our time and money on them.

6. No race is inferior; in fact, some are superior.

7. The Commonwealth will prove, gentlemen of the jury, that this criminal sitting before you, this ruthless enemy of society, shot Meg Hanson in cold blood, with malice aforethought, and should be punished to the fullest extent of the law.

8. Joseph Eliot could not prevent the divorces in his own family; he is hardly a suitable candidate for the honorable office of governor of our state.

9. Houses with shallow foundations should be avoided at all costs, but since this house has an unusually deep, reinforced foundation, you can have no reason for rejecting it.

10. Like Old Hickory Jackson, Stewart Benson stood firm against the fire of the enemy; like Jackson, he will make a fine president.

11. Let pedants quibble about the differences between communism, socialism, and fascism. As all sound-thinking people know, they are only different names for the same thing. If they differ at all, they differ only in degree. There is no room in this country for any ism except one hundred percent Americanism.

12. Anne is a happy woman because she is not troubled by inhibitions.
13. He is a poor speaker. I can barely hear what he is saying.
14. If she does not like the new president, she should resign from the club.
15. Science is the servant of peace and eventually it will outlaw war. Every day the radio, the telephone, fast ships, and so on are bringing nations closer together. Once we were weeks and months apart. Now we are separated literally only by seconds. The day will come when we will speak one language and think similar thoughts. Then war will be impossible because we will be one people.
16. I know a man who had seven years' bad luck because he broke a mirror.
17. Joan's success as a real estate broker is assured; she has a good sense of values.
18. My parents were just like yours: plain, simple hardworking folks; and if you vote for me you can be sure that the rights of the common people will be safeguarded.
19. There is a law against murder in this country, and all murderers ought to pay the full penalty of the law.
20. If everyone on the team would work together, the team would win Saturday's game.
21. Early to bed and early to rise
    Makes a man healthy, wealthy, and wise.
22. The life expectancy in this country has been practically doubled in the past century (from about 35 to about 70). It is likely, therefore, that within another century most people will live to be a hundred and forty.
23. A good school does not limit its efforts to preparation for life, since it is life itself.
24. If politicians can hire ghost writers, a student ought to be allowed to do the same thing.
25. Use Q-Tips because they are safer.

PART THREE

The Special Paper: Using the Range of Writing

The aim of Parts I and II of this book, "The Whole Composition" and "Building a Composition," is to increase the skill in developing an idea through writing—no matter what the particular purpose or application of the composition. That in itself is an important aim. Most educated people need such skill.

But writing is more than the "freshman English theme." It is a practical skill to be applied, in college and beyond college. Some of the special applications are examined here, all building on the general principles presented in Parts I and II. Skill in writing some of these special papers is helpful primarily in college. Writing examinations and summaries and writing about literature fall into this category. The other kinds of special papers are useful in college, of course, but they range far beyond college into various professions.

The educated person is called upon to write many communications. The reference paper or report is useful in many businesses and professions when information must be gathered, evaluated, and presented. Such a paper might be a market analysis, a legal brief, a sociological survey, or a political study.

Many people in industries, engineering, or laboratories of one kind or another are expected to write scientific or technical reports. This kind of paper might be an ecology study, a description of a medical treatment, directions on how to operate a machine, or a feasibility study on running a pipeline over a mountain.

Knowing how to write a business letter is, of course, important for anyone, but particularly for those who are making business their profession. And almost everybody needs to know how to prepare a resume and write a letter applying for a job.

All of these special papers may not be for everyone. Some of them are—such as writing examinations and summaries. The reference paper also has wide application. The student and the instructor may select those special papers most suited to the student's individual needs.

7

The Reference Paper

Using Source Materials

The ability to use source materials effectively is one of the most important skills in the learning process. You may be working with either a single fact or a long paper, but time and again you are called upon to find information, to process it, and to present it to somebody. Knowing basic library sources will aid you in gathering information, and writing a reference paper will give you practice in processing and presenting information.

USING THE LIBRARY

The search for information—such as books, articles, bulletins—usually begins in the library. There you are most likely to use three main guides or indexes to basic materials: (1) The card catalog, (2) indexes to periodicals and (3) reference books.

1. The card catalog The card catalog lists all books and bound magazines held by the library. For most books you will find at least three cards: an *author* card, a *title* card, and at least one *subject* card. Cards may give leads to other books by listing bibliographies or other subject areas.

2. Indexes to periodicals For recent subjects, magazines are the main source of information. Various periodic indexes list every important article in all major periodicals, by author, subject, or both, and sometimes by title. The *Readers' Guide to Periodical Literature,* which lists articles from about 165 magazines, is probably most useful, but other special indexes are helpful.

Author Card

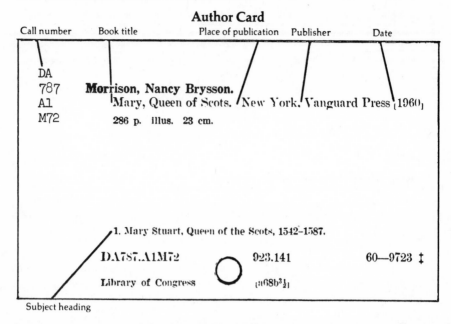

Call number   Book title   Place of publication   Publisher   Date

DA
787
A1
M72

Morrison, Nancy Brysson.
Mary, Queen of Scots. New York. Vanguard Press [1960]

286 p. illus. 23 cm.

1. Mary Stuart, Queen of the Scots, 1542–1587.

DA787.A1M72   923.141   60—9723 ‡

Library of Congress   [a68b³½]

Subject heading

Title Card

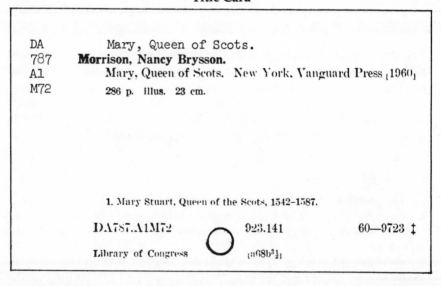

DA   Mary, Queen of Scots.
787   **Morrison, Nancy Brysson.**
A1   Mary, Queen of Scots. New York. Vanguard Press [1960]
M72   286 p. illus. 23 cm.

1. Mary Stuart, Queen of the Scots, 1542–1587.

DA787.A1M72   923.141   60—9723 ‡

Library of Congress   [a68b³½]

GENERAL

Readers' Guide to Periodical Literature. 1900–. Author, title, and subject.

Social Sciences and Humanities Index. (formerly called *International Index*). 1907–74. Continued in *Humanities Index,* 1974–. Emphasizes humanities and scholarly articles.

Bibliographic Index. 1937–. Indexes current bibliographies by subject; includes both bibliographies published as books and pamphlets and those which appear in books, periodical articles, and pamphlets.

Subject Card

```
DA          MARY STUART, QUEEN OF THE SCOTS, 1542-1587.
787      Morrison, Nancy Brysson.
A1          Mary, Queen of Scots. New York, Vanguard Press ₁1960₁
M72         286 p.  illus.  23 cm.




            1. Mary Stuart, Queen of the Scots, 1542-1587.

         DA787.A1M72              923.141              60—9723 ‡

         Library of Congress          ₁a68b³₁₁
```

Book Review Digest. 1905–. Lists books by author and quotes from several reviews for each.

Essay and General Literature Index. 1934–. Indexes collections of essays, articles, and speeches.

New York Times Index. 1913–. Provides dates of events, speeches, and such. It serves as an index to the same events in other newspapers.

SPECIAL

Agricultural Index. 1916–64. Continued in *Biological & Agricultural Index,* 1964–.

Applied Science and Technology Index. 1958–.

Art Index. 1929–.

Business Periodicals Index. 1958–.

Catholic Periodical and Literature Index. 1930–.

Dramatic Index. 1909–1949. Continued in *Bulletin of Bibliography,* 1950–.

Education Index. 1929–.

Engineering Index. 1884–.

Index Medicus. 1899–1927. Continued in *Quarterly Cumulative Index Medicus,* 1927–56; *Current List of Medical Literature,* 1950–59; and *Index Medicus,* 1960–.

Index to Legal Periodicals. 1908–.

Industrial Arts Index. 1913–.

Public Affairs Information Service Bulletin. 1915–. Index to materials on economics, politics, and sociology.

United States Government Publications: Monthly Catalog. 1895–.

Vertical File Index: Subject and Title Index to Selected Pamphlet Material. 1935–. (formerly called Vertical File Service Catalog).

3. Reference books In writing a reference paper, you will usually make many trips to basic reference books such as encyclopedias, dictionaries, yearbooks, indexes, atlases, and guides. They are very helpful for such things as overviews, spot checking of facts and definitions, and statistics. These books cannot be taken from the library, but are usually easily available in open shelves near the main reading room. Reference books are listed in the card catalog, and the call number will tell you where to find each book. Most libraries have reference librarians who are glad to help find books.

ENCYCLOPEDIAS

Columbia Encyclopedia. Perhaps the best single-volume desk encyclopedia. Revised frequently.

Encyclopedia Americana. Supplemented by *Americana Annual.* Revised frequently.

Encyclopaedia Britannica. Supplemented by *Britannica Book of the Year.* Revised frequently.

DICTIONARIES, WORD BOOKS

Evans, Bergen, and Cornelia Evans. *A Dictionary of Contemporary American Usage.* 1957.

Oxford English Dictionary. 1888–1933. 10 vols. and supplement. Reissue corrected, 1933, 12 vols. and supplement. The original issue is known as *New English Dictionary.*

Webster's Third New International Dictionary. 1961.

YEAR BOOKS, CURRENT EVENTS

Americana Annual. 1923–.

Britannica Book of the Year. 1938–.

Facts on File. 1940–. A weekly digest of world events.

New International Year Book. 1907–66.

Statesman's Year Book. 1864–.

Statistical Abstract of the United States. 1878–.

World Almanac and Book of Facts. 1868–.

ATLASES AND GAZETTEERS

Columbia Lippincott Gazetteer of the World. 1962.

Commercial and Library Atlas of the World. Frequently revised.

Cosmopolitan World Atlas. 1962.

Encyclopaedia Britannica World Atlas. Frequently revised.

Rand-McNally Standard World Atlas. Frequently revised.

The Times Atlas of the World. 1972.

Webster's New Geographical Dictionary. 1972.

BOOKS OF QUOTATIONS

Bartlett, John and E. M. Beck, eds. *Familiar Quotations.* 14th ed. 1968.

Mencken, H. L. *A New Dictionary of Quotations on Historical Principles from Ancient and Modern Sources.* 1942.

Stevenson, Burton. *The Home Book of Quotations, Classical and Modern.* 10th ed. 1967.

ART AND ARCHITECTURE

Bryan, Michael. *Bryan's Dictionary of Painters and Engravers.* 5 vols. Rev. ed. by George C. Williamson. 1964.

Encyclopedia of World Art. 1959–1968. 15 vols.

Haggar, Reginald C. *Dictionary of Art Terms.* 1962.

Myers, Bernard S., ed. *Encyclopedia of Painting.* 1955.

Sturgis, Russell. *Dictionary of Architecture and Building,* 1901–02. Repr. 1966.

Zboinski, A., and L. Tyszynski. *Dictionary of Architecture and Building Trades.* 1963.

BIOGRAPHY

American Men of Science. 1910–70. Continued by *American Men and Women of Science,* 1971–.

Current Biography. Monthly since 1940, with an annual cumulative index.

Dictionary of American Biography. 20 vols. plus index and supplements. 1928–74.

Dictionary of National Biography (British). 22 vols. and supplements 1908–71.

Directory of American Scholars. 4 vols. 5th ed. 1969.

Webster's Biographical Dictionary. 1972.

Who's Who (British). *Who's Who in America. International Who's Who.* Separate books containing brief accounts of living men and women. Issued periodically. There are also many specialized "Who's Who" books.

HISTORY

Cambridge Ancient History. 3rd ed. 5 vols. 1970–.

Cambridge Mediaeval History. 2nd ed. 1967–.

New Cambridge Modern History. 14 vols. 1957–.

Dictionary of American History. 7 vols. 1976.

Langer William L., *Encyclopedia of World History.* 5th ed. 1972.

LITERATURE AND DRAMA

Baugh, Albert, C., et al. *A Literary History of England.* 4 vols. 1967.

Bateson, F. W. , ed. *Cambridge Bibliography of English Literature.* 5 vols. 1941–1957.

Funk & Wagnalls Standard Dictionary of Folklore, Mythology, and Legend. 1973.

Gassner, John, and R. G. Allen. *Drama in the Making.* 1964.

Gray, Louis Herbert, John A. MacCulloch, G. F. Moore. *Mythology of All Races.* 13 vols. 1916–32.

Hart, J. D. *Oxford Companion to American Literature.* 4th ed. 1965.

Hartnoll, Phyllis, ed. *Oxford Companion to the Theatre.* 3rd ed. 1967.

Harvey, Paul, ed. *Oxford Companion to Classical Literature.* 1937.

Harvey, Paul, ed. *Oxford Companion to English Literature.* 4th ed. 1967.

Kunitz, S. J., and H. Haycraft. *Twentieth-Century Authors.* 1942. Supplement, 1955.

Nicoll, Allardyce. *The Development of the Theatre.* 5th ed. 1966.

Oxford Classical Dictionary. 2nd ed. 1970.

Preminger, Alex, ed. *Encyclopedia of Poetry and Poetics.* 1965.

Spiller, Robert E., et al. *Literary History of the United States.* 3rd ed. 1963. Rev. bibliography supplement, 1964, 1972, ed. Richard M. Ludwig. Includes extensive working bibliographies of major American writers.

MUSIC

Apel, W. *Harvard Dictionary of Music.* 2nd ed. 1969.

Grove's Dictionary of Music and Musicians. 9 vols. 5th ed. 1955; vol. 10, Supplement, 1961.

Scholes, P. A. *Oxford Companion to Music.* 10th ed. 1970.

Thompson, O. *International Cyclopedia of Music and Musicians.* 9th ed. 1964.

PHILOSOPHY AND RELIGION

Copleston, Frederick. *A History of Philosophy.* 8 vols. 1941–1966.

Cross, F. L., and E. A. Livingstone, eds. *Oxford Dictionary of the Christian Church.* 2nd ed. 1974.

Ferm, Vergilius. *Encyclopedia of Religion.* 1945.

Hastings, James. *Dictionary of the Bible.* 5 vols. 1898–1904. Rev. ed. by Frederick C. Grant and H. H. Rowley, 1963.

Jackson, S. M., et al. *New Schaff-Herzog Encyclopedia of Religious Knowledge.* 12 vols. and index. 1908–12. Supplements, 1955.

New Catholic Encyclopedia. 15 vols. 1967.

Universal Jewish Encyclopedia. 12 vols. 1939–44.

Urmson, J. O., ed. *The Concise Encyclopedia of Western Philosophy and Philosophers.* 1960.

POLITICAL SCIENCE

Bemis, Samuel F., and G. G. Griffin. *Guide to the Diplomatic History of the United States.* 1935. Rpt. 1959.

DeGrazia, Alfred. *Politics and Government: The Elements of Political Science.* Rev. ed., 1962.

Encyclopaedia of the Social Sciences. 15 vols. 1930–35.

Frankel, Joseph. *The Making of Foreign Policy: An Analysis of Decision-Making.* 1963.

Political Handbook and Atlas of the World. 1927–.

Smith, Edward C., and A. J. Zurcher, eds. *Dictionary of American Politics.* 2nd ed. 1968.

Wright, Quincy. *The Study of International Relations.* 1955.

PSYCHOLOGY

Drever, James. *Dictionary of Psychology.* Rev. ed. H. Wallerstein, 1964.

English, Horace B., and A. C. English. *A Comprehensive Dictionary of Psychological and Psychoanalytical Terms.* 1958.

Goldenson, Robert M., *Encyclopedia of Human Behavior: Psychology, Psychiatry, and Mental Health.* 2 vols. 1970.

Harriman, Philip L., *Handbook of Psychological Terms.* 1965.

Hinsie, Leland E., and Robert J. Campbell. *Psychiatric Dictionary.* 4th ed. 1970.

International Encyclopedia of the Social Sciences. 17 vols. 1968.

SCIENCE

Biological Abstracts. 1926–.

Chemical Abstracts. 1907–.

Chronica Botanica. 1935–.

Glenn, James, and R. C. James, eds. *Mathematics Dictionary.* 3rd ed. 1968.

Gray, Peter, ed. *Encyclopedia of the Biological Sciences.* 2nd ed. 1970.

Hawkins, R. R., ed. *Scientific, Medical, and Technical Books Published in the United States of America.* 2nd ed. 1958.

International Encyclopedia of Chemical Science. 1964.

Larousse Encyclopedia of the Earth: Geology, Paleontology, and Prehistory. 1961.

LeGalley, Donald P., and A. Rosen, eds. *Space Physics.* 1964.

McGraw-Hill Encyclopedia of Science and Technology. 15 vols. 3rd ed. 1971.

Physics Abstracts. 1898–.

Thewlis, J., ed. *Encyclopaedic Dictionary of Physics.* 9 vols. 1961–64.

Van Nostrand's Scientific Encyclopedia. 4th ed. 1968.

SOCIOLOGY AND ANTHROPOLOGY

Encyclopaedia of the Social Sciences. 15 vols. 1930–35.

Gould, Julius, and William L. Kolb, eds. *A Dictionary of the Social Sciences.* 1964.

Kroeber, A. L., ed. *Anthropology Today: An Encyclopedic Inventory.* 1953. Extensive bibliographies for work up to 1952.

Mitchell, Geoffrey D. *A Dictionary of Sociology.* 1968.

Social Science Abstracts. 1929–33.

Social Work Year Book. 1929–.

Zadrozny, J. T. *Dictionary of Social Science.* 1959.

Writing the Paper

A reference paper (also called *research paper* or *term paper*) is a formal paper presenting the results of your explorations of a specific subject. It is an experience in learning a body of knowledge by yourself.

(1) You will use and develop five primary skills: your ability to (1) find information, (2) read with critical intelligence, (3) sift evidence with discrimination, (4) organize a large body of material, (5) present your conclusions in readable form.

Writing the paper usually has six steps:

1. choosing and limiting the subject,
2. preparing a bibliography,
3. getting an overview of the subject,
4. collecting material,
5. writing the first draft with footnotes,
6. preparing the final draft.

CHOOSING AND LIMITING THE SUBJECT

Choose a subject which you are interested in and would like to know more about. Interest and curiosity are necessary to keep you happy, for you will be spending a lot of time on the subject. It is best not to start cold on a new subject. You need at least enough knowledge to chart a direction for the paper before the term is over.

Curiosity and preliminary knowledge are not enough to make an appropriate topic for research, though. Some kinds of topics must be ruled out:

1. Personal experience Subjects from personal experience, such as "My Experiences as a Lifeguard" or "My Work in the Hospital" do not require library sources and note-taking, which are part of the reference paper project.

2.   Single-source subjects   If all necessary information on a subject can be found in a single book or encyclopedia article, then research is hardly appropriate. Such subjects might be technical and industrial processes ("Building a Computer"), narratives of a man's life ("Kennedy's Military Career"), or simple narrative histories ("The History of Basketball").

3.   Topics that are too controversial and complex   Time and space decide. You must be able to weigh enough evidence to lead to sound conclusions. These subjects might be too much for the usual reference paper of about 2,000 words:

> The Contemporary Loss of Religious Faith
> Advantages of Socialism over Capitalism
> Are the President's Powers Too Limited?

One aspect of one of these could be explored, however.

4.   Topics that are too broad and general   Subjects such as "The History of Civil Rights," "Ecological Progress," and "Mid-East Crisis" are too large to say anything forceful about in the usual reference paper. But they could be narrowed. A narrow subject developed in detail is more interesting than a broad one sketchily developed. You can also save time in note-taking. The sooner you narrow your subject the sooner you will know which books and articles *not* to read. Note how this general topic has been narrowed:

> The American Novel
> The Novels of Saul Bellow
> The Theme of the Quest in Bellow's Novels
> Henderson's Quest for the Self in *Henderson the Rain King*

Limiting your general topic will continue as you do preliminary reading. Unless you are already fairly well informed, you will need to skim several books and articles before you know just what direction you want your subject to take. This means finding some books and articles and beginning a bibliography.

EXERCISE 7-1
CHOOSING AND LIMITING A SUBJECT

Choose three fields in which you have some interest and knowledge. Then by gradual narrowing, pick a topic in each field which would be suitable for a reference paper of about 2,000 words. Your process may go like this:

> Environment—social problems—population explosion—controls—abortions—recent legislation on abortions

The titles of the essays in Chapters 1, 2, and 9 of this book will suggest general areas. You may get narrowed topics from subpoints in an encyclopedia article, from titles and cross references in the card catalog, or from titles of articles in the *Readers' Guide.*

PREPARING A BIBLIOGRAPHY

Find books, magazine articles, newspaper stories, and other sources to indicate that you will be able to find sufficient information and to give you some special direction for your subject. Make a separate bibliography card (3x5 or 4x6) for each publication that you might use. Put down full information so that you won't have to go back later. The information on this card will be transferred later to the bibliography page of your finished paper. Full information includes these:

1. author,
2. title,
3. facts of publication—place of publication, publisher, date, editor, translator, volumes, edition, and so on.

You may wish to put down the call number to make it easy to find the book on the shelves.

Morrison, Nancy Brysson

Mary, Queen of Scots.

New York: Vanguard Press

1960.

DA
787
A1
M72

Use the standard form of bibliography requested by your instructor. The two most common style sheets are *The MLA Style Sheet* and Kate L. Turabian, *A Manual for Writers of Term Papers, Theses, and Dissertations.* The entries in this book follow the Turabian *Manual.* Whichever form you use, be consistent and accurate. Use commas, periods, colons, italics (underlining), quotation marks, capital letters, volume numbers, editors, and so on exactly as given in the model.

Books

One author

Menninger, K. A. *Man Against Himself.* New York: Harcourt, Brace and Company, 1938.

Two or more authors

Brockway, Wallace, and Herbert Weinstock. *Men of Music.* New York: Simon and Schuster, 1939.

With editor

Isherwood, Christopher, ed. *Great English Short Stories.* New York: Dell Publishing Co., Inc., 1957.

Author and editor

Burke, Edmund. *Reflections on the Revolution in France.* Edited by William B. Todd. New York: Holt, Rinehart and Winston, 1959.

Translation

Camus, Albert. *The Plague.* Translated by Stuart Gilbert. New York: Random House, Inc., 1948.

Two or more volumes

Morison, S. E., and H. S. Commager. *The Growth of the American Republic.* 3rd. ed. New York: The Oxford University Press, 1942. 2 vols.

Essay in edited collection

Pearce, Roy Harvey. "Wallace Stevens: The Life of the Imagination." *Wallace Stevens.* Edited by Marie Borroff. Englewood Cliffs, New Jersey: Prentice-Hall, Inc., 1963.

Magazines and periodicals

With author

Fromm, Erich. "Creators and Destroyers." *Saturday Review,* XLVII (January 4, 1964), 22–25.

No author given

"Women Suicides Increase Due to Social Pressures." *Science Newsletter,* CXXXV (April 25, 1964), 271.

Newspapers

With author

Pinkerton, W. Stewart, Jr. "The Lethal Impulse." *Wall Street Journal,* March 6, 1969, p. 1.

No author given

"Outburst in Trinidad," *Christian Science Monitor*, April 28, 1970, p. 16.

Encyclopedias

With author

Richardson, Robert S. "Astronautics." *Encyclopedia Americana.* 1959. Vol. II

No author given

"The Six Articles." *Encyclopedia Americana.* 1959. Vol. II.

Bulletin, pamphlet

U. S. Library of Congress, Division of Documents. *Monthly Checklist of State Publications:* Washington, D.C.: U. S. Government Printing Office, August, 1950.

Yearbook

U. S. Bureau of the Census. *Statistical Abstract of the United States.* Washington, D.C.: U. S. Government Printing Office, 1969.

Unpublished thesis or dissertation

Tidwell, Patricia. "Isolation and Community in the Works of Hawthorne and Faulkner." Unpublished M.A. thesis, Midwestern University, 1970.

EXERCISE 7-2
BIBLIOGRAPHY

Prepare a bibliography of ten items on 3x5 cards for one of the following subjects. Use a variety of sources, such as books, periodicals, newspapers, reference books, and pamphlets.

National parks
Undeclared wars
Sex education
Negroes in politics
Brain surgery
Exploring the atom
Pollution
Economic conditions in South America

Developing countries in Africa
The drug scene
An important man of the twentieth century
Modern art
Effects of television
Civil rights killings
Rebuilding the cities

GETTING AN OVERVIEW OF THE SUBJECT

Read much of the source material, taking no notes. You don't know what notes to take yet. You need to get an overview of your subject, to become generally informed, to get an idea of limits, subtopics, aspects of the field. You should probably read an encyclopedia article and two or three magazine articles and skim two or three books. Continue reading until several major topics come to mind. Out of these will come the tentative outline of your paper or perhaps the particular area of the general subject you want to concentrate on.

The number of major topics that you choose will depend on the scope of your subject and the length of the paper you are assigned to write. As a very rough guide, you probably should have a major topic for each two pages of longhand of your finished paper.

When you begin to feel at ease with your list of major topics, make a tentative outline (see Chapter 1, pp. 6–8). Only now are you prepared to take notes efficiently.

You may narrow or expand your subject later, at any time you see the need for it. Even after you write the first draft of the paper, you may decide to narrow its scope to include more details on a smaller subject. Your outline will change as your knowledge grows. It is a guide only.

Now you can take notes. You will only be frustrated if you gather material and take notes without knowing what in general you are looking for.

COLLECTING MATERIAL

1. Evaluating sources   You must evaluate your source of information as you prepare a bibliography and as you take notes. Early evaluation may lead you to reject a book without wasting the time of taking notes on it. Or you may find yourself taking notes with reservations. You must evaluate continuously as you gather, sift, and organize your material. But even casual consideration in some specific areas may lead you to either suspect or reject a book.

a. *The author.* Is the author an authority in the field? Ask yourself whether the author has sufficient experience or is a casual observer. Causes of Mid-East tension can probably be better assessed by a known political scientist whose specialty is the Mid-East than by a state governor who toured there or a TV commentator who passed through. Consider what other books authors have written, what institutions they belong to, what their record is. Some information could be found in a biographical dictionary.

b. *The publisher.* Is the publisher known, with a tradition of sound publications and a reputation to maintain? Does the material come from a professional journal or from a magazine circulated for the masses, from a university press or a popular book club? You might suspect a book written by William Jones and published by the Jones Press. An article on "Extrasensory Perception" is probably better if taken from *The Journal of Psychology* or the works of a noted psychiatrist than from a Sunday supplement or the *Reader's Digest.*

c. *The date of publication.* Is the work recent enough to reflect new developments? An essay about the character of George Washington published in 1810 could be quite valid. An article published five years ago on the latest developments in plastic surgery might be antiquated.

d. *The nature of the study.* Does it give valid information? Are opinions and generalizations supported by evidence and sound judgment? Does it seem one-sided, incomplete? Are alternatives considered, other authorities? Has the author sifted evidence and thought as carefully and objectively as you are supposed to be doing now?

2. Taking notes Read and take notes. You should be able to decide what material to take notes on and what to read without taking notes. If you can't decide, quit trying to take notes and go back to general reading. Review again your tentative outline and major topics.

Take brief notes—choice passages you wish to quote, statistics, proper names, dates, definitions, and only enough other material to jog your memory. You are not just transferring bits and gobs of information from books to note cards. You are becoming informed. You cannot write naturally or well if you write just from notes rather than from your knowledge. Take notes as follows:

a. *Follow major topics.* Take only notes that come under one of your major topics. You may, of course, decide that you need to add one or two topics to your list, but don't let your list get too long.

b. *Use note cards.* Take notes on a card (usually 4x6) with the major topic they pertain to written at the top.

c. *List the source.* At the bottom of a note card identify the source from which the notes are taken. This can be done by a number system or by writing the name of the author.

d. *Give page number.* If there is material on the card which will require a footnote—quotations, exact figures, or information or ideas that are not widely known among educated people—be sure to write the page number where this material is found. You will need the page number or numbers for writing the footnotes.

e. *Separate your topics.* Notes for different major topics should always be put on different cards.

f. *Separate your sources.* Notes from different sources should always be put on different cards.

g. *Identify the kind of note.* Distinguish on the card just what kind of note it is—how close it is to a complete passage or an exact quotation. You will need to know when you work the note into the paper. Usually there are four kinds of notes:

1. direct quotation (must be exact)—use quotation marks;
2. paraphrase—can be labeled *par;*
3. summary—can be labeled *sum;*
4. your own comment—brackets are useful.

Notes on the following passage illustrate different kinds of note cards. Each card has sufficient identification of four items:

1. the topic,
2. the source (author, book or article, page number),
3. the note itself,
4. the kind of note (direct quotation, paraphrase, summary, or personal comment).

Up to 50,000 Americans weren't so fortunate last year. They took their own lives, according to estimates by several experts on suicide. While many organic diseases yield to medical science, self-destruction is steadily rising as a cause of death—and as a cause of concern to psychiatrists and other medical authorities.

In eight industrialized nations studied, suicide now is the third most frequent cause of death. In the U.S. it is fourth. There is an alarming increase in suicide among young Americans. For college students, suicide now is the second most frequent cause of death, after accidental fatalities. . . .

About twice as many men as women commit suicide, partly because they choose more violent and lethal means. Women, who favor sleeping pills or barbiturates, often become afraid after taking a few pills. Or they are largely concerned with evoking a sympathetic response from someone close to them, so the dose isn't lethal.

—Pinkerton, "The Lethal Impulse"

Direct quotation, with personal comment

> Men and Women
>
> Women are often "largely concerned with evoking a sympathetic response from someone close to them, so the dose isn't lethal."
>
> — Pinkerton, p. 1
>
> [By contrast, men choose violent means, like guns, which give no second thoughts]

Summary

Number of suicides
    50,000 in 1968, estimates of some
    experts
    In 8 industrialized nations:
        —3rd most frequent cause of death
        —4th in U.S.
        — 2nd among college students

                —Pinkerton, p. 1
                    (Sum.)

Paraphrase

Men and Women
    Half as many women as men commit
    suicide.
        Some reasons:
        1. Because they usually take the
    less sudden means like pills and can
    change their mind in the process.
        2. Women may not be seeking
    death but sympathy.

                —Pinkerton, p. 1
                    (Par.)

EXERCISE 7-3
NOTE-TAKING

Study the paragraph on p. 55, written by Julian Huxley. Using full labeling, write the following three kinds of note cards.

1. Summarize, as briefly as possible, the central idea of the paragraph.
2. Quote verbatim a phrase or idea that you think most interesting.
3. Rewrite the paragraph in your own words. Try to get in all the ideas and attitudes but avoid the style of the original.

WRITING THE FIRST DRAFT AND USING FOOTNOTES

Writing the paper means combining your knowledge with the notes to make a finished expression of your research.

1. Read all your note cards.
2. Think over your material—outline, note cards, general information you have in your head. Get control of all the information so that your paper will not be a collection of notes.
3. Prepare a writing outline.
4. Group your note cards by their major topics and put the groups in the order they come in your outline.
5. Write a rough draft of your paper. Follow these criteria:

1. Make it your paper The writing must be your own. The thoughts must have become part of your knowledge. You may use exact quotations from your sources only if you enclose them in quotation marks and give the source in a footnote. Passing somebody else's work off as your own is called *plagiarism,* a form of dishonesty. If you quote from somebody else, use quotation marks, and acknowledge the source in a footnote. Borrowings of phrases and opinions must also be acknowledged. It is not enough to change a word here and there and then write the passage as if it were your own. If you have made the ideas and phrasing your own, it is your own. But if you are assembling another's work, give the author credit.

2. Use footnoted material correctly The number of footnotes needed will vary from paper to paper. Every direct quotation must have a footnote and so must facts, opinions, judgments that are somebody else's thinking or style rather than yours or that are common knowledge. From two to six footnotes per page are likely for the usual library paper.

1. *Footnote all direct quotations not common knowledge or public property.* The passage from The Declaration of Independence "among these rights are life, liberty, and the pursuit of happiness" is public, common knowledge and needs no footnote. "To be or not to be" is a familiar enough quotation that usually its source in Shakespeare's *Hamlet* does not need to be given.

2. *Quote exactly.* Quotations must be exact down to the last comma, hyphen, capital letter, or abbreviation. Be careful at the note-taking stage and check your paper against your notecard to insure against error.

3. *Use ellipses for omissions.* If you omit material from a quoted sentence, use an ellipsis mark of three spaced periods (. . .). If you omit from the end of a quoted sentence but the part quoted makes a complete sentence in your text, use a period followed by three spaced dots, even if you go on to continue quoting from a following sentence.

Up to 50,000 Americans weren't so fortunate last year. They took their own lives, according to estimates by several experts on suicide.

—Pinkerton

Ellipsis within sentence: "Up to 50,000 . . . weren't so fortunate last year."

Ellipsis and end of sentence: "Up to 50,000 Americans weren't so fortunate. . . ."

Ellipsis overlapping two or more sentences: "Up to 50,000 Americans weren't so fortunate. . . . They took their own lives, according to estimates by several experts on suicide."

4. *Use brackets for your own insertions.*

"Up to 50,000 Americans weren't so fortunate last year [1968]."

5. *Make the quotation a piece with your sentence.* The quotation is part of your style and sentence structure. Use word order, punctuation, and capitalization to fit.

> Pinkerton says that 50,000 "took their own lives, according to estimates by several experts on suicide."

> Pinkerton has this to say about the suicide motives of women: "They are largely concerned with evoking a sympathetic response from someone close to them."

Make small quotations a part of your paragraph. Set off and indent long quotations. When you indent, do not use quotation marks.

6. *Avoid long quotations.* Chunks of quotations much longer than six to ten lines put the burden of interpretation on the reader. It is not the quotation that is important, but your use of it in your paper.

3. Use correct footnote form The footnotes should be numbered consecutively throughout the paper and placed at the bottom of the page on which the cited material occurs (or, if your instructor prefers, in one list at the end of the paper). The first footnote for a source must be complete with author, title, and all facts of publication (based on Turabian, *A Manual*). Later references can be abbreviated. The following sample footnotes illustrate common forms.

FIRST REFERENCES

Books

One author

[1]K. A. Menninger, *Man Against Himself* (New York: Harcourt, Brace and Company, 1958), p. 37.

Two or more authors

[2]Wallace Brockway and Herbert Weinstock, *Men of Music* (New York: Simon and Schuster, 1939), p. 21.

With editor

[3]Christopher Isherwood, ed., *Great English Short Stories* (New York: Dell Publishing Co., Inc., 1957), pp. 86–87.

Author and editor

[4]Edmund Burke, *Reflection on the Revolution in France,* ed. by William B. Todd (New York: Holt, Rinehart and Winston, 1959), p. 44.

Translation

[5]Albert Camus, *The Plague,* trans. by Stuart Gilbert (New York: Random House, Inc., 1948), p. 103.

Two or more volumes

[6]S. E. Morison and H. S. Commager, *The Growth of the American Republic* (3rd ed.: New York: The Oxford University Press, 1942), II, 170.

Essay in edited collection

[7]Roy Harvey Pearce, "Wallace Stevens: The Life of the Imagination," in *Wallace Stevens,* ed. by Marie Borroff (Englewood Cliffs, New Jersey: Prentice-Hall, Inc., 1963), p. 112.

Magazines and periodicals
With author

[8]Erich Fromm, "Creators and Destroyers," *Saturday Review,* XLVII (January 4, 1964), 22.

No author given

[9]"Women Suicides Increase Due to Social Pressures," *Science Newsletter,* CXXXV (April 25. 1964), 271.

Newspapers
With author

[10]Dana L. Spitzer, "Negro Teachers Tell of Job Losses," St. Louis *Post-Dispatch,* July 1, 1970, Sec. D, p. 1.

No author given

[11]"Outburst in Trinidad," *Christian Science Monitor,* April 28, 1970, p. 16.

Encyclopedias
With author

[12]Robert S. Richardson, "Astronautics," *Encyclopedia Americana,* 1959, II, 453.

No author given

[13]"The Six Articles," *Encyclopedia Americana,* 1959, II, 360.

Bulletin, pamphlet

[14]U.S. Library of Congress, Division of Documents, *Monthly Check List of State Publications* (Washington, D.C.: U.S. Government Printing Office, August, 1950), p. 5.

Yearbook

[15]U.S. Bureau of the Census, *Statistical Abstract of the United States.* (Washington, D.C.: U.S. Government Printing Office, 1969), p. 87.

Unpublished thesis or dissertation

[16]Patricia Tidwell, "Isolation and Community in the Works of Hawthorne and Faulkner" (unpublished M.A. thesis, Midwestern University, 1970), p. 87.

SECOND REFERENCES

For second references, use a shortened form, usually the author's last name and the page number:

[17]Camus, p. 271.

To distinguish two works by the same author, add a shortened title.

[18]Camus, *Stranger,* p. 21.

For two references in a row from the same source, use ibid. Ibid. means "in the same place" and can refer only to the immediately preceding source. If the second note refers to the same page, use only ibid. Add the different page number if you need it.

[1]K. A. Menninger, *Man Against Himself* (New York: Harcourt, Brace and Company, 1938), p. 12.

[2]Ibid.

[3]Ibid., p. 28.

[4]Albert Camus, *The Plague,* trans. by Stuart Gilbert (New York: Random House, Inc., 1948), p. 103.

[5]Menninger, p. 87.

ABBREVIATIONS

These are the abbreviations you will ordinarily use in footnotes. Note that abbreviations are followed by a period and that the abbreviations for Latin words are not italicized or underlined (formerly, such abbreviations were almost always italicized, and you will see them that way in many sources).

anon.	anonymous
c. or ca. (*circa*)	about (c. 1935)

cf. (*confer*)	compare
ch., chs.	chapter (s)
ed., eds.	edited by, edition, editor, editors
et al. (*et alii*)	and others
f., ff.	and the following page(s)
ibid. (*ibidem*)	in the same place
l., ll.	line(s)
MS., ms., MSS., mss.	manuscript(s)
n.d.	no date
n.p.	no place of publication, no publisher
op. cit. (*opere citato*)	in the work cited
p., pp.	page(s)
passim	here and there throughout
rev.	revised
tr., trans.	translated by, translator
vol., vols.	volume(s)

PREPARING THE FINAL DRAFT

Study your first draft for correctness, organization, and general effectiveness. Make needed revisions. Check your essay against your outline to see that both have the same organization. If not, decide which represents the better organization and change the other to fit it.

Write the final drafts of your outline and your essay.

Prepare the final bibliography. You have written bibliography cards as you went along. Some of these sources you have used in the paper; some you have not. Those sources that appear in your footnotes must be included in the bibliography. In that case you are likely to have five to ten magazine articles and six to fifteen books. Your instructor may ask you to include every source you have examined or which has had some bearing on the paper. Then your bibliography may include 50 to 100 items.

When you have selected the items to be used, arrange the cards in alphabetical order by author (or title, if there is no author) and copy them in standard bibliographic form. Use one alphabetical list including books, magazines, newspapers, and so on, unless your instructor prefers a different classification. Note that the form is slightly different from footnote form.

Sample Reference Paper

The final library paper has four parts, unless your instructor has directed otherwise:

1. *Title page.* This contains the title, your name, the instructor's name, the course number, and the date.

2. *Outline.*   This is the standard outline of the text of your paper.
3. *Text* of the paper, with footnotes.
4. *Bibliography,*   on a separate page.

These parts are shown in the sample paper that follows.

SUICIDES IN THE UNITED STATES

Karen Hershey

English 1123
Dr. Matthew Burton
December 8, 1977

OUTLINE

I. The variables of suicide

→

A. Male and female suicides

B. Economic depression

C. Wartime

D. Marriage

E. Occupation

F. Season and weather

G. Young people

II. Prevention of suicide

A. Informing the public

B. Learning the danger signals

1. Talk of suicide

2. Depression

3. Intolerable insomnia

4. Sense of futility and worthlessness

C. Getting the suicidal to the psychiatrist

D. Working through prevention agencies

SUICIDES IN THE UNITED STATES

While you are reading this page, several Americans will try to kill themselves. By the time you have read to the end of this paper, two or three will succeed in dying by their own hands.

Americans are destroying themselves at the rapid rate of "one every twenty-four minutes."[1] For every life that is taken by polio, suicide claims seventy-seven. For every five lives snuffed out by breast cancer, suicide takes four. For every two persons killed in automobile accidents, one commits suicide.[2] Day in, day out, every day of the year, three hundred or more Americans attempt to destroy themselves, and every day, sixty or more succeed in doing so.

The "official" estimate by the National Institute of Mental Health of suicides in 1968 was

---

[1] K. A. Menninger, Man Against Himself (New York: Harcourt, Brace and Company, 1938), p. 12.

[2] Edward Robb Ellis, Traitor Within (Garden City, New York: Doubleday and Company, Inc., 1961), p. 3.

about 23,000. But Dr. Edwin S. Shneidman and other experts at that agency, citing the "hidden rate," assert that the actual figure was more than double the official statistic.[3]

The rate is increasing. In 1920, suicide ranked twenty-second on the list of causes of death. In 1973 it ranked ninth,[4] and some authorities put it as fourth.[5]

Suicide is becoming too realistic to be ignored any longer or to be treated as a "taboo." It is a perplexing, constant problem, which must be faced and challenged by the American populace--not tomorrow, or the next day, but right now. ꞋꞋꞋꞋꞋꞋꞋꞋ INTRO 9

To understand the problem of suicide, we need to look at some of the variables and determinants of suicide. Men are more susceptible than women. In the United States three to four times more men than

---

[3] W. Stewart Pinkerton, "The Lethal Impulse," Wall Street Journal, March 6, 1969, p. 10.

[4] U.S. Bureau of the Census, Statistical Abstract of the United States (96th ed.; Washington, D.C.: U.S. Government Printing Office, 1975), p. 64.

[5] Pinkerton, p. 1.

women kill themselves. In 1973, 18,108 men died by their own hands as compared to 7,010 women.[6] One reason for this, according to psychiatrists and sociologists, is that men's roles in society are more active and more demanding, thus keeping them under greater stress than women. SHORT "Men probably have stronger aggressive habits than do women, and thus they generally make more hostile responses to frustrating stimuli."[7] A man is much more likely to succeed in his suicidal attempts with a pistol at his temple, which kills instantly, than a woman who takes sleeping pills, which leaves a large margin of time in which she can be discovered and saved. Three women live through suicide attempts for every man who tries to kill himself and survives.

Naturally, during a time of economic tension there will be more suicides. The best example for this is the year 1932, the depth of the depression. At this time, 17.4 in every 100,000 died by their own hands. This made a record of 20,646, who, because they found

---

[6] U.S. Bureau of the Census, p. 161.

[7] David Lester, "Suicidal Behavior in Men and Women," Mental Hygiene, LIII (July, 1969), 344.

the economic depression unbearable, voluntarily took
their own lives.[8]

It seems quite logical that men should kill
themselves during a depression, but it seems less
easy to understand why fewer men kill themselves in
wartime. But it is a fact that during both world wars
the suicide rate of American men declined sharply.
The explanation for this is that during wartime,
a terribly lonely and suicide-prone person can
identify himself with the national goal to win.
Also, oftentimes the suicidal feelings can be dis-
guised as military heroism, taken out on the
battlefront.

Another interesting factor dealing with the
suicide rate is marriage. Marriage definitely reduces
the suicide threat. In both sexes, of all ages, in
all races, everywhere, fewer married people kill
themselves than single, widowed, or divorced persons.
This is due primarily to the fact that the spouse,
under normal conditions, has a feeling of being loved,
of being secure, and of being wanted. It is also

---

[8] Ellis, p. 21.

interesting to note that children in marriage reduce the suicide danger even further. This can be accounted for in that parents feel they are needed, and that they must live in order to fulfill their obligations of guidance and providence for their children. Divorced persons of both sexes kill themselves more than three times as often as married people. Psychiatrists believe this is because the divorced partner often feels as if he were a failure and so rejected by his mate. Often, a divorced person has been through so many strains of an unhappy partnership that he is horribly depressed. Then after the divorce, there are so many new situations to adjust to that, for the divorced, life seems completely unbearable.

Occupations also play a role in contributing to suicide rates. It has been observed that those who work in the professions kill themselves more frequently than do unskilled laborers. It has also been found that if a person works in an occupation which brings him in close contact with death and provides him with a convenient means to end his own life, suicide poses a greater danger than in more

harmless professions. Physicians, policemen, and
soldiers, for instance, kill themselves more frequently than the general public. An occupation
with a very high suicidal rate is that of the
executioner. An interesting point, worth noting, is
that psychiatrists have quite a high suicidal rate.
So many kill themselves that some authorities consider
suicide as a distinct danger in this field.

A person's economic situation often is a danger
in suicide. Contrary to popular belief, the higher
a person rises on the economic ladder, the greater the
danger of suicide. At least thirty to forty percent
of the so-called economic suicides occur when a man
is successful, not when he is failing. It seems
strange that a rapid rise up the economic ladder can
cause some people to end their lives. But often when
a man has reached his peak of success he has nothing
left to seek, and his life seems meaningless. The
success suicides are definitely more frequent than
most people would expect.

One of the strangest and least understood influences on suicide is the seasons and the weather.
Certain types of weather throw an eerie spell over

many suicidal persons, influencing them to cast the
die. There is a seasonal tide in suicide, and it
never varies. The weather which leads to suicide
is not what most persons would expect. Nine times
out of ten, people think suicide is more apt to be
committed on a cold, gloomy, depressing day in
wintertime. This estimate is wrong. Suicide does
not increase in gloomy weather.

Spring, when nature is at its smiling best, is
the suicide season. It is proven by statistics that
more people kill themselves in spring than at any
other time of the year. In the United States, April
is the peak month, followed by May and March. The
winter months have the least amount of suicides.
December brings the year's low, followed by the
gloomy month of November, and then usually February.
The second upsurge in suicide occurs during September
and October. This autumn increase is as regular as
the rise in spring.

The reasons for spring and autumn being the
suicide seasons are that they are both times of
decisions. In the springtime, everyone changes from
their winter clothes to their spring ones. Spring

is the time for planning summer vacation, and for
deciding to paint the house and do the spring clean-
ing. Autumn is the time when winter clothes are
brought out, and new purchases made. Children must
be gotten ready for school. Autumn is the time to
decide to move, as October shows to be the traditional
moving month. All of these changes play a great part
in piling up uncertainty and problems to the breaking
point for a suicidally inclined person.

If these were the only influences we would
expect spring and autumn to be about equal in their
number of suicides. But since they are not it is
evident that there must be something quite different
about spring which influences people to kill
themselves.

Many of the findings of meteorobiologists--scien-
tists who study weather's effects on human beings--
are controversial. The most generally accepted
explanation, however, of spring's impact is that the
change from cold weather to warm catches our bodies
unprepared. Meteorobiologists have shown conclusively
that every time the temperature changes or the
barometer fluctuates, our bodies have to make an

adjustment. Most of the time this is done easily, automatically, but when the weather makes drastic changes, our bodies and minds are forced to labor. This process requires work and helps to account for the feelings of laziness which is termed "spring fever" in the American society. For the potential suicide the demands that spring make on his body and mind could be the last straw.

It has also been suggested by meteorobiologists and psychiatrists that the suicidally inclined person finds the contrast between his inner despair and nature's exhilaration too great to bear. Many suicidal attempters wait for spring and have hopes that when fine days come with their exhilarating brightness, the cloud of unhappiness will dissolve. But when spring does come, because of the suicidal's depression, things do not seem as bright as in the other springs. Or else, the very perfection of nature with its signs of the life-urge increases the despair of the potential suicide and makes him more willing to die.

Contrary to the popular beliefs of the general public, children and adolescents are not exempt from

suicide. In fact, their suicide rates are astonishing. For American children aged fifteen to nineteen,
suicide is the fifth ranking cause of death. In
1957, 231 boys and 57 girls aged fifteen to nineteen
found life unbearable. In the next lowest age group,
ten to fourteen, suicide ranks thirteenth on the list
of leading causes of death. In 1957, a total of 55
boys and 13 girls of this age were recorded officially
as authenticated suicides. Going back one step
closer to the cradle, the group aged five to nine,
the National Office of Vital Statistics lists three
authenticated suicides of boys at this age level in
1956.[9]

Suicide is not a normal reaction of a child to a
problem. Usually he will run away or dream of death,
but will not actually try to kill himself. Children
who try suicide have inevitably had life histories of
insecurity and lack of love. When they attempt
suicide, they are usually trying to change things,
not escape them, and they normally fantasize that
they will escape death. As would be expected,

[9] Abraham Maurits Meerloo, Suicide and Mass
Suicide (New York: and Stratton, 1962), p. 41.

television and horror comic books have been blamed repeatedly for being the cause of child suicides.

Unlike the younger child, when the adolescent thinks of suicide he generally does not simultaneously believe he will survive. The adolescent's motives and understandings of what will be gained or lost by the act are much closer to those of the adult. Suicides and suicidal attempts in adolescents are for many reasons. They are due to unresolved conflicts, frustrations, disappointments, guilt feelings, loss of esteem, fear of punishment, and the real or imaginary loss of a love object. The unleashing of the sex drive during puberty and the spectacular physical, mental, and emotional changes which accompany this stage in life require difficult adjustments for any adolescent. But when the child has other important fears and problems, the great changes of puberty overwhelm him and life becomes unbearable.

In a study reported by Drs. Benjamin H. Balser and James F. Masterson in the November 1959 issue of the American Journal of Psychiatry, it was found that twelve percent of all suicide attempts in the nation each year were made by adolescents. These

researchers found that ninety percent of adolescent
suicide attempts were made by girls. The group of
attempted suicides did not vary appreciably from the
average population in physical, mental, or emotional
status. Six percent had made previous attempts.
Over fifty percent of the families were in the
medium income bracket. Over forty-two percent were
in the low income group. No adult was at home in
over fifty percent of the suicidal attempts. The
mother was at home in nearly twenty-nine percent of
the cases when the attempt occurred.[10] Disciplinary
measures, emotional upsets, and depression were listed
as the chief causes.

Suicide figures indicate an alarming problem in
our society. But it is a problem we can do something
about. Everyone is able to help a relative or friend
overcome a suicidal urge. Our shocking national
suicide rate can be reduced.

Self-destruction can be defeated because the
vast majority of suicides and suicidal attempts are
caused by emotional states which are temporary and

---

[10] Ellis, p. 57.

remediable. No one becomes suicidal in a day and
there is time in which the suicide attempter can
be helped. Most people in whom a strong suicidal
urge is surging flash clear warning signals of their
danger to the people around them.

If suicide is to be controlled there are several
important things which must be done. The first step
is to make the public aware of the national suicide
problem. The mystery and horror which surrounds
suicide must be cleared up. Statistics must be
publicized. Suicide must concern the public, not
just the specialists, if it is ever to be conquered.

The second thing to be done is to learn to
recognize danger signals. The danger signals of a
suicide-prone person are clear if one knows what to
look for. So many people ignore these signals,
however, that it is no wonder that the suicide rate
is so high. Four of the danger signals are so
simple that any layman can easily recognize them.
First, the potential suicide will almost always talk
of committing suicide. When a person does this it
should never be ignored. It is a common fallacy that
those who talk of killing themselves will never do

so. This is totally wrong. Almost every case of attempted and committed suicide was talked over by the suicidal with someone, but this person failed to recognize the danger signals and to give the help that could have saved the life of a human being.

The second sign is often a deep and lasting depression on the part of the suicidal. Many people feel that to talk to a depressed person about his troubles will only throw him into a state of deeper depression making the risk of suicide even greater. But this again, is false. The confessing of his troubles helps to lighten the load of the suicidal.

Intolerable insomnia is a third signal. Often a suicidal will go to a medical doctor hoping that he will see the signs and offer help. Many times, the doctor, unaware of the signs, will prescribe sleeping tablets, which are later used as a means for the suicide-prone person to kill himself.

As a fourth sign, a person ready to commit suicide will have feelings of futility and an uncalled for feeling of unworthiness. The suicidal person lives in a world of terrible loneliness. If his isolation can be broached, he may be saved. That is why a sympathetic ear and a shoulder to cry on should always be available and can often work wonders.

When these signs are recognized, it is vitally important that the layman give as much help as possible in making the suicidal feel that he is worth something to others and society. But although the advice and counsel of nonprofessional persons is often effective in holding off self-destruction, this is only a stopgap. Psychiatric care is the only real answer. The third step to preventing suicide is to make sure that the suicidal sees a psychiatrist as soon as possible. A psychiatrist can help a person find out what situations and circumstances cause the resurgence of the suicidal's wounds and can help him to avoid them. The suicidal person can learn to recognize the fatal flaw within himself and how to deal with it.

The fourth method of prevention is to work through a suicide prevention agency. There are many church groups and community agencies which can be called upon for help, either by the suicidal himself or a person in contact with him. There also are many little-known organizations which are devoted exclusively to combating suicide. The oldest of these is the National Save-a-Life League, with its headquarters in New York City. Like all the others it is open twenty-four hours a day, seven days a week. Another organization, started by community members in Dade County, Miami, Florida, is FRIENDS. It was claimed that during the twelve-month period from December 1, 1959, when FRIENDS started, to December 1, 1960, Dade County's suicide rate fell from "18.1 to 15.2 per 100,000 population. This is a 13.7 percent decrease."[11] This shows that suicide can be combatted, but it takes interested people, who are willing to give up their time and energy to save a life.

Dr. Ronald S. Mint, Assistant Professor of Psychiatry at the University of California, states that "one hundred percent of those who attempt suicide and are saved are glad they survived."[12] Should this not make it worthwhile for the communities, the

SAME AS #10

_____

[11] Ibid., p. 203.

[12] F. R. Schreiber and Melvin Herman, "Why People Can't Take It," Science Digest, LVI (September 1964), 69.

states, the nation to launch an all-out program against suicide in the United States? Should this not make it worthwhile for individuals to learn the dangers of suicide so they may be better qualfied to recognize a potential suicide and offer help? Suicide is not unconquerable. What it takes is interested and informed people to make the suicide rate go down. The challenge of suicide is here more than ever before. Will it be met?

BIBLIOGRAPHY

Alexander, Shana. "Decision to Die." Life, LVI
    (May 29, 1964), 74-76.

Bahra, R. J. "Potential for Suicide." American
    Journal of Nursing. LXXV (October, 1975), 1782-
    1788.

Balser, Benjamin, and James Masterson. "Suicide in
    Adolescents." American Journal of Psychiatry,
    CXVI (November, 1959), 400-404.

Benson, M. "Doctors' Wives Tackle the Suicide Prob-
    lem." Today's Health, XLIV (May, 1964), 60-63.

Clark, Marilyn. "Suicide in Childhood and Adoles-
    cence." NEA Journal, LIII (November, 1964),
    32-33.

Dublin, Louis Israel. Suicide. New York: Ronald
    Press, 1963.

Ellis, Edward Robb. Traitor Within. Garden City,
    New York: Doubleday and Company, Inc., 1961.

Farberow, Norman L., and E. S. Schneidman, eds. The
    Cry for Help. New York: McGraw-Hill, 1961.

"How to Keep Patients from Jumping Out of Windows."
    Trans-Action, VII (February, 1970), 13.

Hankoff, L. D. "Categories of Attempted Suicide."
    American Journal of Public Health, LXVI (June,
    1976), 558-563.

Lester, David. "Suicidal Behavior in Men and Women."
    Mental Hygiene, LIII (July, 1969), 340-345.

Meerloo, Abraham Maurits. Suicide and Mass Suicide.
    New York: Grune and Stratton, 1962.

Menninger, K. A. Man Against Himself. New York:
    Harcourt, Brace and Company, 1938.

Nott, Kathleen. "Mortal Statistics." Commentary,
    XXXVIII (October, 1964), 64-68.

Pinkerton, W. Stewart. "The Lethal Impulse." Wall
    Street Journal (March 6, 1969), 10.

Schreiber, F. R., and Melvin Herman. "Why People
    Can't Take It." Science Digest, LVI (September,
    1964), 66-69.

Singer, Richard G., and Irving J. Blumenthal. "Sui-
    cide Clues in Psychotic Patients." Mental
    Hygiene, LIII (July, 1969), 346-350.

St. John-Stevas, Norman. The Right to Life. New
    York: Holt, Rinehart and Winston, 1964.

U.S. Bureau of the Census. Statistical Abstract of
    the United States. 1975. 96th ed. Washington,
    D.C.: U.S. Government Printing Office, 1975.

Vinant, M. O. "Suicide and How to Prevent It."
    Christianity Today, XIV (January 16, 1970),
    10-12.

"Women Suicides Increase Due to Social Pressures."
    Science Newsletter, LXXXV (April 25, 1964), 271.

8

Writing About Literature

To write effectively about literature you must first of all understand clearly the piece of literature you are working with. This means, of course, a careful and valid interpretation. Since imaginative literature, such as fiction and poetry, offers many pitfalls to interpretation, it will be helpful for you to keep in mind four sets of materials: (1) the basic rules of literary interpretation, (2) the basic elements of fiction, (3) the basic elements of drama, and (4) the basic elements of poetry.

Some Rules of Literary Interpretation

1. Read from the piece of literature out You must begin with the poem, story, or drama itself and discover what it means or does. A common error is for a reader to come to the piece of literature with a ready-made interpretation and then try to find or force details to fit.

2. Stick to the facts of the piece of literature Free interpretations are not allowed. You must work from the materials in the piece of literature. You must distinguish what the author says from your own wish-fulfillments and private experiences. Generalizations, judgments, and interpretations you make must be supported by evidence from the piece of literature, just as any persuasive paragraph or composition must be supported by pertinent evidence. Base your paper on the text. Don't just gab. The poem or story or drama does not mean what you want it to mean. It means what it means. You may use critics and other thinkers, but the text is the evidence.

3. Distinguish interpretation from implication A good piece of literature will suggest meanings, implications, and applications beyond itself. Such is the nature of a work of art, and it is fair to follow the suggestions. But in writing about a piece of literature, in analyzing and discussing with other people, keep the two areas distinct: first, what the piece of literature itself says, does, and means; and second, what suggestions, implications, and reverberations are set in motion. The first set are in the piece of literature; the second set are outside it.

Elements of Fiction

The elements of fiction and the approaches to analyzing them may be studied on three different levels: the factual level, the thematic level, and the literary level.

Study the following story, "The Open Window," to see how it illustrates the various elements within the three levels.

The Open Window
SAKI

"My aunt will be down presently, Mr. Nuttel," said a very self-possessed young lady of fifteen; "in the meantime you must try to put up with me."

Framton Nuttel endeavoured to say the correct something which should duly flatter the niece of the moment without unduly discounting the aunt that was to come. Privately he doubted more than ever whether these formal visits on a succession of total strangers would do much towards helping the nerve cure which he was supposed to be undergoing.

"I know how it will be," his sister had said when he was preparing to migrate to this rural retreat; "you will bury yourself down there and not speak to a living soul, and your nerves will be worse than ever from moping. I shall just give you letters of introduction to all the people I know there. Some of them, as far as I can remember, were quite nice."

Framton wondered whether Mrs. Sappleton, the lady to whom he was presenting one of the letters of introduction, came into the nice division.

"Do you know many of the people round here?" asked the niece, when she judged that they had had sufficient silent communion.

"Hardly a soul," said Framton. "My sister was staying here, at the rectory, you know, some four years ago, and she gave me letters of introduction to some of the people here."

He made the last statement in a tone of distinct regret.

"Then you know practically nothing about my aunt?" pursued the self-possessed young lady.

"Only her name and address," admitted the caller. He was wondering whether Mrs. Sappleton was in the married or widowed state. An indefinable something about the room seemed to suggest masculine habitation.

"Her great tragedy happened just three years ago," said the child; "that would be since your sister's time."

"Her tragedy?" asked Framton; somehow in this restful country spot tragedies seemed out of place.

"You may wonder why we keep that window wide open on an October afternoon," said the niece, indicating a large French window that opened on to a lawn.

"It is quite warm for the time of the year," said Framton; "but has that window got anything to do with the tragedy?"

"Out through that window, three years ago to a day, her husband and her two young brothers went off for their day's shooting. They never came back. In crossing the moor to their favorite snipe-shooting ground they were all three engulfed in a treacherous piece of bog. It had been that dreadful wet summer, you know, and places that were safe in other years gave way suddenly without warning. Their bodies were never recovered. That was the dreadful part of it." Here the child's voice lost its self-possessed note and became falteringly human. "Poor aunt always thinks that they will come back some day, they and the little brown spaniel that was lost with them, and walk in at that window just as they used to do. That is why the window is kept open every evening till it is quite dusk. Poor dear aunt, she has often told me how they went out, her husband with his white waterproof coat over his arm, and Ronnie, her youngest brother, singing 'Bertie, why do you bound?' as he always did to tease her, because she said it got on her nerves. Do you know, sometimes on still, quiet evenings like this, I almost get a creepy feeling that they will all walk in through that window—"

She broke off with a little shudder. It was a relief to Framton when the aunt bustled into the room with a whirl of apologies for being late in making her appearance.

"I hope Vera has been amusing you?" she said.

"She has been very interesting," said Framton.

"I hope you don't mind the open window," said Mrs. Sappleton briskly; "my husband and brothers will be home directly from shooting, and they always come in this way. They've been out for snipe in the marshes to-day, so they'll make a fine mess over my poor carpets. So like you menfolks, isn't it?"

She rattled on cheerfully about the shooting and the scarcity of birds and the prospects for duck in the winter. To Framton it was all purely horrible. He made a desperate but only partially successful effort to turn the talk on to a less ghastly topic; he was conscious that his hostess was giving him only a fragment of her attention, and her eyes were constantly straying past him to the open window and the lawn beyond. It was certainly an unfortunate coincidence that he should have paid his visit on this tragic anniversary.

"The doctors agree in ordering me complete rest, an absence of mental excitement, and avoidance of anything in the nature of violent physical exercise," announced Framton, who laboured under the tolerably wide-spread delusion that total strangers and chance acquaintances are hungry for the least detail of one's ailments and infirmities, their cause and cure. "On the matter of diet they are not so much in agreement," he continued.

"No?" said Mrs. Sappleton, in a voice which replaced a yawn only at the last moment. Then she suddenly brightened into alert attention—but not to what Framton was saying.

"Here they are at last!" she cried. "Just in time for tea, and don't they look as if they were muddy up to the eyes!"

Framton shivered slightly and turned toward the niece with a look intended to convey sympathetic comprehension. The child was staring out through the open window with dazed horror in her eyes. In a chill shock of nameless fear Framton swung round in his seat and looked in the same direction.

In the deepening twilight three figures were walking across the lawn toward the window; they all carried guns under their arms, and one of them was additionally burdened with a white coat hung over his shoulders. A tired brown spaniel kept close at their heels. Noiselessly they neared the house, and then a hoarse young voice chanted out of the dusk: "I said, Bertie, why do you bound?"

Framton grabbed wildly at his stick and hat; the hall-door, the gravel-drive and the front gate were dimly-noted stages in his headlong retreat. A cyclist coming along the road had to run into the hedge to avoid imminent collision.

"Here we are, my dear," said the bearer of the white mackintosh, coming in through the window; "fairly muddy, but most of it's dry. Who was that who bolted out as we came up?"

"A most extraordinary man, a Mr. Nuttel," said Mrs. Sappleton; "could only talk about his illness, and dashed off without a word of good-bye or apology when you arrived. One would think he had seen a ghost."

"I expect it was the spaniel," said the niece calmly; "he told me he had a horror of dogs. He was once hunted into a cemetery somewhere on the banks of the Ganges by a pack of pariah dogs, and had to spend the night in a newly dug grave with the creatures snarling and grinning and foaming just above him. Enough to make anyone lose their nerve."

Romance at short notice was her specialty.

Let us look at the three levels of fiction and the elements that make them up.

THE FACTUAL LEVEL

This is what the story says—the main ingredients of the story itself. These may be classified into plot, character (or characterization), and setting.

1. Plot Plot is the sequence of events or episodes of which a story is composed. It is the action. But plot seldom consists merely of a series of related actions. The story must have significant actions. That is, the actions are arranged to create excitement or, more maturely, to reveal character or express some theme of life. Usually this excitement and meaningfulness arise out of some sort of conflict—a clash of actions, ideas, desires, or wills.

The main character may be pitted against some other person or group of persons (*man against man*); he may be in conflict with some external force —physical nature, society, or "fate" (*man against environment*); or he may be in conflict with some element in his own nature (*man against himself*). There is conflict in a chess game, where the competitors sit quite still for hours, as surely as in a wrestling match; emotional conflict may be raging within a person sitting quietly in an empty room.

The central character in the conflict, whether a sympathetic or an un-sympathetic person, is referred to as the *protagonist* (one who struggles for); the forces arrayed against the protagonist, whether persons, things, conventions of society, or traits of the person's own character, are the *antagonists* (those who struggle against).

In some stories the conflict is single, clear-cut, and easily identifiable. In others it is multiple, various, and subtle. A person may be in conflict with other persons, with society or nature, and with self all at the same time, and sometimes the person may be involved in conflict without being aware of it.

In reading fiction, pinpoint the various conflicts and identify the protagonist (central character) and the antagonist (the force which the protagonist is pitted against). Classify the different conflicts and see them in terms of the total story. Look for subplots.

Note some of the conflicts in "The Open Window." In the early part of the story, Nuttel is the protagonist pitted against the girl as antagonist. This conflict may be classified as man against man (Nuttel against girl) and is mental. Nuttel later is in emotional conflict with himself, when he is battling his fear. The last episode has the girl as protagonist against her family as antagonist and the conflict is mental as she tries to deceive them with an imaginative story, as she had deceived Nuttel.

In addition to conflict, various devices may be used to advance the plot and appeal to the readers. *Suspense* makes readers ask "What's going to happen next?" or "How will this turn out?" and impels them to read on. *Dilemma, mystery, surprise,* and *foreshadowing* may create suspense.

Various devices may weaken plot by threatening plausibility. Wild *chance,* unusual *coincidence,* or any unmotivated action, such as *plot manipulation* make reader doubt. In "The Open Window," we can at least question whether the perfect timing of the hunting party's arriving home is an unjustifiable coincidence. We ask how improbable is it and how much the author depends on it to resolve the plot. We want a story to be inevitable and logical within itself.

Plot is an important element in fiction. One of the best questions to ask in analyzing fiction is what is the *function* of plot—what is the relationship of each incident to the total meaning of the story? The analysis of a story through its central conflict is especially useful, for it takes us to what is really at issue in the story.

2. Character The term *character* designates individuals in a story and also the quality of humanness which makes up the characters—their interests, desires, emotions, and so on. Plot and character are inseparably bound. We cannot have one without the other. We can emphasize this connection by asking one of the first interpretative questions—who is the protagonist (or protagonists)? Two features will help you identify the central character. This person is usually relevant to every event in the story and usually the events cause some change in the person or in our attitude toward the person.

Besides identifying the protagonist, we want to ask other questions about character. How convincing is it? How complex is it? What changes in character take place?

To be convincing, characterization must also observe three principles. First, the characters must be *consistent* in their behavior: they must not behave one way on one occasion and a different way on another unless there is a clearly sufficient reason for the change. Second, the characters must be clearly *motivated* in whatever they do, especially when there is any change in their behavior: we must be able to understand the reasons for what they do—if not immediately, at least by the end of the story. Third, the characters must be *plausible* or lifelike. They must be neither paragons of virtue nor monsters of evil nor an impossible combination of contradictory traits. Whether we have observed anyone like them in our own experience or not, we must feel that they could appear somewhere in the normal course of events.

In proportion to the fullness of their development, the characters in a story are relatively flat or round. The *flat character* is characterized by one or two traits and can be summed up in a sentence. The *round character* is complex and many-sided and might require an essay for full analysis.

All fictional characters may be classified as static or developing. The *static character* is the same sort of person at the end of the story as at the beginning. The *developing character* undergoes a permanent change in some aspect of character, personality, or outlook. The change may be a large or a small one; it may be for better or for worse; but it is something important and basic: it is more than a change in condition or a minor change in opinion.

In "The Open Window" both Nuttel and the girl are flat, static characters. His essential characteristics are nervousness and insecurity and hers are poise and imagination. Neither changes character during the story.

Obviously, we must not expect many developing characters in any piece of fiction: in a short story there is not usually room for more than one. A common basic plan of short stories, however, is to show change in the protagonist as the result of a crucial situation in the person's life. When this is done, the change is likely to be the surest clue to the story's meaning. To state and explain the change will be the best way to get at the point of the story. To be convincing, a change must meet three conditions: (1) it must be within the possibilities of the character who makes it; (2) it must be sufficiently motivated by the circumstances in which the character is found; and (3) it must be allowed sufficient time for a change of its magnitude believably to take place. Basic changes in human character seldom occur suddenly. The interpretative writer does not present bad men who suddenly reform at the end of the story and become good, or drunkards who jump on the wagon at a moment's notice, but is satisfied with smaller changes that are carefully prepared for.

3. **Setting** Setting is the environment, the time and place in which the story occurs. "The Open Window" takes place in rural England, among the gentry, in the late nineteenth century. Details on setting frequently are

the descriptive passages that many readers are impatient with—they want to get on with the narrative. But the author has a purpose. What you must ask is what the effect or function of these particular details is or why these particular details rather than others are used. Any of several purposes may be helped by setting.

1. The plausibility of plot or character may depend on time and place. In "The Open Window" the action and character of the "nervous" guest and the "self-possessed" young girl are believable for rural England of the late nineteenth century. They would be unbelievable for twentieth century urban America.

2. Setting may influence character, as the effect of war on the young soldier in *The Red Badge of Courage.*

3. Setting may exemplify theme, as the isolated ship in *Moby Dick* suggests Captain Ahab's spiritual isolation.

4. Setting may evoke an emotional tone, an atmosphere, as the decadence and terror in "The Fall of the House of Usher" or the unbearable drabness of *1984.*

All of these functions and more may be served by the setting and they need to be considered in interpreting a story.

THE THEMATIC LEVEL

A story usually has something more to say than just the facts of the story. Most stories have a *theme.* The theme of a story is its controlling idea or central insight. It is the view of life or unifying generalization about life stated or implied by the story.

Not all stories have theme. Horror stories, adventure stories, murder stories may do no more than excite the reader or pose a problem. Humor stories may merely provide laughter, but serious stories do have theme. They bring alive or reveal some segment of human experience broader than the individual facts of the story. The theme may be a particular revelation of human character. It may say something about the nature of all people, the relationship of human beings to each other or to the universe.

The theme of "The Open Window" is not profound, but it is a theme or a central generalization. It can be stated something like this: a self-possessed young girl with imagination can frighten a nervous, insecure young man.

Three principles can help you in discovering the theme of a story.

1. What generalization about life will account for all the details and events of the story? Think of the characters and plot as representative—the same kind of thing happening to people in general. Make specific the general statement "That's the way life is" and you have stated the theme.

2. How has character changed, especially the central character? Classify this change and you have probably formulated theme.

3. What is the central conflict and its outcome? Classify or generalize these situations or events and you have probably formulated theme.

It is best not to state theme as a lesson, a moral, a proverb, or a platitude. Clichés like "Honesty is the best policy" or "Don't judge a book by its cover" are likely to be too narrow to fit the kind of insight provided by a high quality story. It is also best to state theme as a complete sentence. A brief topic like "the evils of greed" or a single word like "love" usually fail to give the essential meaning of a story. Instead, a theme statement might run "Greed produces evil" or "The emotions of a shy young woman may spring almost entirely from imagination rather than fact."

Consider theme carefully. The ability to state theme is a good test of your understanding of a story.

THE LITERARY LEVEL

This level is style. It is the author's method of selecting and arranging details to create meaning and effect. It is a way of controlling and influencing the reader's reaction. There are many devices an author can use to advance a story. We can suggest a few:

1. Patterns   There may be a significant *contrast,* such as a girl dying the day before her wedding, or a *similarity,* such as a sad-faced man with a St. Bernard dog. An author may use a *frame* for the story (a story within a story) to make special emphasis, or a *flashback* to achieve certain effects of time. A minor character may be used as the *foil,* a contrast, to sharpen the character or situation of another character. Many patterns are possible. Look for them and consider what they do for the story. How do they advance the plot, reveal character, or express theme? The plot of "The Open Window" is advanced because Nuttel and the girl are similar in being imaginative but they contrast in poise.

2. Tone   Tone is the particular effect brought about through careful choice of words, through associations, suggestions, and selective details. They may hardly be noticed, but look for them and note the effect.

Elizabeth Bowen's "The Cat Jumps" describes a group of people staying in a house in which a gruesome murder was once committed—a murder involving such items as fingers, flesh, and a woman dragging herself from room to room. Just before the group retire for the night, Bowen writes, "The house, fingered outwardly by the wind that dragged increasingly past the walls, was, within, a solid silence: silence heavy as flesh."

The words "fingered," "dragged," and "flesh" remind us of their former conflict: because of their *associations,* they create an impression of horror and because they are associated with a past murder, we wonder whether something similar is about to happen. Because of the pattern of association, the author makes us feel as she wishes us to feel.

3. Point of view   Point of view is the stance from which the author tells the story. It is whose shoulder we are looking over or whose mind we are looking into or out of. There are many ways to tell a story, and the point of view that the author adopts affects the story. To determine the point of view of a story, we aks, "Who tells the story" and "How much is the teller allowed to know?" To what extent does the author look into the characters and report their thoughts and feelings?

There are four basic points of view:

1. *Omniscient.* Like God, the author sees and knows all; peers inside throughts, hearts, feelings, of all characters; sees thoughts and feelings that even they do not know of. This point of view is the most flexible and allows the widest scope. The reader can be taken anywhere. But if used unskillfully, the omniscient view can make a story lose a sense of authenticity.

2. *Limited omniscient.* The story is told from the eyes, thoughts, or feelings of only one person. We are at that character's side and in that character's mind at all times, but inside no other character's mind. The character may be a major or minor character. The effect is one of authenticity, since this is the view that most approixmates real life. Each of us in real life sees others and the world from our own mind.

3. *First person.* The author tells the story acting as the "I" of the story. The first person may be a major or minor character, but all the reader sees and knows is what the character "I" sees and thinks. The point of view is limited, but it gives a strong sense of immediacy and reality.

4. *Objective or dramatic.* The author becomes a photographer. The camera can go anywhere, but it can record only what is seen and heard— nothing that is thought or felt. The plot and characters are placed on a stage and the reader hears and observes. There can be no interpretation by the author. The strength of this point of view is authenticity and speed of action.

The point of view in "The Open Window" is almost limited omniscient. We see mostly into the mind of Framton Nuttel ("privately he doubted," "wondered"). We see a little into the mind of the girl ("when she judged"). There is some author interpretation in calling the girl "self-possessed."

Considering the point of view of a story can give you a sense of its structure and an insight into some of the special effects of the story.

Elements of Drama

The elements of drama are much like those of fiction. We have plot, character, setting, theme, and stylistic devices, and the work is fictitious. But there are significant differences.

While stories are written to be read, drama are written to be seen and heard. The characters are seen and heard, and the place where the action occurs is visually represented. The author is therefore spared the necessity of most description and narration. What is written is mainly dialogue. This mode of writing has the advantages of vividness and immediacy. But it also has disadvantages. The author can describe settings and characters only in stage directions, which are brief. But the author can never talk about his characters except as they would be expected to talk about themselves to each other, and cannot tell us what they think or feel except as they imply it by their speech and actions on the stage.

So in reading a play, you must make special effort to visualize—to imagine the setting, the appearance of the characters, the tones of their voices, their gestures and movements about the stage. You must see the characters before you on the stage as you observe real people in your life.

As you write about dramas, you must derive implications of plot, character, setting, theme, and stylistic devices from all the nuances of the words of the play, those written for dialogue and for stage directions.

Elements of Poetry

We know immediately that the following description is a poem. It looks like a poem. If we read it aloud, it sounds like a poem. The words act together in a way we recognize as poetry. It has the four commonly recognized elements of poetry: *rhythm, images, metaphors,* and *special diction.*

> An everywhere of silver
> With ropes of sand
> To keep it from effacing
> The track called land.
> —Emily Dickinson

Rhythm is created by sound patterns. We hear or feel rhythm in the recurring beats in the lines. An unstressed syllable alternates with a stressed syllable. Lines 1 and 3 have three strong beats each. Lines 2 and 4 have two strong beats each. Other patterns of sound repetition are the rhymes of *sand* and *land* and the *s* sound in *silver, sand,* and *effacing.*

Images are what we can see, touch, taste, hear, and smell. The specific images here are *silver, ropes, sand, track,* and *land.* These specific images join to create a larger image of a *seashore.*

Metaphors state or imply a comparison between things. They compare an image with an image, an image with an abstraction, or an inanimate thing with a living thing. The word "silver" implies ocean, "ropes of sand" compare sand with ropes to describe the sand's appearance, and land is compared to a track. There is a general metaphor of life and intent, since some power apparently uses the ropes of sand to keep the ocean from effacing the land. "To keep" implies purpose, and therefore a living agent.

Because of the emotional nature of poetry and its compressed form, the individual words are given special attention, that is, *special diction* is employed. Poets will use words for their specific and packed meaning and for emotional effect. Each word carries a lot of weight and must be opened up for its full meaning and effect.

The word "silver," for instance, has very special meanings and effects. It carries the meaning of both the color and the metal to provide an image of beauty and strength. Also, the word "rope" conveys an idea of strength and containment that would not be conveyed by other synonyms, such as "string" or "cord." Again, the term "effacing" suggests an utter annihilation that "covering" or "removing" would not convey.

From the way these four common devices are joined, we may have certain emotional responses, perhaps of two kinds. First, we may enjoy the sounds, images, metaphors, and words themselves, as well as the striking way in which they suggest ideas. Second, as we explore the poem, we may feel a certain tension from the ironies set up. Track implies a way or path as opposed to the unlimited "everywhere" of ocean. The ropes have the purpose of keeping the ocean from effacing the track, but a rope of sand is too weak to protect much of anything. This thought may cause us to shiver a little as we measure the power of the everywhere against such frail protection. The poem gives us a sense of the frailty of humanity against the forces of inanimate nature.

Let us look at further rhythm, images, metaphors, and diction separately to see clearly how they work.

RHYTHM

A poem puts words in patterns of repetition, which produce rhythm. In the following poem we sense the rhythm in the insistent beat, in the rhymes, in the stanza, and in the refrain.

In the Great Metropolis
ARTHUR HUGH CLOUGH

Each for himself is still the rule;
We learn it when we go to school—
   The devil take the hindmost, O!

And when the schoolboys grow to men,
In life they learn it o'er again—
   The devil take the hindmost, O!

For in the church, and at the bar,
On 'Change, at court, where'er they are,
   The devil takes the hindmost, O!

Husband for husband, wife for wife,
Are careful that in married life
   The devil takes the hindmost, O!

From youth to age, whate'er the game,
The unvarying practice is the same—
    The devil takes the hindmost, O!

And after death, we do not know,
But scarce can doubt, where'er we go,
    The devil takes the hindmost, O!

Ti rol de rol, ti rol de ro,
The devil takes the hindmost, O!

The three-line stanza is repeated six times. The last stanza, which breaks the pattern, signals the end. The first two lines of each stanza rhyme, but the last line does not. Each stanza has its own rhyme, but is tied to the other stanzas by its third line, the refrain. Each line has the same number of syllables, except possibly for line 14. In each line a relatively unstressed syllable is followed by a relatively stressed syllable, again except for line 14.

The images are minor, mainly indicating the people in various activities: *school, schoolboys, men, church, husband, wife,* and so on. The main metaphor is the refrain. The other metaphors, such as *game,* are minor. The rhythm, however, is very important in creating the force of the poem.

IMAGES

Images excite our senses and our imagination. The controlling images in the following poem are mentioned in the title: snow and suburbs.

Snow in the Suburbs

THOMAS HARDY

Every branch big with it,
Bent every twig with it;
Every fork like a white web-foot;
Every street and pavement mute:
Some flakes have lost their way, and grope back upward, when
Meeting those meandering down they turn and descend again.
The palings are glued together like a wall,
And there is no waft of wind with the fleecy fall.

A sparrow enters the tree
Whereon immediately
A snow-lump thrice his own slight size
Descends on him and showers his head and eyes.
And overturns him,
And near inurns him,
And lights on a nether twig, when its brush
Starts off a volley of other lodging lumps with a rush.

The steps are a blanched slope,
Up which, with feeble hope,
A black cat comes, wide-eyed and thin;
And we take him in.

Snow is falling. That is the main image of the first stanza. Snow covers the trees, the streets, and the fences, which are the other images. In the second stanza, the poet directs our attention to a sparrow in "the tree." The snow almost overpowers the bird. The third stanza describes a stray cat being admitted to a house, which is covered by the snow like everything else. For the first time, human presences enter the poem in the last line.

The stanzas show a progression from the inanimate to the animate. The images move from the covering snow, to sparrow, to cat, to human presence. Stanza 1 simply describes snow covering various things. Stanza 2 introduces the bird, which is living. We are invited to have a certain sympathy for it through the use of personal pronouns. The bird is referred to in the masculine gender, not the neuter. It is a "he," not an "it." Whoever is looking at him appears to see him as something of a victim, with his "slight size" and the overwhelming snow. Stanza 3 introduces the human action, pity. Admitting the cat brings our attention from the indifferent snow outside to the welcome inside. Thus a series of images leads us from the indifferent but dangerous snow outside to the warm human presence inside.

METAPHORS

A poem uses metaphors to join ideas and images. Such combinations may delight us by their novelty, may clarify an idea, or may startle by an unexpected comparison. In this poem, the metaphors of procreation and knives are the main ones:

Science

ROBINSON JEFFERS

Man, introverted man, having crossed
In passage and but a little with the nature of things this latter century
He begot giants; but being taken up
Like a maniac with self-love and inward conflicts cannot manage his hybrids.
Being used to deal with edgeless dreams,
Now he's bred knives on nature turns them also inward: they have thirsty points
    though.
His mind forebodes his own destruction;
Actaeon who saw the goddess naked among leaves and his hounds tore him.
A little knowledge, a pebble from the shingle,
A drop from the oceans: who would have dreamed this infinitely little too much?

Through the controlling metaphors, the poem describes how man has made nature destructive. The connection called Science is a deadly one. Man creates or procreates on the body of nature ("crossed with," "begot"); yet man does not really understand his mate ("In passage and but a little"). Because he is confused and self-centered, man cannot control his creations, "his hybrids." He has created things with only a limited part of himself, that is, "his mind," not with his whole being.

Knives is the metaphor for man's creations or offspring. Knives, being the creatures of man, have man's own destructive thirst. The children are like the parents. The knives (that is, the metaphor for man's control over nature), being the offspring of introverted man, turn inward, and so destroy the creator. Man is like Actaeon of the Greek myth, who was killed by his own hounds because he was not worthy to look upon or to know the naked goddess Diana (nature) in her reality. The metaphors of procreation and knives join the idea of introversion in the first part of the poem with the idea of destruction in the latter part of the poem.

SPECIAL DICTION

The first step in understanding a word is to be sure of its denotation, often called its dictionary definition. This may be just a matter of clearing up your understanding of an unfamiliar word by checking the dictionary. But since most words can have several definitions, you may have to check the context carefully to see which meaning or meanings are intended. For example, in the phrase, "The guard finally got the old bird locked up," we don't know what kind of animal "the old bird" is. It could be an aged human being or a winged creature with feathers. Only further context can tell us, such as "The guard finally got the old bird locked up and clipped his wing feathers so that he couldn't fly away again."

Words are also used for their connotations or emotional meanings beyond the usual dictionary definition. One denotation of *mother* is a woman who has borne a child. The word has connotations of security, warmth, love, selflessness. The term "female parent" has the same denotation as "mother" but the connotation is quite different. Female Parent Day is not likely to become an important event in our culture. Notice that both denotation and connotation are important in this brief poem:

In a Station of the Metro
EZRA POUND

The apparition of these faces in the crowd;
Petals on a wet, black bough.

We must understand the denotation of "Metro" and "apparition" before we can see the image the poem is developing. "Metro" is the underground railway or subway in Paris. An "apparition" is anything which appears, especially suddenly. These words identify the situation and the station, or, perhaps, the platform. These faces remind Pound of "Petals on a wet, black bough." They are related to the dark mass; yet they seem somehow detached.

Multiple meanings as well as single denotations are important in the poem. Checking the dictionary meanings against the context, we find that "apparition" is used here in both of its common definitions: "anything that appears, especially suddenly" and "ghost or phantom." These connotations add an unworldly tone that the word "appearance" would not give us. Likewise, "petal" gives us a denotation and a connotation that "flower" or "blossom" would not give. A blossom on a black bough is whole and growing, promising life to come. A petal on a black bough is severed, already dead or dying.

With such careful study of denotations and connotations of words in their context, the image acquires meaning and emotion.

Sample Student Compositions on Literature

ANALYSIS OF CHARACTER IN A SHORT STORY

The story: "The Man of the House," by Frank Sullivan
The assignment: Analyze the change in the central character in "The Man of the House."

The student writer follows the assignment; sticks to the subject, developing the basic ideas of character and change; and draws on the text for evidence and illustrative details. The paper itself is well-organized. The opening paragraph states the assignment, pointing out the kind of change in character. Paragraph 2 traces the change through the story, citing particulars. The final paragraph brings the analysis back to the thesis of the opening paragraph.

SULLIVAN'S CHARACTER IN "THE MAN OF THE HOUSE"

When his mother became ill in "The Man of the House," Sullivan suddenly found himself in a position of great responsibility. This responsibility was obviously too much, as his new maturity of character was not consistent throughout the story and he reverted to childlike actions several times while he was supposedly the man of the house.

At the beginning of the story, Sullivan and his mother actually switched roles—he became responsible for her. He stayed home from school to take care of her, and he called for help. Although his actions showed maturity, his fears did not: he had a childish fear of his mother's illness ending in death instead of realizing that she was not seriously ill. As the story progressed, he became more and more dependent on others, though still not irresponsible. To get medicine for his mother, Sullivan volunteered to walk a considerable distance. His character was still that of an adult at this point, but after he got the medicine, he allowed himself to be swindled by a young girl who wanted to "share" his medicine with him as if it were a confection. This was the beginning of his main reversion to a small boy.

After he arrived home, he got sick and allowed himself to be taken care of by his mother, who was not yet completely well. Here the characters were once more reversed and he was once again a young boy.

The following composition on the same assignment is not effective. The analysis develops fairly well up to a point, with a clear thesis statement and use of details from the text to indicate the change in character. Trouble begins at sentence 8. The student gets off the subject and discusses the different kinds of conflict in the story. Conflict is pertinent to the story, but not to the specific assignment on character change. The writer could have made the discussion of conflict pertinent, for example by showing how the boy's maturity or immaturity was revealed by the way he dealt with conflicts. Probably, the writer dragged in extra material from the course in order to pad a short paper.

"THE MAN OF THE HOUSE"

"The Man of the House" is a good example of a character story. The character of the little boy made the whole story. He was trying to show everyone he was a man but he still had the faults of a little boy. When he put his mother in the bed and did all the housework and fixed her breakfast he began to show that he could handle responsibility like a man. Another example of this was his courage to go to the dispensary. The faults of his boyhood began to show up when he let the little girl talk him out of the cough medicine and spend his penny on candy. He showed his manliness once again when he admitted that he drank the medicine. This story shows the different types of conflict which make a good short story. The boy and girl arguing about the cough medicine shows a man against man conflict. When the boy is sitting on top of the hill looking at the school and thinking is a good example of man against himself. An example of man against nature is the boy facing the challenge of walking to the dispensary.

DISCUSSION OF PLOT AND THEME IN A PIECE OF FICTION

The story: *A Clockwork Orange,* by Anthony Burgess
The assignment: Discuss the ending or resolution of *A Clockwork Orange* in terms of the theme of the novel.

The following paper sticks to the subject of resolution and theme. Paragraph 1 clarifies the theme of the novel and paragraph 2 shows how the resolution expresses the theme. The last two lines echo the opening idea of the composition.

THE TWO CLOCKWORK ORANGES

In *A Clockwork Orange,* Burgess is striking not only at violence but at the society which breeds the conditions of violence. There are really two clockwork oranges. One is the original which society bred (that is, Alex and his hoodlum gang). The second is the one which society tried to correct, but by artificial means of no real value—by taking away the self, individualism. That is Alex after he was brainwashed and made sick by any thought of violence. There is really more danger in the second figure. He is utterly without protection, without defenses by which to protect himself, such as when the old men in the library beat him up.

At the resolution of the story, the readers are left at the same place at which they began—with a society breeding violence. Alex has been restored to his original self and can again enjoy Ludwig Van's 9th, but he was restored by artificial means as a pawn of the corrupt minister, who is willing for Alex to continue his brutality. We are torn, and the point is made. A society in which the self is not allowed has more possibilities of horror than a society of violence. Burgess is emphasizing that a solution must be found, but it cannot be one that denies self.

The following student paper on the same assignment illustrates the dangers of personal tastes and emotional evaluations taking over in a paper that should have an objective point of view. The subject matter and idea content of the paper are fairly valid, much like the material of the preceding composition. But the student's emotional evaluations take over.

ALEX AND THE VILLAIN

In this marvelous book (which is not the popular view in this class), we find the author attacking the sick society in which poor Alex is adrift. One solution in the book was to modify the behavior of all the "sickies" in the society. This solution stinks of governmental omnipotence in denying the individual the right of free choice. The ending satisfied me because again Alex has free rein over his choosing of right or wrong even though he may again go out and "tolchock" some poor soul.

ANALYSIS OF IMAGE PATTERN OF A POEM

The poem: "The Wind Has Such a Rainy Sound," by Christina Rossetti
The assignment: Tell how the images of the poem help produce the poem's effect.

Notice that the student writer follows directions, dealing with images and effect and organizing the paper carefully. The opening sentence, or thesis statement, repeats the two terms of the assignment: the large image (storm) and the effect (impending danger). The rest of the paragraph outlines the images, their kinds and relationships to a large image pattern and the effect created.

Paragraph 2 moves piece by piece through the poem, pointing out images and connecting them to the large image and the effect. Specific words and details from the poem are used for evidence and illustration.

The last paragraph is a recap, taking the reader back to the opening thesis.

The Wind Has Such a Rainy Sound

CHRISTINA ROSSETTI

The wind has such a rainy sound
    Moaning through the town,
The sea has such a windy sound—
    Will the ships go down?

The apples in the orchard
    Tumble from their tree.
Oh, will the ships go down, go down,
    In the windy sea?

IMAGES IN "THE WIND HAS SUCH A RAINY SOUND"

In "The Wind Has Such a Rainy Sound," a sense of impending danger is suggested by the image pattern of a violent storm. The main images are wind, sea, ships, and apples; from these Christina Rossetti creates a pattern of storm. A sinister and forlorn tone is suggested by the images of sound (rainy, moaning, windy), and violence is suggested by the images of action (ships going down and apples tumbling from the tree).

Danger is predominant throughout. Rossetti first starts out by describing the wind as it sounds in the town, and builds up this sense of danger as the poem ends. First, the wind has a "rainy" sound, implying a storm. It doesn't sing, but it moans through the town. Second, the sea has a windy sound, still suggesting a storm. Will the ships go down? The question suggests an eerie sense of danger. The image of the apples tumbling from the trees suggests a violent wind, strong enough to knock the fruit off their branches.

Again, she writes "Oh, will the ships go down. . . ." Because the writer states this line twice, it has a stronger meaning. The second time   ·
she continues, as if in a drowning tone "go down, go down. . . ."

Since violence, danger, and fear are all closely related, the poet gets her idea across effectively, by using images of violence (windy, tumble, rainy, moaning) to suggest danger.

Another student paragraph on the same assignment gives a very poor analysis. This student goes around and around, barely saying anything. The writer mentions images of wind and sea, but does not tell how they and other images work to produce an effect. "How each sounds" is not an effect of the poem. Sentences 2 and 3 repeat sentence 1 and move nowhere. The final comparison is little to the point. Basically, the student does not do what the assignment asks for.

ROSSETTI'S IMAGES

Describing the wind and the sea in this manner lets you visualize as well as hear how each sounds. It seems to help you to better visualize things if you can also hear them. It enables you to seem as though you were actually there. One image produces the other to give it a meaningful effect of the two combined at the end—the windy sea. Ships are compared with the falling of apples from a tree as a ship may sink from the windy sea.

STRUCTURE AND THEME IN A POEM

The poem: "The Brain is Wider than the Sky," by Emily Dickinson
The assignment: Show how the pattern of comparisons in the poem helps express the theme.

The student follows the assignment, analyzing carefully from the structure of comparisons. The first sentence states the assignment and forms a thesis statement for the composition. The student moves step by step through the poem, pointing out each comparison in turn and building up to the last comparison, which climaxes the theme of the poem. The citing of details from the poem shows a careful reading of the text, a sticking to the assigned topic, and an adequate support for the analysis of the structure of comparison. The final sentence echoes the opening thesis statement.

The Brain Is Wider Than the Sky

EMILY DICKINSON

The brain is wider than the sky,
  For, put them side by side,
The one the other will include
  With ease, and you beside.

The brain is deeper than the sea,
  For, hold them, blue to blue,
The one the other will absorb,
  As sponges, buckets do.

The brain is just the weight of God,
  For, lift them, pound for pound,
And they will differ, if they do,
  As syllable from sound.

BRAIN, SKY, SEA, GOD

Emily Dickinson's poem "The Brain Is Wider Than the Sky" is structured on a pattern of comparisons to give a feeling of the power and scope of the brain.

Stanzas 1 and 2 compare the brain to the sky and the sea to suggest that man dominates his environment. The phrasing implies man's ability to easily grasp sky and sea within his comprehension.

The brain is greater than the sky because not only can the brain include the sky with ease, it can include "you beside," meaning that there is room for much more than the sky.

In comparing the brain to the sea, the brain appears again to be the greater of the two, as it can absorb many things, as sponges do. In the last stanza, however, the brain is compared with God, and Dickinson indicates that there is not much if any difference in the two. The brain is "just the weight of God," meaning that these two are equal. Both of them are very light and small, but both have great capabilities. Also, the fact that they are compared as "syllable to a sound" shows that, while they are two distinctly different things, they are very much alike. Through the comparisons we get a sense of the greatness of man's brain. The power of comprehension is a divine power.

In the following paper on the same writing assignment, the student violates two of the basic principle of literary analysis. See if you can spot them.

THE BRAIN AND GOD

The first comparison is between the brain and the sky. The brain is wider than the sky, for the brain will include the sky within its thought and knowledge.

The second comparison is between the brain and the sea. The brain is deeper than the sea, for the brain can absorb all of the sea. All the wonders of the sea can be examined by the brain. Eventually the sea has a bottom, but there is no limit to the bottom of the brain.

The third comparison is between the brain and God. God is much greater than the brain, for if it were not for God, we would not have a brain, just as if it were not for syllable, we would not have sound.

Although our brain is wider than the sky and deeper than the sea, nothing is more superior than God. It was God that made all things able to be included or absorbed and to be important, but without him, there would be nothing.

The paper is fairly good through the first two paragraphs, analyzing the first two comparisons. The writer points out the terms of the comparison and evaluates validity. The student goes awry at the third comparison—violating at least two rules of interpretation. (1) The student has not carefully stuck to the facts of the poem, has not actually read and accepted the simple word "just," which would have made clear that the poet is saying that God and the brain are equal, not that God is superior. (2) The student is diverted from accurate interpretation, probably by prejudice or other personal training about what we are allowed to believe about God. Whether God *is* superior to the human brain is beside the point. The poem *says* they are equal. In interpreting a poem, you must not violate the facts of the material.

9

The Scientific and Technical Report

Writing a scientific or technical report requires all the general skills and methods used in writing any other composition. You need a limited subject, a clearly defined thesis statement, adequate development of the separate ideas in the paragraphs, and connective devices for smooth flow of thought. The purposes are usually to clarify or confirm—to report and describe a body of information or to give evidence and reasoning to validate a hypothesis or a conclusion.

Methods of adequate development are the same as for other compositions; examples, definitions, classification of kinds, descriptive detail, comparison and contrast, tracing causes and effects, statistics, reasoning, and so on. The general principles for writing scientific reports follow the principles of all good composition. However, two features of scientific reports are distinctive: (1) *The scientific attitude* and (2) *specialized reports.*

The Scientific Attitude

The scientific attitude is not ruled out of other kinds of writing, but the scientific writer must place special premium upon it. It is the dominant approach and it is a constant. The following features make up the scientific attitude.

1. **Impersonal or objective viewpoint** The pronoun "I" is seldom used. The third person objective is standard, or the "we" as in "from these facts we can see that. . . ." The writer's taste, preference, personal likes and dislikes have no place in the scientific report.

2. Factual accuracy   To deliberately report inaccuracies is, of course, unscientific. Beyond that, one must make all efforts to check, double check, and report facts accurately. There might be a place for inaccuracies in advertisements, political speeches, and love letters, but not in scientific reports.

3. Valid sources of information   The chief sources of information for scientific reports are observation and experiment. The information must be verifiable.

4. Carefully drawn conclusions   Any interpretation of facts or conclusion drawn from them must indeed be drawn from the facts.

5. Opinions and hypothesis used sparingly   Generalizations and hypotheses are to be made, for they form the basis for science—the laws and the theories. Generalizations reduce the chaos and uncertainty of the universe to order; hypotheses lead to the future of science through exploration. But generalizations and hypotheses must be based on evidence and go only as far as the evidence allows.

6. Distinctions made between kinds of materials used   Facts, opinions, theories, and hypotheses must be clearly distinguished for the reader. The two excerpts that follow demonstrate the features of the scientific attitude.

> A root system is a really incredible thing. Many studies have been made of its extent. In one study, a plant of winter rye grass was grown for four months in a box with less than two cubic feet of earth. In that time the plant grew twenty inches high, with about 51 square feet of surface above the ground. But underground the root system had developed 378 miles of roots and an additional 6,000 miles of root hairs! This meant an average growth of three miles of roots and 50 miles of root hairs for each day of the fourth-month growing season. The growth rate varies with different plants, of course, but this gives us some idea of the activity that goes on under the surface of a quiet-looking meadow, while the grass prepares food that will later become milk and meat and butter for us.
>
> —John H. Storer, *The Web of Life*, Devin-Adair, 1953.

The paragraph starts out with an apparently unscientific, emotional term in "really incredible," but after we read through such facts as "6,000 miles of root hairs," we are ready to accept "incredible" as "seeming too unusual or improbable to be possible."

Four main features of the scientific attitude can be seen:

1. *Impersonal.* The viewpoint is third-person objective.
2. *Valid sources of information.* Experiment ("one study") and careful observation ("the careful calculations") form the basis for the report.
3. *Opinions, conclusions, and hypotheses.* There is no opinion at all except "incredible" and the safe interpretation of averages in sentence 4.
4. *Factual accuracy.* The measurements suggest accuracy and are certainly verifiable.

> Slowly as the sun rotates, it still does so in a remarkable manner: it spins faster at the equator than at the poles, so that its surface must be in a state of

shear—that is, some parts of the surface must continually be slipping past others. Possibly the differential rotation plays some part in producing sunspot vortexes. And if even the slowly turning sun spins faster at the equator than at the poles, what of the stars that turn on themselves in a few hours, and are highly distorted? What, too, of the internal rotation of the sun? We can see the surface only; and a different internal rate of rotation is not only possible but likely. A star that turns very slowly will probably not churn up its interior and mix its constituents; but one that is spinning fast may be much better mixed. The degree of mixing of the materials within a star may well be a crucial factor in its history.

—Cecilia Payne-Gaposchkin, "The Sun," *Stars in the Making,* Harvard University Press, 1952.

The paragraph begins with an apparently unscientific term in "remarkable" (as the previous excerpt used "incredible"); the facts and reasoning of the paragraph easily support the term and show several main features of the scientific attitude.

1. *Impersonal.* The term "we" is used; otherwise the stance is fully third-person objective.

2. *Carefully drawn conclusions, opinions, and hypotheses.* Certain terms indicate that the writer is not interpreting beyond the evidence: "must be," "probably," "possibly," "may," "play some part" (not all), "a factor" (not the full explanation). The use of questions further shows that the author is inquiring about possibility within the evidence, not asserting an actuality beyond the evidence.

3. *Distinctions made between kinds of material.* Facts are distinguished ("spins faster at the equator than at the poles," "can see the surface only") from hypotheses and opinions ("must be in a state of shear," "different internal rate of rotation . . . likely").

With such use of the scientific attitude, the author persuades us of the validity of her theories.

Specialized Reports

The scientific writer is called upon to write some very specialized reports because of the required scientific attitude and because of the nature of the subject matter itself. Studying eight of the common structure patterns and thought patterns of typical scientific reports will help you arrive at a framework and develop your own scientific subject.

STAGES IN A DEVELOPMENT

Tracing the changes in something from one stage to another is one of the main studies of science. This form of analysis is sometimes called *functional analysis.* With anything where there is life or movement or change, functional analysis can be used. It picks the subject up at one significant point and describes it through various discrete stages to another significant point. For instance, in biology one may use this thought pattern to trace from egg to caterpillar to pupa to butterfly.

According to our point of interest, we shift points of significance. Instead of tracing the stages from egg to butterfly, we might wish to trace the stages in the butterfly's emerging from the cocoon. Or we might trace just the larva preparing the cocoon.

We observe and describe how something changes, grows, moves, noting the various stages of the development.

The following report, "Ecological Succession," traces the stages a natural community goes through to become a climax community. The composition follows a definite structure. First is the definition of the key term. Then the paragraph traces an ecological succession through four stages from black bass and sunfish to no fish—in this case, a climax community. Paragraph 2 describes the observation of a similar succession in a controlled laboratory experiment with bacteria in an aquarium, tracing a succession from bacteria through Protozoa to a balanced aquarium—a climax community.

The article ends where it began—climax community—having traced two sequences of changes from one significant point to another. Transitional words are used to help keep the stages distinct: "for example," "later," "still later," "finally," and so on.

Ecological Succession

ROBERT W. HEGNER AND KARL A. STILES

When a community has reached comparative stability it is called a **climax community**. But every climax community has had a history of changes; such changes constitute ecological succession. A new habitat, as for example, a pond resulting from the overflow of a river, may contain certain types of fish, including black bass and sunfish. Later the sides of the pond become overgrown with vegetation and the clean bottom becomes covered with deposits; the black bass and sunfish disappear because such an environment is not suited to them, but bullheads may persist. Still later, just before the pond becomes a swamp, the mud minnow and the mud pickerel make their appearance. Finally, conditions become such that no fish are able to live in the habitat. Here are several successions, each differing in the type of fishes present. Each succession differs also in other animal types. The final stage in the series of succession is a climax community. Ponds at the same stage in their development tend to contain the same kinds of animals; lakes of the same size and depth have similar faunas; and so on for each type of community.

Ecological succession can also be observed in the laboratory. For example, if a few pieces of hay are placed in a beaker of water, countless bacteria will appear in the water in a day or two. Soon minute flagellated Protozoa make their appearance, feeding on the bacteria and on the products of bacterial decomposition. Next, ciliated Protozoa (often *Colpidium* and *Colpoda*) become numerous; these eat bacteria but are themselves eaten by larger ciliates which soon become dominant. After all the smaller organisms are eaten, the large ciliates die unless green plants are added to the community. If this is done the plants and animals become adjusted to one another and a comparatively stable condition is established which we call a balanced acquarium, which is essentially a climax community.

SUGGESTIONS FOR WRITING

Trace the stages in the development of some process or function from one significant point to another. Define necessary terms and keep the stages distinct and clear. Do not leave out an important stage in the sequence. You may do as the authors of "Ecological Succession" have done and describe parallel sequences—natural and in the laboratory—or you may use either one.

SUGGESTED TOPICS

Making a field fertile	Eruption of a volcano
Erosion	Birth of a planet / an island / a coral
From seed to fruit	reef
A storm	Tooth decay
A rock breaks down into soil	

DEFINITION OF A PRINCIPLE

Science works hard at establishing and clarifying principles, or natural laws, and then uses these laws as bases for making sense out of new data that comes along. For these principles to be applied, they must be defined clearly.

The following report, "The Doppler Effect," makes clear a common scientific principle. The report has a three-part structure: the definition, examples for clarification, and application to indicate the significance of the principle. Note that the examples are taken from common experience to really clarify.

The Doppler Effect

CARL CAMPBELL

When a vibrating source of waves is approaching an observer, the frequency observed is higher than the frequency emitted by the source. When the source is receding, the frequency observed is lower than that emitted. This is known as the Doppler effect, or Doppler's principle, and is named after an Austrian physicist who lived in the first half of the 19th century. When a whistling locomotive, for instance, approaches a stationary observer, more density concentrations reach his ear than when both the sound source and the observer are stationary. Since the pitch depends on the frequency (number of vibrations per second), the sound from the approaching locomotive's whistle has a higher pitch than the sound coming from the same whistle when the locomotive is stationary is relation to the observer. Similarly, when the locomotive is receding, its whistle sounds with a lower pitch. At the instant when the locomotive passes the observer, the whistle is heard to change to a lower pitch. The same effect is observed when we are passed by a fast-moving hooting car in the street, or when the observer is moving fast in relation to a stationary sound source, for example, a motorcyclist approaching a siren.

The Doppler effect is widely used in astronomy for measuring the velocity at which distant stars or nebulae are approaching or receding. These motions produce a shift in the position of lines in their spectra. A particular spectrum line corresponds to a certain definite light wavelength. If the star emitting the light is moving away from us, its light rays have a longer wavelength (lower frequency) by virtue of the Doppler principle, and this effect is manifested in a general shift of the spectrum lines towards the red end of the spectrum. This is known as the "red shift." Similarly, in the spectrum of a star moving towards us, the characteristic lines would show a "blue shift," that is, they would be displaced towards the blue end of the spectrum, corresponding to shorter wavelengths and higher frequencies. A remarkable thing about the spectra of the spiral nebulae (the galaxies of stars far out in space beyond our own Milky Way system) is that they all display the red shift and must therefore—on the basis of Doppler's principle—all be moving away from us. The theory of the "expanding universe" is based on this phenomenon.

SUGGESTIONS FOR WRITING

Define a scientific law or principle. Your purpose is to make clear, so use examples, illustrations, comparisons, explanations, or whatever material will help your reader to understand the principle.

SUGGESTED TOPICS

Brownian movement	Osmosis
Buoyancy	Einstein's theory of relativity
Fission	Inertia
Fusion	Gravity

METHOD ANALYSIS: HOW TO DO OR MAKE

In explaining how something is made or done, the writer describes methods or steps toward a product or predetermined end. Some question is usually understood. "How do you do it?" "How is it made?" A report of this kind presents an orderly, step-by-step, chronologically arranged description of how a process of some kind takes place. It tells how to dissect a frog, how to cure tobacco, how to build a Foucault pendulum, how to make a bomb.

At its simplest, method analysis is giving directions, such as how to adjust a microscope. A more complex form may tell how to perform an appendectomy.

The essential structure in any case is the same. We move from a beginning point through a sequence of steps *in a necessary order* to the end product.

In the following report, the author tells how to make a simple solar cell. In paragraph 1, he defines the basic principle of the light energy of the solar cell. Then, in paragraph 2, he traces the steps in making a solar cell to apply the principle explained in paragraph 1. The process moves through three steps: doping the crystal of silicon with arsenic, cutting it into wafers, heating the wafers and doping them with boron. Final product: a thin wafer with its own electrical field.

The Solar Cell
SHERMAN LINDLEY

A solar cell operates on the principle that photons of light energy striking atoms of certain materials will dislodge electrons from the atoms. If these electrons are segregated before they can return to their former locations, they can be drawn off as electric current. The vacancies or "holes" left by the electrons when they are dislodged constitute positive charges and will also conduct a current.

For many years, the problem with solar cells was how to build an electric field inside the individual cell. After much experimenting, researchers hit upon the way to build an electric field right into the crystals. They made single crystals of silicon which were rich in positive charges on one side and rich in negative charges on the other. They did this by "doping" the crystals with arsenic—one part arsenic to a million parts of silicon. This created what is called an n-type silicon crystal, one having an excess of negative charges.

This n-type crystal was cut into thin wafers with a diamond-cutting wheel. Finally, these wafers were placed in an electric furnace and heated to more than 1,000C. While being subjected to this heat, one side of each wafer was "doped" with boron. Boron, when it penetrates a silicon crystal, creates a p-type substance having an excess of positive charges. The final product of this complex process was a thin wafer of silicon that had two layers with different electrical characteristics. This wafer produced its own electrical field, which kept negative charges on the "n" side and positive charges on the "p" side.

SUGGESTIONS FOR WRITING

Write a composition in which you describe the steps in doing or making something.

SUGGESTED TOPICS

Preparing a microscopic slide	Setting a broken bone
How to finish a gemstone	How to adjust a microscope
Building an aquarium / terrarium	How to cure tobacco

A NATURAL PROCESS: HOW SOMETHING FUNCTIONS

A common type of analysis is to tell how something in nature carries on a characteristic function. The writer moves through a series of stages in the movement or process of something until the total function is described. A function analysis is similar to a method analysis in that both describe a sequence of events that must follow one another in a necessary chronological order. But, while method analysis arrives at a predetermined product or end, function analysis is concerned just with the system or function itself and how the parts work together to perform the whole.

The circulation of the blood is a good example. We could begin logically with the heart and its function, then trace the blood as it moves from the right ventricle through the pulmonary artery to the lungs, from the lungs through the pulmonary vein to the left atrium, and so on, describing what happens to the blood at each stage along the whole system until it is back again at our starting point.

In writing effectively about a function, keep these principles in mind:

1. No significant stage must be omitted.
2. The function or relationship of each stage to the whole must be explained.
3. Any significant principle must be defined or made clear to the reader.

In the following account, "The Voyage of an Air Mass," the writer traces a whole cycle of nature. He starts with a mass of cold, dry air and describes it through many stages or changes until it is back to cold, dry air.

The Voyage of an Air Mass

DAVID C. HOLMES

A specific illustration is perhaps the best way of explaining the weather changes resulting from the voyage of an air mass. Continental polar air will often surge through the United States from its Canadian breeding ground. At the beginning of its journey, temperatures range downward to −40°, and the citizens of Minnesota huddle against their stoves. As the air travels southeast, it absorbs heat from the land. By the time it reaches the southern states, temperatures are rarely below freezing. At this point it is shunted seaward over the warm Gulf Stream by the tropical maritime masses swirling north from the equator. Once over the Gulf Stream, our wandering air mass picks up both heat and moisture. In the normal course of events, driven by the westerlies, it will reach the European continent. As it encounters that cool surface, it will lose heat. Since cold air cannot hold as much moisture as hot, clouds will form and the water vapor will condense into rain. Finally, our air mass will return to what it started out to be: cold, dry air.

—from *The Story of Weather*, Pyramid Publications, 1963.

SUGGESTIONS FOR WRITING

Describe the stages in a natural function or process.

SUGGESTED TOPICS

How plants manufacture chlorophyll
How plants manufacture oxygen
How we see/hear/maintain balance
What makes a rainbow
Radioactivity

A cycle of water
The tides
Sunspots
The respiratory system

CAUSAL ANALYSIS

The laws of cause and effect are at the base of scientific study. We ask "Why?" "How did this come about?" "What will happen if I do this?" "What causes the tides?" "What makes the sky blue?" "How did this pond become polluted?" "What will happen if we continue our heavy use of insecticides?" "What makes the earth revolve around the sun?" With such basic questions as "why?" and "what will be the result?" scientists are trying to make sense of their world.

In analyzing causes and effects for scientific reports, you should follow the same principles used for tracing causes and effects in any other area. These principles are defined in Part I of this book, "The Whole Composition" (pp. 1–41). Review especially pages 27–29, noting the four guides to thinking clearly about causes and effects:

1. Distinguish immediate cause from remote cause.
2. Look for several causes.
3. Don't leave out any links in a sequence.
4. Don't confuse causal relationship with time relationship.

In the following report, "Radioactivity and the Future," the writer analyzes a cause and consequence pattern. Beginning with radioactive substances, he first moves back to two causes of them: atomic bomb explosions and atomic energy waste. He then moves the other way to trace probable consequences of radioactive substances on the human being. Since germ cells are influenced by radioactivity and the effects of radioactivity are cumulative, it is likely that human mutations will occur.

The report offers a possible structure to follow in your own writing. From a given condition or event, trace backward to causes (to give your selected event significance) and then move the other direction to consequences.

Radioactivity and the Future

KARL von FRISCH

Whenever an atom bomb is exploded, the atmosphere is likely to be polluted with a great quantity of radioactive substances, which remain active for long periods of time and reach plants and ultimately animals through fallout and in rain and snow. The exploitation of atomic energy for peaceful purposes also results in radioactive waste, the removal and safe storage of which are still great problems, quite apart from the possibility of their liberation by accident. It has been established that all over the earth Man is exposed to a considerably higher degree of radiation than was the case before the time of atomic explosions, and it is obvious that this will get worse and worse if human reason does not prevail. It is known that germ cells can be influenced by the smallest doses, in proportion to the applied radiation, and that the effects of exposure are cumulative. This means that the germ cells, which cannot "forgive and forget," hand on the sum of our sins against them from one generation to the next. They live on, while the individual dies. As time goes on a great increase in mutations may take place, and we know that most of them will be unfavorable. This ever-present danger now threatens the life of future generations, although years or even several decades may pass between the first exposure to radiation and the appearance of the final dire consequences in the human race.

—from *Man and the Living World*, Harcourt, Brace and World, 1962.

SUGGESTIONS FOR WRITING

Write a composition in which you make a causal analysis. There are several thought patterns to select from, depending on your subject:
1. cause to effect (or multiple),
2. effect to cause (or multiple),
3. a causal chain (A is the cause of B, which is the cause of C, and so on).

SUGGESTED TOPICS

Why the sky is blue	Hiccoughing
What made coal / oil / petrified wood	The appearance of the stars at night
The seasons	A kind of cloud formation
Hay fever	A specific disease or illness

HYPOTHESIS AND EXPERIMENT

The process of forming a hypothesis and conducting an experiment to test it is a standard tool of science. It is one of the necessary ways of establishing meaning from the observations of science. Is this substance acid or base? Will this substance dissolve in water? Will the addition of nitrogen to the soil increase the growth rate of the plant? Does smoking cause cancer? Will changing the shape of the wings improve the efficiency of the airplane?

In writing on a project involving hypothesis and experiment, you follow fairly closely the standard steps in the scientific method.

1.   *Observe.* Usually what is observed is the result of a deliberately contrived experiment or a controlled search.

2.   *Form a hypothesis.* A hypothesis is a suggestion explanation of some sort to account for the facts that have been observed.

3.   *Experiment.* The scientist conducts an appropriate experiment to test the hypothesis. If the result of the experiment is different from what was expected, the hypothesis is at once rejected as wrong. If the experiment agrees, the hypothesis is accepted tentatively. Further experiments are done. The hypothesis is continually put to the test of experiment, perhaps by other scientists, and if it survives a large number of experiments and can explain all of them, it comes to be called a theory. A theory is simply a well-tested hypothesis.

The following article, "Habit as a Block to Reasoning," follows the two-point structure of hypothesis and experiment. The first three paragraphs define the hypothesis that "habit limits our ways of thinking about a problem." The next three paragraphs describe the controlled experiment set up to test the hypothesis and state the results. As a tie, the next to last sentence restates the hypothesis: habit blocks thought.

Habit as a Block to Reason

FRANK A. BEACH

Many times we encounter a new problem that bears a superficial resemblance to some we have solved before. Then we are likely to persist in attacking the novel difficulty with unsuitable methods just because they have been successful on other occasions. More than once an amateur has solved some problem that had been puzzling experts for years. Sometimes the amateur is smarter than the experts, but more often his only advantage is a fresh point of view. His approach to the solution is not cluttered up with habitual modes of thought about the problem.

From early childhood we build up habits that guide our day-to-day lives. It is fortunate that we can do so. Imagine how troublesome life would be if we had to solve every problem anew each time it arose. In 99 out of every 100 of the little problems confronting us each day, habit provides a ready-made answer, and original thinking is unnecessary. It is only when old habits will not serve that reasoning makes its appearance.

Habit limits our ways of thinking about a problem, and this is a very real block to successful reasoning. The trouble may originate at a very simple level. The way in which we "see" a problematical situation has a powerful control over our ability to solve it.

In one experiment young men and women were led into a bare room and given three candles, three thumbtacks, and three small boxes. They were instructed to fasten the candles to the door of the room in any way they could devise. There was only one solution, but it was simple. The boxes were fastened to the door with thumbtacks, and one candle was placed upright in each box. Every individual discovered this method in short order.

Then the experiment was repeated, using a new group of "subjects" and introducing one minor change in the setup. This time the little boxes contained matches. The rest of the equipment was the same, and so were the experimenter's instructions. Less than half of the men and women solved the problem.

What was the difference? In the second version of the experiment, most of the people "saw" the boxes as containers for matches, and this blocked the possibility of "seeing" them as potential candleholders. Furthermore, the presence of matches was distracting, for they suggested (due to habit) lighting the candles. A burning candle suggested (due to habit) the use of hot wax as an adhesive. The problem had been designed so that no such solution would work. Nevertheless, the force of habit was so strong that many individuals stubbornly persisted in trying minor variations on the same futile theme. The little boxes continued to be match containers, and the thumbtacks were simply ignored.

SUGGESTIONS FOR WRITING

Write a report about some hypothesis you have tested through experiment. Or describe somebody else's hypothesis and experiment.

SUGGESTED TOPICS

Einstein and relativity
Thor Heyerdahl's trip across the ocean
A chemical substance
Growing a plant
People's reaction to a peculiar action or condition of another person
Discovering what was wrong with the automobile
What caused the power failure

COMPONENT PARTS AND FUNCTION: A TECHNICAL OPERATION

Explaining how tools, machinery, and other technical appliances operate is a special form of functional analysis in that it deals with a process or a system—a sequence of events that follow one another in chronological order. Describing a technical operation usually makes use of structural analysis—that is, laying the whole thing out into the component parts that make up its structure. The purpose, though, is to explain how each part functions in the whole operation or system.

For instance, in explaining how a thermostat works, you might structurally separate the main component parts into regulating device, heat sensing unit, heating medium, valve, and heating unit. Then you would explain how each functions in the total system to regulate heat, probably doing so in terms of the natural laws involved—the main one the fact that liquid and metal expand when heated. The function of each component part may also need to be explained in terms of the natural law underlying it.

The following report describes the function of the overheat/fire detection and warning system of a jet engine. Paragraph 1 of the report states the function of the detection system and lists the component parts. Paragraph 2 states the function of the fire warning signal system and lists the component parts. Then paragraph 3 begins with the first element in the sensing system and moves part by part through the total system, explaining the function of each part in the whole, until we are back where we began and the "fire condition is corrected."

Paragraphs 4 through 6 give secondary but important information about breaks in the system and tests of the system.

Because clarity is of first importance, the description uses short, simple sentences and avoids emotionally toned words. It is a straightforward detailed description of a straightforward mechanical function.

Engine Overheat/Fire Detection and Warning System

UNITED STATES AIR FORCE

The overheat and fire detection system senses the presence of an overheat condition in each of the engine nacelles, and the presence of fire in each of the nacelles. A separate system is provided for each of the nacelles. The systems consist of sensing element loops, control units, two fire warning relays, and fire emergency handles. Each engine system also contains a keyer. Master FIRE warning lights are located on the pilot's and co-pilot's instrument panels. Each of these lights is common to all four nacelle detector systems. A fire emergency handle for each engine is on the fire emergency shutdown panel above the main instrument panel.

An audible fire warning signal system provides a fire warning signal through the interphone system at each crew station and at the loudspeaker within the flight station. The audible warning system consists of a fire warning generator, audible signal silencing relay, audible fire warning silencing switch and an amplifier at each crew station, except the navigator's.

The sensing elements for each engine are attached to the forward and aft cowl doors on both sides of the engine. There are three elements on each side. One is attached to the aft cowl door behind the vertical firewall, one is attached to the aft cowl door forward of the vertical firewall, and one is attached to the forward cowl door. Another element connected in series with these elements is attached to the pylon structure. The elements are attached to the cowl by means of clamps. The sleeving in the clamps is made of Teflon-impregnated asbestos, Walter Kidde No. 245284. Each sensing element is a thermistor device which has a negative temperature coefficient of resistance. The element consists of an inconel tube enclosing two wires which are separated by and imbedded in a special ceramic core. The electrical resistance of the core decreases as the temperature increases permitting a small current flow between the parallel wires. When the temperature in the nacelle reaches a certain value, the resistance between the two wires in the element decreases enough to trigger an overheat relay in the control unit. This relay completes circuits to the fire handle and master fire warning lights through the keyer, which causes the lights to flash on and off indicating an overheat condition. If the temperature increases above this point, as it would in the event of a fire, the resistance would decrease sufficiently to allow enough current flow to trigger a relay in the control unit. This relay completes a circuit to the fire warning relays. With the fire warning relays energized, the circuit to the lights in the fire handle and master fire warning

ENGINE FIRE EMERGENCY CONTROL PANEL

MASTER FIRE WARNING PANEL

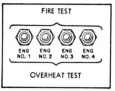

FIRE TEST SWITCHES

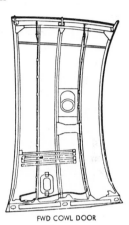

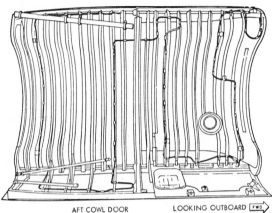

lights is completed, but the circuit bypasses the keyer and the lights remain steady indicating a fire. The fire warning relays also energize the audible fire warning generator and an audible signal is directed to the flight station loudspeaker, and to the amplifier at each crew station except the navigator's. An audible fire alarm silencing switch on the fire emergency panel, when actuated, completes a circuit to the audible fire alarm silencing relay. With this relay energized, the circuit to the fire warning relays is broken and the audible fire warning stops. A holding circuit maintains the audible alarm silencing relay energized through a ground in the control unit, until the fire condition is corrected.

Since the current flow in the sensing elements is not around the element loop, but between the parallel wires in the loop, a break in the sensing element would not cause a malfunction or failure of the system. If two or more breaks occurred in the element, the portion of the element still connected to the control unit would still detect a fire or overheat condition.

The sensing elements are isolated from ground to prevent false alarms due to single grounds in the sensing element loop or aircraft wiring to the loop. The control unit monitors the resistance between the parallel wires rather than between one of these wires and ground. A single ground will not affect the system. A discriminator circuit within the control unit prevents false alarms due to a ground between either wire of the element and the aircraft or between both wires in the element. However, when the discriminator circuit is actuated the detection system for that engine is inoperative.

A switch on the pilots' control pedestal tests the circuit for both a fire and an overheat condition. This system does not operate when the test switch is actuated if there is a break in the sensing loop or a double ground in the loop. It does not detect a single ground, since a single ground has no adverse effect on the system operation. Placing the switch in the "OVHT" position decreases the resistance of the circuit sufficiently to trigger the overheat relay in the control unit. Placing the switch in the "FIRE" position allows enough current flow in the system to trigger the control unit fire relay.

—from *PIMO Technical Manual*, USAF Series C-141s, Aircraft, Vol. 4, January 1, 1968.

SUGGESTIONS FOR WRITING

Describe a technical operation, showing how something works. You will likely have to make a structural analysis too as you lay the whole operation out into its component parts. A diagram can be useful, but is not necessary.

SUGGESTED TOPICS

A gasoline engine	A calculator
A television set	An irrigation system
A laser	An oil well
An elevator/escalator	An automatic garage door opener
Sonar/radar	An X-ray machine
A thermostat	

DESCRIPTION OF A NATURAL EVENT

Sometimes the scientist wants to combine scientific observation and interpretation with standard description and to describe a natural event or phenomenon not just for factual accuracy but to bring the scene to life for the reader. The writer does not violate the principles of the scientific attitude, but just adds to it or moves a little beyond it. The writer is still accurate, uses valid sources of information, and draws no conclusion beyond the facts. The impersonal tone may be set aside, but the writer remains objective. Having once made the scientific observations, the writer humanizes to some extent. Impressed by the observations, the writer wants others to be impressed too, and says, as does the writer of description, I have observed something worth observing and I want you to see it and feel what I felt about it. To bring the scene to life, the technique used is that of good description, as explained in Chapter 2(pp. 25–26):

1. Use concrete details
2. Create a dominant impression

In the following description of army ants, the writer steps in personally as "I" and wants the reader to step in and see, but the observations and interpretations are scientific. After an introductory paragraph, the author states a scientific principle or interpretation that "instinct is too fine to hope for any initiative." Then the writer describes the incident of the army ants to validate the principle. After the event is described, the writer restates the thesis: "there was no Eciton with individual initiative enough to turn aside an ant's breadth from the circle."

Though the writer brings himself in as human and the reader in as human, the report is an account of scientific observation, factual accuracy, and carefully drawn conclusions based on the evidence.

The Ant Circle

WILLIAM BEEBE

On my first tramp each season in the tropical jungle, I see the legionary army ants hastening on their way to battle, and the leaf-cutters plodding along, with chlorophyll hods over their shoulders, exactly as they did last year, and the year preceding, and probably a hundred thousand years before that. The Colony Egos of army and leaf-cutters may quite reasonably be classified according to Kingdom. The former, with carnivorous, voracious, nervous, vitally active members, seems an intangible, animal-like organism; while the stolid, vegetarian, unemotional, weather-swung Attas, resemble the flowing sap of the food on which they subsist—vegetable.

Yet, whatever the simile, the net of unconscious precedent is too closely drawn, the mesh of instinct is too fine to hope for any initiative. This was manifested by the most significant and spectacular occurrence I have ever observed in the world of insects. One year and a half ago I studied and reported upon, a nest of Ecitons or army ants. Now, eighteen months later, apparently the same army appeared and made a similar nest of their own bodies, in the identical spot near the door of the out-house, where I had found them before. Again we had to break up the temporary colony, and killed about three-quarters of the colony with various deadly chemicals.

In spite of all the tremendous slaughter, the Ecitons, in late afternoon, raided a small colony of Wasps-of-the-Painted-Nest. These little chaps construct a round, sub-leaf carton-home, as large as a golf ball, which carries out all the requirements of counter shading and of ruptive markings. The flattened, shadowed under surface was white, and most of the sloping walls dark brown, down which extended eight white lines, following the veins of the leaf overhead. The side close to the stem of the leaf, and consequently always in deep shadow, was pure white. The eaves catching high lights were black. All this marvelous merging with leaf tones went for naught when once an advance Eciton scout located the nest.

As the deadly mob approached, the wasplets themselves seemed to realize the futility of offering battle, and the entire colony of forty-four gathered in a forlorn group on a neighboring leaf, while their little castle was rifled—larvae and pupae torn from their cells and rushed down the stems to the chaos which was raging in Eciton's own home. The wasps could guard against optical discovery, but the blind Ecitons had senses which transcended vision, if not even scent.

Late that night, our lanterns showed the remnants of the Eciton army wandering aimlessly about, making near approach impossible, but apparently lacking any definite concerted action.

At six o'clock the following morning I started out for a swim, when at the foot of the laboratory steps I saw a swiftly-moving, broad line of army ants on safari, passing through the compound to the beach. I traced them back under the servants' quarters, through two clumps of bamboos to the out-house. Later I followed along the column down to the river sand, through a dense mass of underbrush, through a hollow log, up the bank, back through light jungle—to the out-house again, and on a large fallen log, a few feet beyond the spot where their nest had been, the ends of the circle *actually came together!* It was the most astonishing thing, and I had to verify it again and again before I could believe the evidence of my eyes. It was a strong column, six lines wide in many places, and the ants fully believed that they were on their way to a new home, for most were carrying eggs or larvae, although many had food, including the larvae of the Painted Nest Wasplets. For an hour at noon during heavy rain, the column weakened and almost disappeared, but when the sun returned, the lines rejoined, and the revolution of the vicious circle continued.

There were several places which made excellent points of observation, and here we watched and marveled. Careful measurement of the great circle showed a circumference of twelve hundred feet. We timed the laden Ecitons and found that they averaged two to two and three-quarter inches a second. So a given individual would complete the round in about two hours and a half. Many guests were plodding along with the ants, mostly staphylinids of which we secured five species, a brown histerid beetle, a tiny chalcid, and several Phorid flies, one of which was winged.

The fat Histerid beetle was most amusing, getting out of breath every few feet, and abruptly stopping to rest, turning around in its tracks, standing almost on its head, and allowing the swarm of ants to run up over it and jump off. Then on it would go again, keeping up the terrific speed of two and a half inches a second for another yard. Its color was identical with the Ecitons' armor, and when it folded up, nothing could harm it. Once a worker stopped and antennaed it suspiciously, but aside from this, it was accepted as one of the line of marchers. Along the same route came the tiny Phorid flies, wingless but swift as shadows, rushing from side to side, over ants, leaves, debris, impatient only at the slowness of the army.

All the afternoon the insane circle revolved; at midnight the hosts were still moving, the second morning many had weakened and dropped their burdens, and the general pace had very appreciably slackened. But still the blind grip of instinct held them. On, on, on they must go! Always before in their nomadic life there had been a goal—a sanctuary of hollow tree, snug heart of bamboos—surely this terrible grind must end somehow. In this crisis, even the Spirit of the Army was helpless. Along the normal paths of Eciton life he could inspire endless enthusiasm, illimitable energy, but here his material units were bound upon the wheel of their perfection of instinct. Through sun and cloud, day and night, hour after hour there was found no Eciton with individual initiative enough to turn aside an ant's breadth from the circle which he had traversed perhaps fifteen times: the masters of the jungle had become their own mental prey.

Fewer and fewer now came along the well worn path; burdens littered the line of march, like the arms and accoutrements thrown down by a retreating army. At last a scanty single line struggled past—tired, hopeless, bewildered, idiotic and thoughtless to the last. Then some half dead Eciton straggled from the circle along the beach, and threw the line behind him into confusion. The desperation of total exhaustion had accomplished what necessity and opportunity and normal life could not. Several others followed his scent instead of that leading back toward the out-house, and as an amoeba gradually flows into one of its own pseudopodia, so the forlorn hope of the great Eciton army passed slowly down the beach and on into the jungle. Would they die singly and in bewildered groups, or would the remnant draw together, and again guided by the super-mind of its Mentor lay the foundation of another army, and again come to nest in my out-house?

Thus was the ending still unfinished, the finale buried in the future—and in this we find the fascination of Nature and of Science. Who can be bored for a moment in the short existence vouchsafed us here; with dramatic beginnings barely hidden in the dust, with the excitement of every moment of the present, and with all of cosmic possibility lying just concealed in the future, whether of Betelgeuze, of Amoeba or —of ourselves: *Vogue la galère!**

SUGGESTIONS FOR WRITING

Write a description of some natural event that has moved you. Bring the scene to life, but do not violate the scientific attitude. The possible subjects to write on are practically endless. Look anywhere at nature for a moment and you have a subject. The list below offers a few suggestions.

SUGGESTED TOPICS

A flight of birds
A spider making a web
The birth of a baby
A meteor shower
Life in a stagnant pond / fresh-water pond
An animal procuring food
A flood
The structure / growth of a plant

Insects attacking a plant
Corrosion at work
The movement of the planets
A leaf
A grasshopper
A diatom
A crystal
Lichen on a rock

---

*Come what may!

10

Business Letters

The Total Message: Clarity and Character

A written business communication has a double message. Its reader gets meaning out of *what* is said and out of *how* it is said. The primary message is the information, the factual material presented. The secondary message is the manner in which the letter delivers the message.

The reader gets both messages, or, rather, the combination of the two is the total message. It is like a face-to-face conversation. Your tone of voice, your manner of speaking, the urgency or calmness of your voice, the frown or smile on your face, the glint in your eye, all tell something beyond what your words say. Sometimes the secondary message reinforces the words; sometimes it contradicts. A severe contradiction can nullify the verbal message, and the manner becomes the primary message. "I hear what you are (or mean), not what you say."

We call these two messages the *informative message* and the *character message.* Why is it important to keep these two messages in mind? Because with the business letter you are trying to evoke a certain reaction from the reader. So you must make sure that both the clarity of the letter (that is, *what* the letter says) and the character (that is, *how* the letter says it) help to bring about that reaction. Since a letter is written for a specific purpose in business, its message cannot be neutral. It will work either for you or against you. Give attention to *clarity* and *character* and you can make them work *for* you.

Clarity and character are products of techniques in five areas:

1. format, - *Shape - Form*
2. factual precision, - *write facts*
3. grammar and usage, *✓*
4. style, *use good sentences*
5. tone. - *Attitude*

1. Format Physical precision means following the standard format—making a letter look right. The illustrative letters in this chapter are models. Include the following items: letterhead (if available), heading, inside address, salutation, body, signature block, and IEC block (initials, enclosures, and carbon copies).

2. Factual precision The reader must grasp the contents immediately with absolute clarity. A business letter is precise only when it communicates the necessary ideas, down to the smallest relevant detail, with accuracy and clarity.

Note the lack of preciseness in thse sentences:

Omission of important detail: Please send a copy of your brochure to my old address. (exact title, exact address)

Ambiguity: All large orders must be approved by the head buyer. (What does he buy besides heads?) *two diff meanings*

Contradiction: We do not advocate violence, but we believe it is the only way for minority groups to get their rights.

3. Grammar and usage Sloppy, incorrect use of the language just does not make sales and keep customers, or get any other job done. You must check carefully for misspellings, incorrect verb forms, misuse of pronouns, sentence fragments, and such.

4. Style Style must be forceful. Beyond mere grammatical correctness, you must use effective sentences that will put your point across and impress your reader. To learn to use clear, direct, emphatic style, see Chapter 4 (pp. 64–101) of this book.

5. Tone No matter what you have to say in your letter, if the reader does not like the way you say it, your letters will fail. The character of the letter is part of the total message.

Achieving effective tone is a complex business, but most of it grows out of your awareness of the reader as a human being. You must sharpen your sensitivity to the interests, the motives, the possible reactions of anyone with whom you are communicating. If the person is a businessman, you must write from a businessman's point of view. If your reader is a teacher, a doctor, a housewife, then you must write from these points of view.

This sympathy for the reader is labeled the "you-attitude." Instead of writing "*We* are shipping your order immediately," you appeal more to the reader if you write, "*Your* order is being shipped immediately and should reach *you* no later than Monday, June 8." Use mostly the pronouns "you," "your," "yours" rather than "I," "my," "mine," "we," "ours."

Tone is not achieved merely by pronouns. It is a product of your real respect and consideration for the reader as a human being. This attitude will be reflected in three features: *courtesy, sincerity,* and *positiveness.*

a.　*Courtesy.* Courtesy is more than a well-placed "please" or "thank you." It is a combination of cordiality and tact. You must show warmth and friendliness as well as sensitivity and discretion. Courtesy is destroyed in a letter if your reader thinks you are being sarcastic, curt, angry, suspicious of the reader's motives, condescending, familiar, or presumptuous. Check carefully the wording of your letter to see that blunders in courtesy have not crept in. Here are some examples:

> **Suspicion:**　If the electric iron was defective at the time of purchase, as you claim, we will definitely replace it with a new one. We do think it strange, however, that you waited so long to inform us that . . .
>
> **Condescension:**　It will soon be time to renew your credit privileges. You will be needing them in the summer months ahead.
>
> **Sarcasm:**　Congratulations, men. I'm proud to announce that, because of your superb and tireless efforts last month, we fell only $17,000 short of our sales quota. Be sure to pick up your medals on the way out this evening.
>
> W.A. Morgan
Sales Manager

b.　*Sincerity.* A courteous attitude is successful only if it is believed. The tone must be genuine. Check your writings for marks of insincerity such as over-humility, obvious flattery, exaggeration, and gushiness. Here are some examples:

> **Over-humility:**　Our most sincere apologies for the foolish error we made in handling your last order. Our distribution coordinator, our driver, and myself all wish to say we are extremely sorry . . .
>
> **Obvious flattery:**　Only you, Mr. Nelson, can handle this difficult assignment for us.

c.　*Positiveness.* To evoke the desired reaction, you must appeal to your reader's best side and let the reader see the best side of your idea or message. Positiveness is the knack of presenting an idea in its most positive, favorable light.

Here are two basic rules for achieving the highest positive tone in your business letter:

1. Stress what things are or what they will be, rather than what they aren't or won't be. And stress what you have done, what you can do, or what you will do, rather than what you haven't done, can't do, or won't do.

2. Wherever possible, avoid using words with negative connotations, as in these examples:

I'm sorry we blundered on your order.
We regret the inconvenience you've been caused by the broken mixer.

Some examples of positive tone:

Negative or Neutral	Positive
Because of recent heavy demand, we will not be able to deliver your goods before August 12.	Although recent demand has been heavy, we will be able to deliver your goods by August 12.
The only work experience I have is two summers as a camp counselor.	I have had supervisory responsibility as a camp counselor for two full summers.
This unfortunate incident will not recur.	Future transactions will be serviced with the utmost care.
The box is half empty.	The box is half full.
We do not have any black convertibles in stock.	At present, we have only one blue, one gray, and two green convertibles in stock.
If you will submit your bid right away, you will be able to . . .	By submitting your bid right away, you will be able to . . .
If your references prove satisfactory, we shall gladly . . .	As soon as your references are checked, we shall gladly . . .
If you would like us to send you a sample . . .	We would be happy to send you a sample . . .
We hope you find this adjustment satisfactory.	We are glad to offer you this adjustment.

Typical Letters

There are many types of business letters, each seeking a certain kind of reaction from the reader and each making special demands upon the writer's ability. Every letter is in some way unique, but all letters can be classified into eight types according to function.

1. *Routine request*—everyday letters and memos which initiate some exchange of information or ideas.
2. *Routine reply*—everyday letters and memos which respond to someone else's initiating communication.
3. *Goodwill communications*—letters and memos written primarily to enhance the recipient's good feeling toward the writer or the writer's organization.

4. *Good-news communications*—letters and memos which convey information the recipient will be happy to read.
5. *Demand communications*—letters and memos which demand, rather than just ask for, something.
6. *Conciliatory communications*—letters and memos which are written to repair the recipient's ill feeling toward the writer or the writer's organization.
7. *Bad-news communications*—letters and memos which convey information displeasing or disappointing to the recipient.
8. *Persuasive communications*—letters and memos which must induce a new way of thinking in the recipient's mind or bring about a previously unanticipated action from the recipient.

Some of the more common types of letters are illustrated here.

ROUTINE REQUEST

Here are some guidelines for effective writing of an inquiry, a request, or an order.

1. Begin and end positively, especially if rapport between you and your respondent will induce a more satisfactory response.
2. Unless it is self-evident, make clear early in the communication who you are (what position you hold or what situation you are in that has caused you to write).
3. State specifically and completely what you want.
4. Unless self-evident, state why you want it. The reason or reasons you give make it easier for the respondent to provide precisely what you need.
5. Unless self-evident, indicate why you are writing to the person you address. People like to know why requests or inquiries are being made of them.
6. Ask for as little information as you have to. It is annoying to be asked for information which is readily available elsewhere or which is obviously superfluous.
7. If possible, time your requests, inquiries, and order letters to coincide with your respondent's least busy period.
8. Write with as much empathy as you can, injecting the everyday courtesies into your communications.

   1. Inquiry for information   In Letter 1, the writer is correct, congenial, and factually precise, and is likely to receive the information he asks for.
   2. Credit check   Matters of credit can be sensitive, but Letter 2 handles this inquiry in a warm, positive tone. The proper factual material is given. The "you" of the letter is clearly more prominent.

22 Crimson Road
Wichita Falls, Texas 76308
October 14, 1977

Dixson Supply Company
3002 Lomita Street
Fort Worth, Texas   76119

Ladies and Gentlemen:

Through conversations with your south-
western regional representative, Loren Fast,
I have learned of the manual which Dixson
Supply provides for its secretaries and other
correspondents. Judging by Mr. Fast's comments,
the manual is a real success.

As a student of business communications in
my senior year at Midwestern State University, I
am writing a term report entitled "Communications
Problems in Big Business" and I would much
appreciate receiving a copy of the Dixson Supply
Company Correspondence Manual for material upon
which to draw.

Yours truly,

David White

David White

Letter 1   Traditional indented format

DIXSON SUPPLY COMPANY

3002 Lomita Street
Fort Worth, Texas 76119

April 5, 1977

Gifford Electronics, Inc.
877 Third Avenue
Columbus, Ohio 43210

Ladies and Gentlemen:

We were pleased to receive your order of April 1
for six Model TP18 speakers.

So that we can fill your order on account as
quickly as possible, will you please send us
the names of three firms from whom you purchase on a credit basis.

Six Model TP18's are being held aside to assure
you quick delivery. We enjoy the opportunity
of being able to serve you and will process the
information you provide us with immediately.

Sincerely yours,

Barbara Thomas

Barbara Thomas
Credit Manager

BT:ab

Letter 2 Full block format

J. D. HOOPER & CO., INSURANCE

708 Cedar Rd.

Lincoln, Nebraska 68508

August 30, 1977

Ms. Linda Barnett
3609 Shady Lane
Lincoln, NE 68504

Dear Ms. Barnett:

On August 3, we sent you insurance claim forms
and requested that you complete said forms and
return to this office. To date, we have received no reply from you.

Unless we hear from you within ten days regarding
this matter, we will assume that you have no claim
to present and will close our file accordingly.

Very truly yours,

Nancy Ramson

Nancy Ramson
Claims Consultant

NR:lg

Letter 3 Modified block format

J. D. HOOPER & CO., INSURANCE

708 Cedar Rd.
Lincoln, Nebraska 68508

August 30, 1977

Ms. Linda Barnett
3609 Shady Lane
Lincoln, NE 68504

Dear Ms. Barnett:

We haven't yet received the insurance claim
forms we sent you on August 3.

I don't want to press you, but if you wish to
make any claim, it will be necessary for you to
complete these forms and send them in to us
within the next ten days.

Sincerely yours,

Conrad Johnson

Conrad Johnson
Claims Consultant

CJ:cd

cc: Charles Henson
    Bill Brady

Enclosure

Letter 4 Modified block format

3. **Request: offensive or courteous** The writer of Letter 3 was probably not deliberately offensive, but the tone is cold, antagonistic, and self-concerned. Ms. Barnett will dislike the company and perhaps take her insurance account elsewhere.

Letter 4 says exactly the same thing, but in a better manner. It has a positive opening and closing; it gives necessary precise factual information; it does not accuse Ms. Barnett of neglect (as the other writer did). It has a "you-attitude"; yet it firmly indicates that the next step is entirely up to Ms. Barnett.

EXERCISE 10-1
ROUTINE REQUESTS

1. Thumb through a national magazine or your local newspaper and locate a mail-order advertisement for some relatively low-priced item you would like to own. When you find one, write a letter ordering that item. Assume that you are enclosing a check in payment for your order. Clip the ad and attach it to your letter when you submit it to your instructor.

2. Assume that six weeks have passed since you sent a letter to Harper & Row, Publishers, Inc. (10 East 53rd Street, New York, N.Y. 10022), ordering a copy of *Introduction to the Humanities* by Doris Van De Bogart. You had attached a check for $10.95 to your order letter in full payment for the book. You have received no response to that order. Write a letter to Harper & Row asking about the delay.

3. You are working as credit manager for the McClurkan Company, a large department store handling only high-quality merchandise. This morning you received Letter 5. The store would very much like to open a charge account for Mrs. Rushia, but first it must look into her credit rating. Your job is to write her a letter enclosing the store's standard credit inquiry form, which asks questions about spouse's employment, banking affiliations, and other charge accounts presently held.

   In the letter, you should request that Mrs. Rushia complete the form and return it to you as soon as possible. It's not a difficult letter to write, but if you imply in any way that Mrs. Rushia's credit record might not be satisfactory, you may offend her, and instead of gaining a credit customer you'll lose a cash one.

4. You work at Wilson, Baker, Inc., a large mail-order house. Letter 6 comes to your attention. You would like to fill the order right away, but Jenkins' letter does not indicate whether he wants silk shirts or cotton-blend. Write a reply to Jenkins which requests the additional information without disappointing him over the delay.

1120 Valley View Road
Eastchester, New York   10709
September 8, 1977

The McClurkan Company
498 Madison Avenue
New York, New York   10022

Ladies and Gentlemen:

    After purchasing from your store for the last eighteen months, I would like to open a charge account in my name. Please send the charge card to me at the above address.

              Very truly yours,

Cynthia Rushia

              (Mrs.) Cynthia Rushia

Letter 5

329 Mountain View Road
Denver, CO   80220
January 10, 1977

Wilson, Baker, Inc.
3905 Harrison Street
Colorado Springs, CO   80901

Ladies and Gentlemen:

    Please send me 4 light green, Colliers dress shirts, size 16, with short sleeves.

              Yours truly,

Ralph Jenkins

              Ralph Jenkins

Letter 6

ROUTINE REPLY

Here are some general guidelines for the writing of effective routine replies:

1. Read very carefully the communication to which you're replying. As you read it, it may be advisable to circle all the points you want to answer. An incomplete reply is an ineffective reply.
2. Begin and end every routine reply as positively as is necessary to establish a congenial tone.
3. If the communication to which you are replying contains significant particulars, be sure to acknowledge those particulars. For example, when acknowledging a purchase order, be sure to restate the details of the order (unless those details are so long they'll make your reply clumsy). Restatement is a courtesy which assures your reader that his or her communication has been fully understood.
4. If the communication contains a remittance, acknowledge it.
5. If your reply does not answer all the questions which were put to you, explain why those questions are unanswered.
6. If necessary to make a reply complete, give more information than requested. If you reply contains enclosures, be sure it tells the reader where in the enclosed material any questions are answered.
7. When your reply is potentially disappointing (for instance, when a price has risen or there is a shortage) treat the situation as positively as you can, and with empathy.
8. Always reply as empathetically as you can, keeping the recipient's point of view uppermost in your message. If you read the initiating communication carefully, there's a lot you can learn about the writer and his or her interests.
9. Always reply as promptly as you can; if possible, immediately. Promptness is not only a courtesy, it can keep your recipient from losing interest or thinking you are slow.

1. A confirmation A first-time order should always be acknowledged, to insure the customer's continuance. The tone of Letter 7 is positive from beginning to end. It gives the essential facts. It expresses genuine appreciation. It identifies the customer with the product and the company. The letter does two things at once. It appeals to "you" throughout and it uses the brand name, Durall, four times to build product identification into the reader's mind.

The most attractive idea, cost, gets its own single-sentence paragraph, the third.

2. A negation It is risky to say "no" in any way to a customer. The customer is almost sure to feel some ill will. Extra effort must be made to create good will. Letter 8 is not totally bad, but it falls short. The first paragraph is negative and the whole letter is didactic (as if giving the "amateur" a lecture) and self-centered.

DURALL PRODUCTS, INC.

347 State St.

Fort Worth, Texas 76102

May 16, 1977

Parker-Timberwood, Inc.
418 Parker Square
Wichita Falls, Texas 76308

Ladies and Gentlemen:

Just a note of thanks for your recent order and for your check for $368.20 in prepayment. We've already shipped your fifty cartons of Durall's Vanishers. They should reach you within a few days.

We feel sure you'll find the same rapid turnover that other dealers have found with Durall. Housewives find their multipurpose value and disposability hard to resist, to say nothing of the attractive package.

Needless to say, for you there is Durall's substantial mark-up.

Enclosed is a handy reorder blank for your convenience when your Durall stock gets low.

Sincerely,

Mary Gerlack

Mary Gerlack
Distribution Manager

MG:ld

Letter 7

MODERN SOUND, INC.
587 Waller Avenue
Detroit, Michigan   48202

January 24, 1977

Mr. Jay Beeman
3280 Eastlake Avenue
Glenview, IL   60025

Dear Mr. Beeman:

In answer to your inquiry, we wish to inform
you that we do not market reprocessed magnetic
sound tape of any length. We believe that its
quality is wholly substandard, and we advise that
you do not use it if you want satisfactory
results on your home tape recorder. Often,
reprocessed tape is nothing more than outdated
tape or the ends of tape used at professional
sound studios. The studios would not think of
using it, and it is certainly not suited to the
needs of the amateur.

We suggest that for satisfactory results,
you use Modern Lux 6K sound tape. It is available at your local dealer for only $9.50--
actually not much more than reprocessed tape.
And it is fully guaranteed.

Very truly yours,

Carl Hamilton

Carl Hamilton
Customer Service Department

CH:dk

Letter 8

MODERN SOUND, INC.

587 Waller Avenue
Detroit, Michigan   48202

January 24, 1977

Mr. Jay Beeman
3280 Eastlake Avenue
Glenview, ILL   60025

Dear Mr. Beeman:

We were glad to receive your inquiry regarding reprocessed sound tape. Many of our customers have expressed curiosity as to its real quality.

Modern Sound has decided, after careful investigation, not to market reprocessed tape. We want to be able to guarantee fully any product we put on the market. Because reprocessed tape often consists of outdated tape or the ends of tape used professionally, we are unable to guarantee the quality of its reproduction. Some of our customers have tried reprocessed tape and have been dissatisfied with it.

Actually, the tape we recommend--Modern Lux 6K sound tape--costs little more than reprocessed brands. And we fully guarantee it. We are eager to provide only the best in recording supplies because we know how much its dependability can mean to you.

Sincerely,

Kenneth Benson
Customer Service Department

KB:lg

Letter 9

224

Letter 9 is an improvement. The opening and closing are positive. The tone of lecturing is totally absent. The arbitrary tone is avoided, giving Mr. Beeman an easy and positive option.

EXERCISE 10-2
ROUTINE REPLIES

1. You are sales manager of Barnes Enterprises, Inc. During lunch with your friend Joe Wilson, he ordered 10,000 ballpoint pens imprinted with the slogan "Morley for Mayor" at 3½ cents each. You promised delivery within three weeks. Write a confirmation letter to Joe to avoid any confusion over the terms of the oral agreement, as well as to convey a friendly attitude.
2. Your company, the Valley Real Estate Company of Charleston, West Virginia, today received Letter 10 from a prospective client. Obviously,

```
            1800 Third Avenue
            Charleston, West Virginia   25301
            December 6, 1977



Valley Real Estate Company
3408 W. Greenville Avenue
Charleston, West Virginia   25301

Ladies and Gentlemen:

     I am interested in purchasing a home with at
least five acres of land in Kanawha County, some-
where in the $32,000 to $40,000 range.  I under-
stand that such properties are frequently avail-
able and that you are the outfit most likely to
be handling them.  Please let me know what you
have.  I will reply immediately by phone or in
person.

                    Very truly yours,

                    Elizabeth Grauerholz

                    Elizabeth Grauerholz
```

Letter 10

you would like to sell property to Ms. Grauerholz and you have several Kanawha County listings of over ten acres. Because of a recent boom in land prices, however, none of these properties can be purchased for less than $45,000.

Write a letter to Ms. Grauerholz informing her that there is property available in Kanawha County, and that although the prices are higher than her suggested range, the properties are among the best values still available in the county. The likelihood is that county real estate prices will continue to rise. Tell her, too, that you'd like very much to show her these choices properties.

Your task isn't simple. Consider the reactions you desire from Ms. Grauerholz. Your primary objective is to maintain, or even enhance, Ms. Grauerholz's enthusiasm for buying property in Kanawha County, in spite of the fact that she underestimated how much it would cost.

3. Assume that you are the manager of the mail order department at Fashion Interiors, Inc., of Urbana, Illinois. You received Marilyn Dickerson's order letter, Letter 11, and have just filled the order and shipped it via freight express as Ms. Dickerson requested. Now, because it's your policy to acknowledge all orders with a letter, write an effective letter of acknowledgment to Ms. Dickerson. This is the first order you've received from Ms. Dickerson. And remember to acknowledge the check she included with her order.

CONCILIATORY LETTERS

Conciliatory letters are among the hardest to write because, obviously, somebody has complained and his or her confidence in you is impaired. Maybe it's poor service, or damaged merchandise, or an overcharge; but the person is at least disturbed, perhaps angry. You will need all the help you can get from effective use of tone. The three techniques to consider in a conciliatory letter are an apology, an explanation, and a positive close (perhaps an offer of adjustment).

1. **Apology-explanation-adjustment** With a letter like Letter 12 from a long-time customer, the problem is clear. You have to soften his anger, offer an adjustment, and keep his patronage. The answer, Letter 13, follows the pattern of apology-explanation-adjustment. Positive tone and customer identification are maintained throughout.

2. **Apology-explanation** When no adjustment is possible or necessary, conciliation must be brought about by apology and explanation, as in Letter 14. There is nothing tangible to offer the customer, such as a discount on a piece of merchandise. Conciliation is managed by good will and explanation. Note the special appeal to the customer by writing "You are correct."

3. **Apology** In some conciliatory situations, there is no tangible remedy and even an explanation is meaningless or unnecessary. In Letter 15,

CROSSROADS ANTIQUES AND GIFTS
Route 4
Ludlow, Vermont   05149

November 1, 1977

Fashion Interiors, Inc.
2118 Emmett Road
Urbana, Illinois   61801

Ladies and Gentlemen:

Please ship the following prepaid order via freight express:

12 Antique Copper Kettles @ 16.50	198.00
12 Cross-Stitch Pillows (4 red, 4 blue, 4 olive) @ $8.50	102.00
6 Early American Johnny Seats @ $19.75	118.50
6 15" x 5" Decorated Butter Molds @ $3.25	19.50
Total	$438.00

My check for $475.20 is attached to cover both the goods ($438.00) and the freight charges ($37.20). I would very much appreciate your sending out this order in time to reach me by November 12, 1977.

Sincerely yours,

Marilyn Dickerson

Marilyn Dickerson
Manager

MD:cd

Letter 11

1680 Ranch Road
Philadelphia, Pennsylvania 19103

June 14, 1977

Evinrude Motor Co.
3407 Perch Street
Philadelphia, Pennsylvania 19103

My dear Sir:

   To call it like it is, you sure fouled up
delivery of my Evinrude outboard motor. If I told
you once, I told you five times you should deliver
it to my week-end place at Lake Arrowhead, not to
my regular address. So there I sat, with the wife
and kids who were going boating with the thing,
while you tried to deliver it to the regular
address. If the neighbors hadn't seen your
delivery man with the motor, we still wouldn't
know what happened. I've got a good mind to
cancel my charge account and take my business
someplace else where they've got ears!!

                    Disgustedly yours,

                    Fred Stuart

                    Fred Stuart

Evinrude Motor Co.

3407 PERCH ST.

PHILADELPHIA, PENNSYLVANIA   19103

June 17, 1977

Mr. Fred Stuart
1680 Ranch Road
Philadelphia, Pennsylvania   19103

Dear Mr. Stuart:

Please accept our most sincere apologies for the
delivery mix-up on your Evinrude outboard motor.
Upon receiving your letter this morning, I checked
the delivery slip and found that, in completing
it, our shipping department had copied the address
straight from your account folder. When your
neighbor told our delivery man that you were on
vacation, he brought the outboard motor back to the
store assuming he would redeliver it as soon as
you got back. We in the sales department
assumed delivery had been made to your summer
residence. Both departments are indeed embarrassed.

Having purchased from us for many years, you know
that we do our best to avoid these slip-ups in
communications. Somehow, this one got away from us.

What we'd like to do is deliver your Evinrude to
you at either address you wish. And, because we
didn't get it to you in time for your vacation,
we'd like to pay for your not having had it by
delivering it at a thirty percent discount. By
doing this, we can say we're sorry _and_ still
provide you with the finest in recreation equipment for your many summer vacations to come.

Mr. Barker, our shipping manager, has said that he
will call you for your "OK" on a delivery time
that will meet your earliest convenience.

Sincerely yours,

Thomas Walton
Sales Manager
TW:kr

Letter 13

Thompson Furniture Store

3518 Carlton St.
Pierre, SD 57501

November 21, 1977

Ms. Helen Monahan
4493 Carta Road
Yankton, SD 57078

Dear Ms. Monahan:

We sincerely apologize. Upon receiving your
letter, we rechecked your invoice of November 10.
You are correct. Your check for $420.50 does cover
the charges fully. Shipping costs incurred by
another customer had been mistakenly added to your
account.

You have our assurance that, however cross-
eyed from overtime our bookkeepers may become, our
policy is still to make your bills as low as we
possibly can.

Cordially yours,

Janet Stillwell

Janet Stillwell
Vice-President

JS:me

conciliation is brought about with just an apology. But the right tone is used, along with a little chatter to humor the customer and keep her identified with the company. If Braun had written only the very brief Letter 16, he would have been guilty of compounding the offense with curtness.

EXERCISE 10-3
CONCILIATORY LETTERS

1. Think back to the last time you were dissatisfied with a product or service you purchased, and wanted to write a sharp letter of complaint to the appropriate higher-ups. Now is your chance. Write that letter. Besides expressing your discontent with tactful firmness, you might also mention that you are active in a number of organizations and will gladly pass along the news of your dissatisfaction to your friends and fellow members to protect them from the same kind of dissatisfaction. If you don't remember the name and address of the company you're complaining to, make them up.

2. Assume that you are the public relations consultant for The Pelican. The Pelican is an expensive but highly recommended restaurant, the recipient of a number of international awards for its cuisine. The restaurant has received a letter from a disenchanted customer accusing the restaurant of "trading on its reputation." It seems that the customer and his party of fifteen had Prime Rib of Beef Deluxe last Friday night and found it "terribly fatty." He also said "the vegetables were all dried out." The Pelican has never received a complaint like this before, and unless this disappointed customer is effectively conciliated, he could really hurt the restaurant's reputation.

   The management has asked you to write the customer a letter. "Do anything within reason for him," they say, "just make him happy." Make him happy.

3. Write a proper apology and explanation rather than the tactless one shown as Letter 17.

   What actually happened (and George Humbolt never took the trouble to track down what had happened) was that a warehouse assistant, upon being asked to bring five thousand blue retractable pens to the imprinting room, knew there was a case of five thousand old pens which had been sitting around for three years and took it upon himself to "finally get them out of the way." With these facts in mind, rewrite Humbolt's conciliatory letter to Mr. Kornman.

4. Improve the tone of Letter 18.

TEXAS STORES, INC.

5001 North Stennons
Dallas, Texas 75247

November 27, 1977

Ms. Debra Thomson
4376 Webster Lane
Nacogdoches, Texas 75961

Dear Ms. Thomson:

I am so sorry! I know personally how it
feels when someone misspells my name--they
usually spell it o-w.

Please forgive the typist's mistake. The
intention of our letter--to say thanks for your
patronage--still stands. We appreciate it.

Sincerely yours,

William Braun

William Braun
Manager

WB:jr

TEXAS STORES, INC.

5001 North Stennons
Dallas, Texas 75247

November 28, 1977

Ms. Debra Thomson
4376 Webster Lane
Nacogdoches, Texas 75961

Dear Ms. Thomson:

We're sorry we misspelled your name.

Yours truly,

William Braun

William Braun
Manager

WB:jr

Letter 16

BARNES MANUFACTURING, INC.

27 Main St.
Houston, TX 77002

January 11, 1977

Mr. Everett Kornman, Purchasing
Gulf Enterprises
228 Townsend Blvd.
Houston, TX 77004

Dear Sir:

We were shocked to read in your recent
letter that the imprinted ballpoint pens we
shipped were unsatisfactory to you.

You claim that most of them were tarnished
and that many of them would not write. In the
event this is true, we cannot understand how
such deterioration could have occurred. We
observe very strict quality control procedures,
and these pens were manufactured only last
month.

But since you have been a customer of ours
for such a long time, we will take back the pens
and send a replacement order to you soon. I
hope this solution will be satisfactory to you.

Yours truly,

George Humbolt

George Humbolt
Sales Manager

GH:sr

Letter 17

Continental Wholesalers

BOX 1718
LOUISVILLE, KENTUCKY 40201

November 22, 1977

Wilson Furniture
2372 East Third Street
Atlanta, Georgia 30303

Attention: B. J. Bloomfield

Ladies and Gentlemen:

We were quite surprised to read your letter of last week in which you state that you wrote "Rush" on your order blank. There was no such notation on the order form we worked from. So we sent your order by rail freight just like we usually send all orders.

We have a policy here at Continental that says the customer is always right. So we are certainly sorry for any inconvenience you might have been caused.

Sincerely yours,

Margaret Maxwell

Margaret Maxwell

MM:vr

Letter 18

JOB APPLICATION

To land a good job, you must have qualifications—and must effectively communicate those qualifications to a prospective employer. The two components are the *resume* (pronounced rez-uh-may) and its *covering letter*.

1. The resume The usual *resume* has several blocks of information:

1. *Personal information*

   Name
   Address and phone number
   Birth date
   Height and weight
   Marital status
   Health
   Willingness to relocate (if applicable)

2. *The education block*

   Specific degree
   Name of school
   Date of graduation
   Overall grade average (if B or higher or if class standing is in the top third or better)
   Specific courses related to the job
   Extracurricular activities
   Academic awards, scholarships, honors

3. *The experience block.* Any kind of work experience (if honest) is an asset. List jobs in reverse chronological order—most recent first.

   Job title
   Name and address of company
   Dates of employment
   Number of hours per week (if part time)
   Special responsibilities

4. *Personal interests.* Activities, interests, and experiences to indicate well-roundedness as an individual. It is best not to include religious or political organizations. Also, do not list activities that might indicate temperamental oddities, such as sky diving, motorcycle racing, or fire-eating.
5. *Military block.* (If any)
6. *References.* You have two options. Either indicate that references will gladly be provided upon request or give a list of names of three or four persons who will speak for you. Include titles and addresses. Be sure to check first with each person you use as a reference.

Guidelines of format

For neatness, be sure to maintain a "picture-frame" effect, with one inch or more of white space at top and bottom, left and right.

Richard Sodders

4638 El Capitan Street
Wichita Falls, Texas   76320
817 692-9476

Age: 23
Height: 6'1"
Weight: 180 lbs.
Single
Willing to relocate

Education

B.S. in Industrial Engineering, Midwestern State
University, June 1977
Top five percent of class, with special courses:
business law, statistics, motivational psychology, and communications.

Won Pittsburgh Plate Glass Scholarship 1975, 1976
Member of Industrial Relations Club
Elected Secretary of Student Council
On Dean's Honor Roll since 1974

Experience

Staff supervisor, Quichita Boys' Club Camps,
Lawton, Oklahoma, Summer 1976; responsible
for housing, activities scheduling, and
occasional discipline of fourteen counselors
and 110 campers.

Camp counselor, Quichita Boys' Club Camp,
Lawton, Oklahoma, Summer 1974 and 1975.

Personal Interests

Politics, world affairs, camping, tennis, Junior
Chamber of Commerce, and volunteer hospital
worker.

References

Will gladly be provided upon request.

4638 El Capitan Street
Wichita Falls, Texas   76310
February 14, 1977

Mr. James Kable
Director of Personnel
National Industries, Inc.
4920 Turner Blvd.
Oklahoma City, Oklahoma   73069

Dear Mr. Kable:

With graduation only months away, I would like
very much to apply for a position in this year's
Executive Training Program at National Industries.
My Midwestern State University degree will be in
Industrial Engineering. I will finish in the top
five percent of my class.

For the past three summers, I've been employed
on the staff of the Quichita Boys' Club Camp.
During the first two years, I served as a counselor. Last summer I became a supervisor responsible for fourteen counselors and their
campers. The enclosed resume will give you
fuller details of this experience and the rest
of my background.

With my college training almost completed, I
have anticipated this year as a time of beginning.
The career beginning which interests me most is
one with National Industries. May I hear from
you regarding my qualifications, and come to see
you at your convenience?

                              Sincerely yours,

                              Richard Sodders

                              Richard Sodders

Be sure, as well, that your heading and subheadings will be clear to the reader at a glance.

That a resume must be physically flawless to be successful goes without saying.

Be sure to confine it to a single page in length. Anything longer will be considered wordy and wasteful of the reader's time.

When you prepare to mail out more than one application package, do not use carbon copies of a resume. A carbon copy carries the implication the neater original has gone elsewhere.

2. The covering letter The resume presents a detailed, factual, and largely impersonal view of the applicant. It tells your qualifications for the job. The purpose of the accompanying covering letter is to humanize the applicant and interest the employer. It gives the employer a view of your motives, goals, personality, and ability to express yourself.

More specifically, any covering letter your write must perform these functions:

1. It must introduce you and state your specific reason for writing: your interest in a particular position in the employer's organization.
2. It must highlight your background by mentioning your major qualifications, then invite the employer to consider the details in the resume.
3. It must ask specifically for the response you desire: an interview for the job. Not one employer in a hundred will offer a job without first seeing you; consequently, you appear quite naive if you ask directly for the job. *At Employers conv.* —

Letter 19 is a sample written to accompany the resume of Richard Sodders. The letter is brief, complete, and articulate, and it seems to reveal a warm and sensible personality.

11

Examinations

Students frequently lose points on examinations not because they don't have the information, but because they don't put it down right. If the exam calls for discussion that requires at least a few sentences, then attention to the principles of sound thinking and effective writing will help you get the highest grade for your information.

Here are some guides to keep in mind when you write extended answers on examinations.

1. Read the question or topic Read carefully to be sure you understand what it is the instructor wants. The instructor is probably asking for a *specific* aspect or area of information.

2. Answer the question Write to the point. Don't wander. Don't try to tell everything you know about the general subject area. Remember: the instructor is probably looking for a specific aspect. Just to be sure, occasionally go back to read the question again and be sure you are still on the specific subject.

3. Plan your answer Don't just gush whatever comes to mind. A good examination answer, just like a paragraph or larger composition, is not merely a jumble of information. Review the principles of good paragraphing. A good paragraph has a topic sentence stating the central idea, it has adequate supporting material to back up the idea, and it has devices to connect the parts. The specific subject asked for in the exam question is your central idea. State it clearly and use details to put it across. Have enough connective devices to show the relationships between the pieces of information in your answer paragraph. The instructor will see that you have done more than memorize, that you comprehend the meaning and implications of the material.

Here are some examples of student answers for three typical kinds of examinations—identification, brief discussion, and extended discussion.

Identification

Question: Identify the following: "Declaration of the Rights of Man and the Citizen"
Answer

The Declaration of the Rights of Man and the Citizen:
This document was issued by the National Constituent Assembly in France on August 26, 1789. It was written by Thomas Paine and asserted that the rights of man were liberty, property, security, and resistance to oppression.

Note some specific features of the answer. It identifies the term as the title of a document. It gives the author, the date, and the occasion. It indicates the contents, backing up the information by giving four specifics.

Compare the following answer to the same question. The information is not incorrect; there is just not much of it.

The Declaration of the Rights of Man and the Citizen was the French Declaration of Independence written when they had their Revolution. It is similar to the Americans' Declaration of Independence.

Brief Discussion

Question: Discuss the four types of analysis [International Relations].
Answer

The four types of analysis a student may use in approaching international relations, or any subject, are (1) descriptive, (2) normative, (3) predictive, (4) prescriptive. All have some aspects of descriptive, but which one a student chooses pertains to his goal. He chooses descriptive if his goal is merely to describe a situation and tell what happened. He uses normative analysis if he wishes to convince his reader of something or change an opinion. Predictive analysis allows him to predict future events and is often used in foreign policy. Finally, prescriptive analysis allows him to state what he thinks should be done or changed in the future, and is also prevalent in foreign policy.

The answer is not just a list of labels. It follows the principles of writing an effective paragraph. There is an opening topic sentence, which repeats the question and lists the four kinds. Then, in turn, each type of analysis is defined more largely, indicating the special function of the type. Notice how the connective devices in the last sentence ("finally," "also") round off the paragraph and give a sense of control. The answer has a central idea, organization, and development.

Another student's answer uses about the same number of words to give vague and inaccurate information. Compare sentence 2, which says "descriptive" is descriptive. The term "normative" is inaccurately defined, and "postscriptive" is a hodge-podge word made up by the writer, also inaccurately defined.

> People in foreign policy use four types of analysis to tell what is going on, has happened, or will happen in the field. They use descriptive analysis to describe events. They rely on normative analysis if they are trying to explain an international event to the normal population who has little contact with international affairs on the whole. They use predictive analysis to predict what will happen in the field of international relations. Foreign policy makers use postscriptive analysis when they want to analyze what has taken place recently on the international scene.

Extended Discussion

Question: Describe the High Middle Ages as an explosive period.
Answer

The High Middle Ages, the period between A.D. 1000 and 1300, was probably the most explosive period in western history. In 1000 the society was feudalistic with an agriculture base. There were hardly any towns and less than half the lands were cultivated. The majority were wastelands and moorlands. Between 1000 and 1300, however, the population tripled, and the society had to bring these lands under cultivation. Technology expanded, although the tools were primitive. The people brought back the use of the windmill, which had been used in Rome (but not extensively), to drain the swamplands. Around 1000 the people became fascinated with labor-saving devices because labor in this society was scarce. The serfs were just slipping away from the manors at night and going to the towns where they could be free. The low-scale technology developed during this period led to the scientific discoveries of the eighteenth, nineteenth, and twentieth centuries.

Also between 950 and 1000 there was a great gap between the east and the west, and a massive population expansion to the east began. In this area of the gap there was no one living but pagans, Slavs, Poles, etc. The Germans really began the expansion and there was a great frontier spirit. People were eager to go because they could be free and have twice as many lands as they had in the west. The only areas that were really taken into western society, however, were the areas that were Germanized. The Teutonic Knights were a German religious order who fought rather than prayed. During this expansion they conquered Prussia, intermarried with the survivors, and became the most German of Germans.

Another explosive factor during this period which contributed to commercial expansion was that in 1095 the Crusades began. They were underfinanced and supported only by the clergy for the most part. Only the first one was even close to being successful; yet they lasted for 300 years. Out of them grew many trade routes and goods for trade.

From the great commercial expansion during the high middle ages came extensive urbanization. Towns grew where none had been and already existing towns expanded rapidly. This was true especially along the Baltic and the river systems of Europe, because all trade had to be waterborne. Northern Italy began to monopolize the trading industry. By the 1300s all the goods had to be shipped on Italian vessels and all the merchants at Constantinople were Italian. The Venitians were the first to build a shipyard, the arsenal, and to adapt cannons to ships.

With all this rapid population expansion and population growth the society was undergoing changes of unmatched proportions. Medieval society could never really be called urbanized but townsmen did become a major factor in the politics of the time. They were able now to pay the kings to leave them alone and the kings lost much of their effective control. This was so because the feudalistic society of the early middle ages was designed to govern a military elite on an agricultural basis. It was just simply not equipped to handle the rapid population, commercial, urban, and technological expansion of the high middle ages.

The preceding answer has all the features of a well-written essay. It states a thesis or central idea ("The High Middle Ages were explosive.") and then develops the idea with clear organization and abundance of detail for support. The essay contains more than specific facts and information. Causes, effects, and relationships are pointed out. The essay moves through different forces of expansion—technological, population, commercial, urban.

The final sentence of the essay echoes the opening thesis of the essay and recaps the four major forces that brought about the explosion.

Compare the following answer with its empty words. In about as many words as used in the preceding essay, this student manages to say almost nothing.

Question: Select one of the poets (Eliot or Jeffers) and two of the prose writers (Hemingway, Steinbeck, Faulkner) and show in detail how a selection in the textbook is representative of the author.

Answer

THOMAS STEARNS ELIOT'S <u>THE WASTE LAND</u>

To say that <u>The Waste Land</u> is representative of T. S. Eliot is an understatement. The poem illustrates many of his techniques, the least of which is his ability to write so long a poem with so little deviation from the theme which he establishes in the first few lines of his poem, which may be said which makes it the best example of the Eliot style. The following illustrates some of the factors which make the poem so representative.

Eliot writes so fully and with such insight in the poem that one might expect some deep underlying (and often exclusive) meaning to be forthcoming. As with most of Eliot's writing, <u>The Waste Land</u> is no exception. Here Eliot combines the seriousness of the bang-whimper tradition with the lighter insights into man's character as a lost and forgotten creature who needs to be remembered. Once a reader has sampled the clarity of the Eliot language in <u>The Waste Land</u>, he should have little difficulty in picking Eliot's poems from those of other poets. In <u>The Waste Land</u> especially, moreover, the Eliot style manifests itself in one major respect: Eliot is here able to combine the pathos of the situation with his own ethos and the whole poem seems to result in an air of logic.

It is not so much his analysis of the situation nor his use of multilingual passages that make this poem representative of his works. What does make this poem representative is the fact that Eliot herein makes final and vast use of all that is good in his poetry: terseness of language, complexity of style, completeness of imagery, fullness of tone, intensity of color, and finally, timelessness of thought. Whereever and whenever he is read, Eliot will always stand as a great poet.

(<u>The Waste Land</u> is underlined throughout. In my opinion this poem fits well into the category established by grammarians for "underline book-length poems.")

12

Summaries

There are three qualities to an effective summary, whether it is of a piece of fiction, of an essay, or of a poem. A summary is brief, complete, and objective.

   1. Brief   A summary is the whole work condensed, and much condensed. Yet nothing significant can be left out.

   2. Complete   A summary will usually contain the following:

    a.   Central idea, theme, or impression.

    b.   The main points or basic structure or central images and metaphors (for a poem).

    c.   Emphases and relationships. Causes, effects, priorities, proportion, and so on must be noted.

    d.   Attitude of the author, if any, such as sarcasm, approval, preference, and so on.

   3. Objective   A summary deals with what the author says. It condenses the work itself. Your own tastes, criticisms, emotions, preferences, evaluations, and applications are out of place. Express only what the piece of writing expresses.

An Essay

The following summary of "Harvest of the Seasons" (p. 29) is brief, complete, and impersonal. It states the central idea or thesis of the essay and identifies the thought structure and idea relationships as causes and effects. The idea pattern is traced throughout, essentially leaving out the supporting material. No essential idea, subpoint, or idea relationship is left out. The summarizer's own tastes, emotions, or evaluations are not brought into the summary.

"HARVEST OF THE SEASONS"

The essay "Harvest of the Seasons" by J. Bronowski traces a sequence of causes of the change from nomad life to village agriculture, as illustrated by the ancient people of Jericho. The big stages are from wild wheat, to Emmer, to bread wheat, to agriculture. The wild wheat with its small 14-chromosome grains that scatter in the wind crossed with a goat grass of 14 chromosomes to make Emmer, a larger 28-chromosome grain that scattered in the wind. Emmer crossed with another 14-chromosome goat grass to make bread wheat, an even plumper 42-chromosome grain that did not scatter in the wind, but must be planted. The need for planting and harvesting brought about the need for the permanent settlement. Hence village agriculture.

The following summary has several weaknesses. On the strong side, it does point out the central idea and the subpoints, and it is objective. On the weak side, the summary lacks brevity (about 230 words to the 115 of the preceding summary), it unnecessarily includes supporting material (such as references to Garstang and to the Natufian civilization), and it does not make sharply clear the idea relationship of cause and effect.

"HARVEST OF THE SEASONS"

The largest single step in the ascent of man was made possible by both man and nature. This step is the change from nomad to village agriculture. A hybird wheat appeared at the end of the Ice Age in many places, one of which is Jericho. The first people in Jericho harvested wheat, but did not know how to plant it. John Garstang substantiates this by the tools he found here in the 1930s that were made for wild harvesting. This wild wheat and type of harvesting of the Natufian pre-agricultural civilization no longer survives. Agriculture happened next on the Jericho tel. Two forms of wheat produced the turning point to the spread of agriculture in the Old World. Through a genetic accident a plumper, more fertile hybrid, Emmer, was formed that spread naturally by scattering its seeds in the wind. This hybrid, Emmer, then crossed with another grass. This produced a larger hybrid, which is bread wheat. This hybrid does not spread naturally. It must be planted. So man and the plant have come together. The life of each, man and plant, depends on the other. It can be considered true that a fairy tale of genetics produced the change from pre-agricultural to agricultural civilization.

This summary fails to give the sense of the essay. It misses the main idea-structure of the cause and effect pattern tracing the development of village agriculture from hybrid wheat. At best the stages in the process are muddled, scarcely seen as a process. For instance, the summary does not mention the final need for planting, which meant men must be settled. From the summary, we get only a jumble of ideas without relationships.

"HARVEST OF THE SEASONS"

"Harvest of the Seasons" by J. Bronowski is a short, informal history of science in agriculture. Jericho was an ancient oasis. The people who settled in the oasis harvested wheat, but they did not know how to plant it. The wheat no longer exists there. This was the first edge of agriculture. It was a turning point in the history because two types of crop turned up, both with full, large seeds. Wild wheat accidentally crossed with goat grass and came up with a rare hybrid because it was fertile. This produced 28-chromosome Emmer. Because of a second genetic accident, a 42-chromosome Emmer was produced—which is bread wheat. These accidents came through air travel of seeds—but today the ear is too tight to break up. If it is broken up, the grain falls to the ground where it grew. The fairy tale at Jericho is a fairy tale of genetics, a fairy tale of coming civilizations.

A Short Story

The following summary of the short story "The Open Window" (p. 172) traces the thought structure (or plot), points out the characters with the characterization and relationships, and indicates the central idea or theme (the last line of the story). The one major piece of summarized interpretation is "Both of the stories of the niece are pieces of imagination," although the statement is obvious from the plot, the theme, and the character of the girl.

"THE OPEN WINDOW"

A nervous and sickly young man, Framton Nuttel, visits a country house in late nineteenth-century England, with letters of introduction to several people in the area. Nuttel hopes that a retreat to the restful country will act as a nerve cure.

'A "self-possessed" girl of fifteen entertains Nuttel until her aunt arrives. When the girl learns that the visitor is a stranger to the area, she tells him about her aunt's tragedy. She explains that the French window in the room is kept open because three years ago the aunt's husband and her two brothers went through the window on a hunting trip. They fell into a bog and never returned. The aunt's mind snapped and she keeps the window open, expecting the hunters to return.

At this point the aunt arrives and talks cheerily about the open window and the expected return of the hunters. When indeed the hunters with their dogs do appear out of the twilight and walk across the lawn toward the window, Nuttel flees.

When the others ask about why the young man fled the girl says she supposes it was fear of dogs. He had told her, she says, that he had once been kept all night in an open grave by a pack of wild dogs in India.

Both of the stories of the niece are pieces of imagination. As the last line of the story states, "Romance at short notice was her specialty."

The following summary is weak in several ways. It misinterprets the theme—which is not terror, but romance, as stated in the closing line. The summarizer seems to have missed the author's tone—Nuttel's flight is not to be considered tragic, but amusing. The summarizer also fails to indicate that the girl made up the tragedy of the death of her uncles. Finally, the essential character of Nuttel and the girl should have been delineated, since their characters are the prime conditions for motivating the plot.

"THE OPEN WINDOW"

The terror that children are capable of inflicting on the people around them is perhaps the greatest of all terrors. This is illustrated in the short story "The Open Window" by H. H. Munro (Saki). In this story you encounter Framton Nuttel, a man undergoing a nerve cure, and a very unusual girl. The girl is the niece of Mrs. Sappleton, who tells Mr. Nuttel of her aunt's tragedy. The tragedy was the death of her uncles, who died snipe shooting in the moors. It is the third anniversary of their death. When talking to Mrs. Sappleton, Mr. Nuttel finds the conversation on her husband and brothers. He shoots the niece comprehending looks, until at twilight, three figures appear crossing the moor—Mr. Sappleton and his brothers-in-law returning from their day's hunting. The niece tells them that Mr. Nuttel had a fear of dogs. Perhaps the terror a child can inflict is because children always seem to be innocent and believable.

A Poem

The summary of the following poem, a sonnet, indicates the basic structure, the central idea ("permanence of love"), the main points (the three distinct quatrains and the couplet), and the developing metaphors and images (ship, star, fool, sickle). The summarizer keeps it objective, saying nothing about liking or disliking the poem or whether it is a quality poem.

Sonnet 116

WILLIAM SHAKESPEARE

Let me not to the marriage of true minds
Admit impediments. Love is not love
Which alters when it alteration finds,
Or bends with the remover to remove.
O, no! it is an ever-fixèd mark
That looks on tempests and is never shaken;
It is the star to every wand'ring bark,
Whose worth's unknown, although his height be taken.
Love's not Time's fool, though rosy lips and cheeks
Within his bending sickle's compass come;
Love alters not with his brief hours and weeks,
But bears it out even to the edge of doom.
    If this be error, and upon me proved,
    I never writ, nor no man ever loved.

"SONNET 116"

With the typical structure of a Shakespearean sonnet, this sonnet is composed of three quatrains that build up the idea and the final couplet which resolves or affirms the idea. The poet asserts, in lines 1–4, the permanence of love based on the union of minds. Though the loved one may show alteration, love will not change. Lines 5–8 express this permanence in the metaphor of the fixed guiding star of the navigators. Though the worth of the star be not known, its "height" can be used for navigation. Lines 9–12 express the permanence of love through the metaphor of time as the reaper with a sickle. Though time may destroy "rosy lips and cheeks," love will last till the end of time. The end couplet emphasizes these beliefs.

The following summary is weak on four counts: (1) it does not give a clear sense of the idea-structure or image-structure of the poem—we do not clearly see the parts and development; (2) it leaves out the important item of love's not altering; (3) it is wrong about what the poem really says—love is the star, not the ship; and (4) the personal judgments are out of place—the word "best" in the first sentence and the entire last sentence.

"SONNET 116"

The poem says that the best kind of love is the marriage of true minds. In storms and tempests it is like a ship in the sea following its star, even though we don't know how much the star is worth. Though time will cut down the rosy cheeks and lips, love will last on to the "edge of doom." It is a good poem because that is the way real love is.

Appendix

Punctuation

QUICK-CHECK

TO END
{
Period
Question mark
Exclamation point
}

1. **Statements**
2. **Indirect questions**
3. **Commands and requests**

4. **Questions**
5. **Exclamations**

TO SEPARATE
{
Comma   Dash   Parentheses
Semicolon   Colon   Brackets
}

1. **Pairs of main statements**
{
Period
Semicolon
Comma
Dash
Colon
}

2. **Introductory elements**
{
Comma
Dash
}

3. **Parenthetical items**
{
Comma
Dash
Parentheses
Brackets
}

4. **Lists and series**
{
Dash
Comma
Semicolon
Colon
}

5. Final items 〔 Comma
Colon
Dash

6. Parts 〔 Comma

SPECIAL EFFECTS 〔 Italics   Period
Quotation marks   Capital letter
Apostrophe

1. **Quotations**
2. **Titles**
3. **Possession**

4. **Special words**
5. **Numbers**
6. **Abbreviations**

Checklist

TO END

1. Statements. Use period.

A storm blew in from the east.
The man asked us where we were going.

2. Questions. Use question mark.

What will the population be in 1990?
He asked, "How can we prevent pollution?"

3. Indirect questions. Use period.
These are not questions, but statements about questions.

Indirect question: The driver asked where we wanted to get off.
Direct question: The driver asked, "Where do you want to get off?"

4. Commands and requests. Use period or exclamation point.

Stop by and pick up your free gift.
Drive carefully!

5. Courtesy requests. Use period or question mark. Courtesy questions, often used in business letters, may end with either a period or a question mark. They are not really questions, which require answers, but imperatives in question form. A phrase like "Will you" is often equivalent to "Please."

Will you kindly answer the enclosed questionnaire?
Will you kindly answer the enclosed questionnaire.

6. Exclamations. Use exclamation point. Set pattern with exclamation point: with *how, such, what.*

What a great opportunity!
How many times I have heard that excuse!

Words of emotional intent. The words themselves must convey the emotion. The exclamation point will not create the emotion; it will only signal the intent.

"Look out!" Glen yelled. "Are you trying to cause an accident?"

If the words themselves do not convey the emotion, the exclamation point is a poor crutch. Use a period, or revise the sentence.

> **Questionable:** I could hardly believe it! "Honest Joe" was actually trying to cheat!
>
> **Improved:** I could hardly believe that "Honest Joe" was trying to cheat!
>
> **Revised:** What a shock! "Honest Joe"—I could hardly believe it—old "Honest" himself was trying to cheat!

TO SEPARATE

1.　Pairs of main statements

a. *Full break, stressing equal importance.* Use a period.

She smiled as sweetly as she could. // Still I did not trust her.

b. *A break, but close relationship.* Use a semicolon.

She smiled as sweetly as she could; // still I did not trust her.
She smiled as sweetly as she could; however, I did not trust her.

c. *Separate statements, but two parts of one idea.* Use a comma with coordinating conjunction (*and, but, or, nor, for.*)

She smiled as sweetly as she could, but still I did not trust her.

d. *Suspense or abrupt break.* Use a dash.

She smiled as sweetly as she could—still I did not trust her.

e. *Balance—the second statement echoes or amplifies the first.* Use a colon.

To study for grades only is to prepare for the end of a term: to study to understand is to prepare for life.

2.　Introductory elements

a. *For ordinary separation.* Use a comma. The subject begins the main idea of the sentence. Unless the subject of your sentence stands out clearly, put a comma after introductory elements to mark where the subject begins.

Yes, men of ability will be noticed.
As long as I remained, the policeman watched me suspiciously.
Although the car was actually a wreck, the eager young man thought it was a bargain.
Having many people to see, the women canvassed the neighborhood voters ten hours a day.

Clear without a signal
On the fence sat three crows.
On Sunday he rests.

b. *For a double start.* Use a dash to separate a beginning list from a summary word.

Oil, wheat, cattle—these are the state's main products.
Taxis, buses, trains—all forms of transportation were on strike.

List only, without a second start

Taxis, buses, trains, and all other forms of transportation were on strike.

3. Parenthetical items

a. *Slight interruption:* Use a comma. The parenthetical material can be removed from the sentence without changing the meaning of what remains.

Julie Vielkind, who led the peace march, is a philosophy major.

A word or a group of words necessary to identify or distinguish the word it refers to is part of the main thought, not an interruption. No punctuation is used.

Any person who leads a peace march must be a pacifist.

b. *Abrupt or violent interruption.* Use a dash

Then Tommy—good old idiot Tommy—threw back his head and began to laugh.

An interruption in full statement form, unless it is an idiom ("it seems to me," for example) takes dashes, not commas.

Jeff called early for Nanette—nobody knew what she was up to then, of course—and the two of them started out for Santa Fe on his trail bike.

4. Lists and series

a. *Two equal adjectives.* Use a comma. Equal adjectives modify the noun separately. They are not equal if each adjective in turn modifies the total idea that follows it.

Equal: Carl is an unselfish, courageous man.
Not equal: The girls are planning an exciting summer camping trip.

Two adjectives are equal if you can reverse them or connect them by *and*.

Equal: Carl is an   unselfish / courageous   man.

Carl is an unselfish *and courageous man.*
—*a courageous, unselfish man.*
—*an unselfish, courageous man.*

Not equal: —*an exciting summer camping trip*
—*an exciting and* summer *and* camping trip.
—a camping summer exciting trip.

b. *Any three or more items in a series.* Use a comma.

> The car is cheap, it is well-built, and it is economical.
> He grabbed his hat, jumped from his seat, and ran from the room.

Journalistic English often leaves out the comma before *and* if there is no danger of misreading.

> Swimming appeals to men, women and children.

Commas are not needed for separation if all items are joined by *and.*

> He worked and fought and cheated his way to the top.

c. *Commas within items.* Use a semicolon.

> **Simple:** The search party was made up of James Wilson, Thomas Crampton, and Jack Billings.

> **Complex:** The search party was made up of James Wilson, a lawyer; Thomas Crampton, an industrialist; and Jack Billings, a city councilman.

Freshmen are known for their greenness; sophomores, for their moronic behavior; and juniors and seniors, for their snobbery.

d. *A formally announced list.* Use a colon. Such words as *these, those,* and *the following* are signals. Use a colon only after a grammatically complete statement—with subject-verb-direct object or predicate noun, and so on.

> The essay listed our problems as these: poverty, civil injustice, and urban paralysis.

Journalistic English often uses a colon before a list whether it is formally announced or not.

> The essay listed our problems as: poverty, civil injustice, and urban paralysis.

e. *A series as a parenthetical group containing commas.* Use dashes.

> Three problems—poverty, civil injustice, and urban paralysis— are most important.

5. Final items. Items tacked on to the end of your main statement can be separated from it by a comma, a colon, or a dash.

a. *Parenthetical items.* Use a comma to set off items not necessary to the direct line of thought, often afterthoughts, such as modifiers and tag questions.

> The pioneers have been gone for a hundred years, haven't they?
> Truman was President then, if I am not mistaken.
> The police arrested Tim Riley, whom they charged with reckless driving.

b. *Formal announcement of something to follow.* Use a colon. Such words as *these, those,* and *the following* are signals. The colon signals "Watch this space: special information to follow."

> Enclosed you will find copies of the following: the original order, our follow-up letter, and your answer.

  c. *Informal introduction of summarizing word or emphatic words.* Use a dash.

> He wanted to walk on the railing—a ridiculous notion.
> She wanted only one thing out of her students—hard work.

  d. *Sudden change in thought or break-off of the sentence.* Use a dash.

> I had to read a novel, work nine pages of math, learn 30 Spanish words, and—ugh! what a weekend!

6. Parts
Parts of items must be separated by commas to prevent misreading and to give clarity.

  a. *Dates.* Use two commas.

> On June 6, 1976, he joined the army.
> On Thursday, June 6, 1976, he joined the army.
> At 11 A.M., Thursday, June 6, 1976, he joined the army.

If no day of the month is given, no comma is necessary.

> In June 1968 he joined the army.

  b. *Addresses.* Use two commas.
  She lived in Tilman, New York, for two years.
  She lived at 138 Main Street, Tilman, New York, for two years.

  c. *Titles.* Use two commas.

> Bud Jameson, M.D., was appointed to the Advisory Commission.
> Bud Jameson, Jr., was appointed to the Advisory Commission.
> Bud Jameson, Jr., M.D., was appointed.

  d. *Reference.* Use two commas.

> The phrase "to be or not to be" is from Act 3, Scene 1, of *Hamlet.*

  e. *Statistical material:* Use commas to separate thousands.

> He drives about 12,000 miles a year.
> I still think $2,800,320 is a lot of money.

SPECIAL EFFECTS

1. Quotations
  a. *Direct quotations from written or spoken source.* Use a pair of double quotation marks around just the quoted parts.

> She asked, "What will we do after the game?"
> "What will we do," she asked, "after the game?"
> The dictionary says, "*Ain't* should be shunned by all who prefer to avoid being considered illiterate."

Note that the parenthetical unquoted part is left out of the quotation marks. It is punctuated according to the rules of "To Separate" and "To End."

> "That's my name," he said, "such as it is."
> "That's my name," he said. "Take it or leave it."

b. *Quotations within quotations.* Use single quotation marks.

> "After that," Joe went on, "the policeman said, 'I'd better see your driver's license.'"

Except in journalistic and British English, single quotation marks are never correct alone. Use them only within double marks.

> **Incorrect:**　He thought 'darn' was a swear word.
> **Correct:**　He thought "darn" was a swear word.

c. *Indirect quotations.* No quotation marks.

> The policeman said that he had better see my driver's license.

d. *Other marks with quotation marks.*
1. Period and comma: inside.

> He called the performance a "flop."
> That common expression, "dog eat dog," refers to Darwin's theory.

2. Semicolon and colon: outside.

> He came to the door and said only one thing: "She's dead"; then he left.

3. Dash, question mark, exclamation point: Inside when part of the quote, outside when not part of the quote.

> He asked, "Would you vote for him again?"
> Didn't General Losser say, "I'll keep us out of war"?
> We heard him cry "Help!"

If the mark applies to both the quote and the whole sentence, use it only once.

> Did she ask, "How many accidents can we afford?"

2. Titles
(In handwritten and typed papers, underlining takes the place of italics.)

a. *Publications and works of art*
Works issued separately. Use italics for titles of books, plays, magazines, newspapers, bulletins, pamphlets, paintings, musical compositions, movies.

> *Treasure Island*　　*Beethoven's Fifth Symphony*
> *The New York Times*　　*The Sound of Music*
> *Playboy* magazine　　the *Mona Lisa*

Parts of other works. Use quotation marks for titles of short stories, poems, essays, subdivisions of books, articles in a magazine, a song in a musical, a movement in a symphony.

> Hawthorne's short story "The Minister's Black Veil" was published in *Twice-Told Tales.*
>
> The article "Priorities for the Seventies" appeared in *Saturday Review.*

b. *Ships, trains, aircraft.* Use italics.

> the *Queen Elizabeth*
> the *Santa Fe Flyer*
> United Airlines' *Sky King*

c. *Other signals with titles.*
The.   Do not italicize *the* unless it is actually part of the title.

> *The Red Badge of Courage*
> the *Saturday Review*

Books of the Bible.   No italics or quotation marks.

> He memorized the Sermon on the Mount from the book of Matthew.

3. Possession

a. *Singular nouns.* Add apostrophe and *s.*

> the driver's side   a day's wait
> a woman's rights   a stone's throw

b. *Plurals ending in s.* Add only apostrophe.

> the girls' team   three days' wait
> the Joneses' house   two dollars' worth

c. *Singular nouns ending in s or z sound.* Add apostrophe and *s* or only apostrophe, whichever form you pronounce.

> Burns' poems   Burns's poems
> Moses' laws
> James' hat   James's hat

d. *Indefinite pronouns.* Add apostrophe and *s.*

> anybody's guess
> everybody's responsibility

e. *Plurals that do not end in s.* Add apostrophe and *s.*

> men's suits
> children's playgrounds

f. *Compound expressions used as a single noun.* Add apostrophe and *s.*

> my sister-in-law's car
> the Queen of England's throne
> Thomas and Hedges' sale
> somebody else's seat
> Jack and Bill's neighbors (same neighbors)

g. *Separate possession with a compound.* Add apostrophe and *s* after each item.

Jack's and Bill's neighbors (different neighbors)

h. *Personal pronouns.* Use the special possessive form of the pronoun —*your, his, hers, its, ours, theirs, whose.*

The cat caught its own food.
It's a serious situation. (contraction of *it is,* not a possessive pronoun)

Whose job is it?
Who's going to do it? (contraction of *who is*)

4. Special words
a. *Words used as words.* Use either italics or quotation marks.

The word "receive" is often misspelled.
The word *receive* is often misspelled.

b. *Letters and numbers used as words.* Use italics.

The *a* and the *o* in the sign looked alike.
He doesn't dot his *i*'s or cross his *t*'s.

c. *Foreign words which have not become accepted as English.* Use italics.

femme fatale, tempus fugit
menu, rodeo, blitz

Check the dictionary for confirmation.

d. *Words used in special context.* Use quotation marks. For definitions, single quoted words, words out of normal context (such as slang in standard writing).

He defined "ego" as "awareness of one's self."
Mr. Jackson did not appreciate having his Jaguar referred to as a "hotrod."

e. *Plural of letters, words used as words.* Add apostrophe and *s*.

He used too many *but*'s and *if*'s.

f. *Plural of numbers.* Add *s* only.
The 1920s were called the Jazz Age.

g. *Words in combination.* Connect by hyphen.

semi-independent, shell-like, a do-it-yourself kit, self-sufficient

Usage changes. Check the dictionary to see if words should be written solid (*blackberry*), hyphenated (*tough-minded*), or as two words (*high school*).

h. *Special emphasis.* Use italics.

She couldn't understand that *to want* is not *to get.*
Avoid italics as a crutch. The best way to get emphasis is to make the

right word combinations.

> **Weak:** But is he *really* living?
> **Better:** But is he really happy with that way of life?

5. Numbers

a. *Spell out numbers that require only one or two words.*

twenty-eight dollars $28.95
in four days   in 104 days
about four thousand people   exactly 4,228 people

b. *Spell out numbers that begin a sentence.*

Two hundred eighty-two people were drowned in the flood.

c. *Spell out ordinal numbers, except in addresses.*

The tenth of August
The third person to arrive
1020 85th Street

d. *Use figures* for dates, street numbers, decimals and percentages, pages and divisions of books, the hour of the day when used with A.M or P.M.

May 13, 1972
13 May, 1972
Unemployment rose $5^1/_2$ percent.
I read from page 4 to page 12 in eight minutes.
The doors open at 8:30 P.M.
The doors open at eight-thirty.
3412 Taft Road
341 89th Street
a .32 caliber bullet

Note: The endings -st, -nd, -th are not added to the day of the month when the year follows. May 4 (not May 4th), 1972

6. Abbreviations. In general, don't abbreviate often. Spell out words in Standard English.

a. *Standard abbreviations*
Titles before and after proper names. Dr., Mrs., Jr., Sr., M.D., B.A.

Dr. Wilson examined me.

Signs for hours, numbers, dollars, and "and." Abbreviations and signs are correct only with the numerals.

8:30 A.M.   at Gate No. 2   about $750

The ampersand (&) is correct only when it is part of a title.

A & P Company   Benson & Hedges

Names of organizations and agencies usually referred to by initials.

YMCA   NAM   FBI   UN

b. *Spell out* names of persons, countries, states, courses of study, months, days of the week, and the words *avenue, road, street, park, company, high school, university.*

Capitalization

Checklist

The main principle of capitals is: proper nouns are capitalized along with their abbreviations and derivatives. Common nouns are not capitalized. A proper noun names a particular person, place, or thing. A common noun names one or more members of a class of persons, places, or things. In a sense, a proper noun (capitalized noun) says there is only one in existence. A pentagon is one of any five-sided figures. The Pentagon with all the military brass in it is the only one.

1. Persons, groups, title, positions

Betty Chapman   a woman
Judge Thompson   a judge
the President (of the nation)   the mayor (of any town)
Indian, Negro, Caucasian   a member of a race
Father (for me, his name)   my father (my one out of many fathers)

2. Organizations and members

The Western Steak House   a restaurant
First Methodist Church   a church
a Presbyterian   a church member
FBI   a government agency
Democratic party   a democratic attitude

3. Historical documents and events

the Declaration of Independence
the Treaty of Paris
the Battle of Hastings

4. Places—but not directions or seasons

the North, the East
Mars, North Star (but not sun, moon, earth, unless used as astronomical names)
Nile River
Brazil

5. Publications and works of art.

Capitalize the first word, the last word, and all other words except articles, coordinating conjunctions, and short prepositions.

The Last of the Mohicans

Check the original title to see if *the* or *a* are part of the title.

A Clockwork Orange
Ship of Fools
The New York Times

6. Days of the week, month, and holidays

Friday   April   Christmas   spring   summer

7. Academic courses when numbered or otherwise indicated as proper nouns

Philosophy 412   American history   American History 316

8. Derived words   from capitalized nouns

Spanish   Darwinian

Spelling

Checklist

The following lists contain the most commonly misspelled words. The 350 words are arranged in alphabetized groups for easy reference and study.

GROUP 1

1. allot
2. allotted
3. barbarians
4. barbarous
5. beneficial
6. benefited
7. changeable
8. changing
9. commit
10. committed
11. committee
12. comparative
13. comparatively
14. comparison
15. compel
16. compelled
17. competent
18. competition
19. compulsion
20. conceivable
21. conceive
22. conception
23. conscience
24. conscientious
25. conscious
26. courteous
27. courtesy
28. deceit
29. deceive
30. deception
31. decide
32. decision
33. defer
34. deference
35. deferred
36. describe
37. description
38. device
39. devise
40. discuss
41. discussion
42. dissatisfied
43. dissatisfy
44. equip
45. equipment
46. equipped
47. excel
48. excellent
49. explain
50. explanation

GROUP 2

1. apparent
2. appearance
3. attendance
4. beggar
5. brilliant
6. calendar
7. carriage
8. conqueror
9. contemptible
10. coolly
11. descent
12. desirable
13. dictionary
14. disastrous
15. eligible
16. equivalent
17. existence
18. familiar
19. grammar
20. guidance
21. hindrance
22. hoping

23. imaginary
24. incredible
25. indigestible
26. indispensable
27. inevitable
28. influential
29. irresistible
30. liable
31. marriage
32. momentous
33. naturally
34. nickel
35. noticeable
36. nucleus
37. obedience
38. outrageous
39. pageant
40. permissible
41. perseverance
42. persistent
43. pleasant
44. possible
45. prevalent
46. resistance
47. similar
48. strenuous
49. vengeance
50. vigilance

GROUP 3

1. accept
2. across
3. aisle
4. all right
5. amateur
6. annual
7. appropriate
8. argument
9. arrangement
10. association
11. awkward
12. bachelor
13. biscuit
14. cafeteria
15. career
16. cemetery
17. completely
18. convenient
19. cruelty
20. curiosity

21. definite
22. desperate
23. diphtheria
24. discipline
25. disease
26. distribute
27. dormitories
28. drudgery
29. eighth
30. eliminate
31. ecstasy
32. eminent
33. enemy
34. except
35. exercise
36. extraordinary
37. fascinate
38. fraternity
40. grandeur
41. height
42. hypocrite
43. imitation
44. interest
45. livelihood
46. loneliness
47. magazine
48. material
49. messenger
50. mischievous

GROUP 4

1. accidentally
2. accommodate
3. accompanied
4. achieved
5. address
6. aggravate
7. anxiety
8. barren
9. believe
10. ceiling
11. confident
12. course
13. disappear
14. disappoint
15. dissipate
16. efficiency
17. emphasize
18. exaggerate
19. exceed

20. fiery
21. finally
22. financial
23. forehead
24. foreign
25. forfeit
26. grief
27. handkerchief
28. hurriedly
29. hypocrisy
30. imminent
31. incidentally
32. innocence
33. intentionally
34. interest
35. legitimate
36. likely
37. manual
38. mattress
39. misspell
40. niece
41. parallel
42. psychiatrist
43. psychology
44. occasion
45. organization
46. piece
47. receive
48. religious
49. severely
50. villain

GROUP 5

1. obstacle
2. operate
3. opinion
4. pastime
5. persuade
6. piece
7. politician
8. practically
9. presence
10. professor
11. propeller
12. quantity
13. recommend
14. region
15. relieve
16. representative
17. reservoir

18. restaurant
19. ridiculous
20. sacrifice
21. sacrilegious
22. safety
23. salary
24. scarcely
25. science
26. secretary
27. seize
28. separate
29. shriek
30. siege
31. similar
32. suffrage
33. supersede
34. suppress
35. syllable
36. symmetry
37. temperament
38. temperature
39. tendency
40. tournament
41. tragedy
42. truly
43. tyranny
44. unanimous
45. unusual
46. usage
47. valuable
48. wholly
49. yoke
50. yolk

GROUP 6

1. hesitancy
2. hesitate
3. instance
4. instant
5. intellectual
6. intelligence
7. intelligent
8. intelligible
9. maintain
10. maintenance
11. miniature
12. minute
13. ninetieth
14. ninety
15. ninth
16. obligation
17. oblige
18. obliged
19. occur
20. occurred
21. occurrence
22. omission
23. omit
24. omitted
25. procedure
26. proceed
27. picnic
28. picnicking
29. possess
30. possession
31. precede
32. precedence
33. preceding
34. prefer
35. preference
36. preferred
37. realize
38. really
39. refer
40. reference
41. referred
42. repeat
43. repetition
44. transfer
45. transferred
46. tried
47. tries
48. try
49. writing
50. written

GROUP 7

1. arctic
2. auxiliary
3. business
4. candidate
5. characteristic
6. chauffeur
7. colonel
8. column
9. cylinder
10. environment
11. especially
12. exhaust
13. exhilaration
14. February
15. foremost
16. ghost
17. government
18. grievous
19. hygiene
20. intercede
21. leisure
22. library
23. lightning
24. literature
25. mathematics
26. medicine
27. mortgage
28. muscle
29. notoriety
30. optimistic
31. pamphlet
32. parliament
33. physically
34. physician
35. prairie
36. prejudice
37. pronunciation
38. recede
39. recognize
40. reign
41. rhetoric
42. rhythm
43. schedule
44. sentinel
45. soliloquy
46. sophomore
47. studying
48. surprise
49. twelfth
50. Wednesday

Subject-Verb Agreement

Checklist

Most errors in subject-verb agreement are caused by two difficulties: (1) finding hidden subjects, and (2) determining whether the subject is singular or plural.

1. *Finding hidden subjects.* You are likely to make errors in using the s form of the verb because you are looking at the wrong word for subject. These five kinds of patterns tend to hide the true subject.

a. *Words between subject and verb*

A study of these riots shows that they have several causes. (A *study . . . shows . . .*)

b. *Inversion of subject and verb* (subject coming after verb)

Lying in a corner were the mother dog and her two puppies. (A mother *dog* and her two *puppies were. . .*)

c. *Introductory subjects.* The word *there* may point to either a singular or a plural subject (*there is, there are*).

There *is* one *cause* of war.
There *are* two *causes* of war.

d. *Predicate nouns.* The verb links two nouns or pronouns that refer to the same thing, but one noun may be singular and the other plural. Whichever noun comes first is the subject.

Her greatest *expense was* records.
Records were her greatest expense.
What we need most is better leaders.
Better *leaders are* what we need most.

e. *Subject with or, nor.* Two or more subjects are joined by *or, nor, either-or, neither-nor, not-but.* The verb agrees with the closer subject.

Neither you nor *he* is welcome.

2. *Determining whether a subject is singular or plural.* Even after you have found some subjects, it can be hard to tell whether they are singular or plural. Here are the common trouble spots.

a. *Everyone, anyone, and other singular pronouns.* The following words are singular. Their present tense verbs use the s form.

one	everybody	each
everyone	anybody	every
anyone	nobody	many a
no one	somebody	neither of
someone	either of	

Everyone in the boat *was yelling* for help.
Many a man and *many a* woman *has heard* that story before.

b. *Who, which, that.* Check the nouns they take the place of; they should have the same person and number.

A man *who* loses his temper usually regrets it later.
Men *who* lose their tempers usually regret it later.
It is I *who* am to blame.
It is you *who* are to blame.

c. *One of and only one of.* The words *one of* generally link *who* to a plural word. The words *only one of* generally link *who* to a singular word.

Tim is one of the *swimmers* who *have* won two medals.
Tim is the *only one* of the swimmers who *has* won two medals.

d. *Some, none, any, more, most, all.* These may refer to one or more than one. Especially check the object of *of* as a sign of singular or plural.

None of the roads *were* paved.
None of the road *was* paved.

e. *Collective nouns.* A collective noun, which designates a group, is singular if you think of the group as a unit, plural if you think of the separate members of the group. Some common collective nouns: *band, class, committee, couple, crowd, family, jury, majority, team.*

That so-called blissful *couple fight* one another continually.
That *couple is* the first one to win a prize.

f. *Nouns in -s*

Usually singular *economics, mathematics, measles, mumps, news, linguistics, semantics, billiards, checkers, summons.*

The *summons is* sure to come.
The *news is* hilarious.

Usually plural: *acoustics, pliers, riches, scissors, thanks, trousers, tweezers.*

His *trousers are* torn.

Case of Pronouns

Checklist

Problems with pronouns arise because the personal pronouns and the pronoun *who* use one form when they are subjects and a different form when they are objects.

1. Subject forms are used for subjects and for words that rename subjects. *I, he, she, we, they, who.*

She worked in a shoe store.
Bill and *I* often went to see Mary.

2. Object forms are used for objects and for words that rename objects. *me, him, her, us, them, whom.*

> The customers liked *her.*
> She liked to talk with Bill and *me.*

3. Two steps for working with pronouns

Step 1: Make a fast check of the bones of the sentence: verb, subject, object of verb, object of preposition.
Step 2: To which word does the pronoun connect?

John asked Bill who/whom the crowd was cheering for.

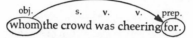

Pick out subjects and objects for practice:

Mary and I *were* the only ones left.

The real *students are they* who understand.

They *sent* Anderson and *me* to the peace rally.

Awards were won *by two* of us, John and *me.*

Most of the problems of case arise from five major sentence patterns:

1. Compounds. If a subject or an object consists of two or more parts, all the parts will be in the same case.

> John and *I* went there. (subject)
> (John went there. I went there. John and I went there.)

> They invited Bill and *her* to the game. (object)
> (They invited Bill. They invited her. They invited Bill and her.)

> I bought it for Mary and *him.* (object)
> (I bought it for Mary. I bought it for him. I bought it for Mary and him.)

2. Appositives. A pronoun in apposition to a noun is in the same case as the noun. Three types of expressions are most troublesome:

Appositions in compounds

> Two of us, Tom and *I,* went.
> (Two went. Tom went. I went. Two of us, Tom and I, went.)

> They sent two, Tom and *me.*
> (They sent two. They sent Tom. They sent me. They sent two, Tom and me.)

Expressions like "we boys" and "us boys"

> *We* girls laughed.
> (We laughed. Girls laughed. We girls laughed.)

They asked *us* men to go.
(They asked us to go. They asked men to go. They asked us men to go.)

Expressions like "Let's you and me"

Let's *you* and *me* try.
(Let us try. Let you try. Let me try. Let's you and me try.)

3. Comparisons with than and as. Comparisons with *than* and *as* usually imply words understood but not stated. Test for case by thinking of the implied words.

He is taller than *I.*
(He is taller than I am.)

She needs him more than *me.*
(She needs him more than she needs *me.*)

We are as efficient as *they.*
(We are as efficient as they are.)

4. After inflected form of to be. The inflected forms of *to be* (such as *is, am, are, was, were, will be,* and *could have been*) do not take objects. In formal speech and writing, pronouns following such words are in the subjective case.

I believe it is *he.*
It is *I* (*he, she, we, they*).
Was it *I* (*he, she, we, they*)?
It will be *I* (*he, she, we, they*).
It may be (*could be, would be, should have been*) *he.*

Note: Some authorities approve the use of the objective case in informal speech and writing after parts of the verb *to be.*

"Is that you, Joe?" "Yes, it's me."
That's her in the blue sweater.

5. Who and whom. The words *who* and *whoever* are subjects. The words *whom* and *whomever* are objects. Pick the word according to how it is used in the clause in which it occurs.

Who saw you?
Whom did you see?
Who do you think saw you?
Whom do you think you saw?

Four aids in working with who and whom

a. *In your mind, put the clause in normal order of subject-verb-object. Whom as a question-type word usually comes before the verb, when you expect a subject, like who.*

Which one: *Whom/Whom* do you think Jim meant?
Change order: You do think Jim meant *whom.*
Correct: *Whom* do you think Jim meant?

b.   *Mentally shift* whom *to* him *and* who *to* he. What word do you need, subject or an object?

Who/Whom do you think Jim meant?
You do think Jim meant *him*.
Whom do you think Jim meant?

c.   *Mentally cross out intervening phrases like* I think, we believe. Then see whether the main verb needs a subject or an object.

Who/Whom do you suppose will win?
Who/Whom will win?   Who   will win?
                do you suppose

d.   *Isolate the* who *clause*. The *who* clause is its own unit. Pick *who* or *whom* for that clause.

Get money from *whoever/whomever* will give it to you.
Get money from [*whoever/whomever* will give it to you.]
         s.   v.
. . . *whoever* will give it to you.

INDEX

Notes

Notes

Notes

Notes